THE APOSTLE ◆ PAUL ◆ HIS LIFE AND HIS TESTIMONY

SIDNEY B. SPERRY

Sidney Branton Sperry, a pioneer in Latter-day Saint religious education, believed sincerely that one must be learned both by study and by faith. His own career began with a mission, followed by a degree at the University of Utah in chemistry and geology. His acquaintance with Dr. John A. Widtsoe, Dr. James E. Talmage, Dr. Frederick J. Pack, and others led him to prepare himself to give understandable answers to reasonable questions, to build faith and counter skepticism. Thus after a few years' work as a chemist and then as a teacher in early LDS seminaries and institutes of religion, he enrolled at the University of Chicago for graduate study in archaeology, Egyptology, and biblical languages and literature, without baccalaureate preparation in those subjects. As a young man with his wife, Eva Lila Braithwaite Sperry, and the beginning of large family, he earned the master's and doctoral degrees and did a year of postdoctoral work at the American Schools of Oriental Research in Jerusalem. He went to Brigham Young University in 1932, where he became a distinguished and beloved teacher, counselor, and administrator and where he worked for forty-five years. He has left a heritage in a multitude of writings, and his works live on in his many students and the students of his students, "unto the third and fourth generation."—Ellis T. Rasmussen

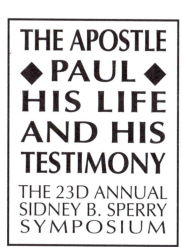

THE APOSTLE ◆ PAUL ◆ HIS LIFE AND HIS TESTIMONY

THE 23D ANNUAL SIDNEY B. SPERRY SYMPOSIUM

DESERET BOOK COMPANY
SALT LAKE CITY, UTAH

OTHER VOLUMES IN THE SPERRY SYMPOSIUM SERIES
FROM DESERET BOOK COMPANY:

Thy People Shall Be My People (1994)

The Heavens Are Open (1993)

Doctrines of the Book of Mormon (1992)

The Lord of the Gospels (1991)

A Witness of Jesus Christ (1990)

Doctrines for Exaltation (1989)

Library of Congress Cataloging-in-Publication Data

Sperry Symposium (23d : 1994 : Brigham Young University)
  The Apostle Paul, his life and his testimony : the 23d annual Sidney B. Sperry Symposium.
    p.   cm.
  Includes bibliographical references and index.
  ISBN 0-87579-887-X
  1. Paul, the Apostle, Saint—Congresses. 2. Paul, the Apostle, Saint—Teachings—Congresses. 3. Church of Jesus Christ of Latter-day Saints—Doctrines—Congresses. 4. Mormon Church—Doctrines—Congressess. I. Title. II. Title: Apostle Paul.
  BS2506.S63   1994
  225.9'2—dc20   94-38322
                                                                CIP

Printed in the United States of America

10 9   8   7   6   5   4   3   2

CONTENTS

PREFACE...vii

1 PAUL'S WITNESS TO THE EARLY
HISTORY OF JESUS' MINISTRY 1
Richard Lloyd Anderson

2 PAUL'S EARNEST PURSUIT OF SPIRITUAL GIFTS 34
Robert C. Freeman

3 "AN HEBREW OF THE HEBREWS":
PAUL'S LANGUAGE AND THOUGHT 47
C. Wilfred Griggs

4 PAUL AMONG THE RHETORICIANS:
A MODEL FOR PROCLAIMING CHRIST 65
Gary Layne Hatch

5 HEBREW CONCEPTS OF ADOPTION AND
REDEMPTION IN THE WRITINGS OF PAUL 80
Jennifer Clark Lane

6 THE JERUSALEM COUNCIL..96
Robert J. Matthews

7 PAUL AMONG THE PROPHETS:
OBTAINING A CROWN 110
Michael W. Middleton

8 WALKING IN NEWNESS OF LIFE:
DOCTRINAL THEMES OF THE APOSTLE PAUL 132
Robert L. Millet

9 WHAT IS A MORTAL MESSIAH? 151
Craig J. Ostler

10 THE HOLY GHOST BRINGS TESTIMONY,
    UNITY, AND SPIRITUAL GIFTS 166
    Rex C. Reeve Jr.

11 A TRIUMPH OF FAITH: PAUL'S
    TEACHINGS IN SECOND TIMOTHY.....................................178
    John G. Scott

12 THE JEWISH AND GENTILE MISSIONS:
    PAUL'S ROLE IN THE TRANSITION.......................................188
    Gaye Strathearn

    INDEX..207

PREFACE

Paul's life touched all the strands of the New Testament. Born a Roman citizen in the city of Tarsus, Paul was educated by the great Jewish rabbi Gamaliel. He became a staunch defender of what he must have considered the legitimate Israelite heritage, but then in an instant on the road to Damascus his direction was changed completely, and he became a most ardent advocate for Jesus Christ and his gospel. For the rest of his life, Paul weathered the storms caused by his former Jewish allies, by well-meaning but ill-informed members of the Church, and by Roman administrators and petty bureaucrats. In the end he freely sealed his testimony with his blood.

Those who are curious about Paul as well as those who take a deep interest in one of the chief contributors to the New Testament will find *The Apostle Paul, His Life and His Testimony,* a source of knowledge and inspiration. Paul was the conduit for many doctrines, including those on the nature of the mortal Messiah, the work of the Holy Ghost, spiritual gifts, and missionary work among non-Israelites. This volume addresses various aspects of Paul's life, including his own use of spiritual gifts. Also explored are Paul's Jewish background, with new ideas about Jewish culture in the Jerusalem of his day; his use of Greco-Roman culture in his missionary labors to further the kingdom of God; his use of Old Testament traditions and language to teach the plain and precious truths of the gospel to Jewish converts; his efforts to bring Gentiles into the fold and the ensuing questions that arose about the conversion process; and his part in the council held in Jerusalem and the principles of Church government and policy that came out of it. The chapters on these and other topics demonstrate that the lessons and principles of Paul's life and testimony are just as pertinent today as they were some two thousand years ago.

It is our hope that this volume will add to the legacy of Dr. Sidney B. Sperry, to whose memory it is gratefully dedicated.

Paul Y. Hoskisson

Editor

CHAPTER ONE

PAUL'S WITNESS TO THE EARLY HISTORY OF JESUS' MINISTRY

RICHARD LLOYD ANDERSON

The fiftieth anniversary of the Allied invasion of Normandy was observed in June 1994.[1] Venturesome survivors revisited their beaches, and the daring parachuted again in reenacting their small part of the miraculous crusade to break apart an evil dictatorship. Do able minds match bodies of such surprising tenacity? I saw no article claiming that multinational veterans had invented exploits or misstated their experiences. Though these aging warriors believed deeply in their cause, modesty rather than exaggeration was the rule in published interviews. Their recollections were in surprising agreement with reports republished from a vanished era. Spontaneous stories dovetailed with each other, given a commonsense allowance for many points of view in many sectors. The parts had to be harmonized to repicture the whole operation. Certainly there were discrepancies in some details of sequence, exact times, precise numbers, and so forth. But no one doubts the blend of oral and documentary history that enables us to make a quality reconstruction of the most spectacular sea-to-land attack in history.[2]

PAUL AND THE SCHEME OF LATE GOSPELS

Such living sources might inject caution into many armchair speculations on how the Gospels were written. Christianity invaded the Roman Empire. Jewish participants numbered in the hundreds, and scores passed on their experiences to writers of the Gospels. On their face, these narratives of Jesus' ministry embody memories of those who originally walked with him in Galilee and Jerusalem. But what of the time lag? Jesus went to

□ □ □ □ □

Richard Lloyd Anderson is professor of ancient scripture at Brigham Young University.

the cross about A.D. 30. Mainstream Christian scholars think the religious biographies of Christ came to their present form in about the last three decades of the first century: Mark no earlier than A.D. 65, Matthew and Luke around 80, and John 90 or beyond. These figures are out-and-out estimates; Christ's prophecy of Jerusalem's destruction is supposedly recorded so accurately by Matthew and Luke that their Gospels must have been written after the Roman siege in A.D. 70, prompting a well-informed critic to remark, "It is surprising that on such inconclusive evidence . . . there should be such widespread acceptance of a date between A.D. 75 and 85."[3] My view agrees with a minority that sees Luke as the third Gospel, written by the year 63. Matthew and Mark would necessarily be among the "many" who had already narrated the miraculous events of the days of Jesus (Luke 1:1–2; Acts 1:1–2). These first full-scale Gospels would then fall between the expansion of the Church beyond Israel in the forties and the increase of urban, literate converts in the fifties. On this more compressed evaluation, fifteen to thirty years would separate the composition of the synoptic Gospels from the Crucifixion. On the more prevalent scheme, this gap would at least double.

According to ancient sources near the apostle John, he wrote a fourth Gospel to add his recollections of events not already in the synoptic Gospels.[4] *Synoptic* of course refers to the first three accounts of Christ's ministry in the New Testament. Because they have interdependent characteristics, they "see together," the Greek meaning behind *synoptic*. Paul's information about Jesus correlates mainly with the synoptic Gospels, so that relationship is under discussion here. But to return for a moment to the analogy of the Normandy invasion, a number of soldiers who live to age eighty-five will have memories that reach back accurately to the expedition sixty-five years before. Early Christian sources put the apostle John in this situation, writing after other apostles were gone.[5] So in terms of late authorship alone, John's Gospel has a minor relationship with Paul's letters. Yet in a long lifetime John would have widely shared his treasured knowledge of the Master. Some themes in John's writing have intriguing counterparts in Paul's letters and speeches, but that is a more subtle study.

How was the written history of Jesus formed between A.D. 30 and 90? Could his life and message have been accurately handed down through this period? The obvious solution is to read the Acts of the Apostles, which covers what the Galilean Twelve and Paul taught up to about 63. But mainstream professionals reshape Acts with the same technique they apply to the Gospels. Their theory is that both the history of the Savior and the history of the apostles were written by later generations that inherited and enhanced faith-promoting legends. In Acts the apostles personally testify of the divinity and doctrine of Christ right after the resurrection.

But here the important perspective of Acts must be largely set aside for another focus—what Paul had learned of Christ's life and teachings from his conversion about A.D. 35 until writing his early letters fifteen or twenty years later. In other words, Paul wrote during the critical years when faith-stories were supposedly replacing true history of Jesus. The convert-apostle tells more about Christ's mission and teachings than is apparent. This field of study has been productive recently, though conduits of information from Jesus to Paul are minimized by theologically correct scholars.

My purpose is to review Paul's expressed knowledge of Christ in a fresh framework, paying attention to the difference between data and speculation that was defined by Stephen E. Robinson in profiling the work of faithful Latter-day Saint scripture scholars: "They accept and use most objective results of Bible scholarship, such as linguistics, history, and archaeology, while rejecting many of the discipline's naturalistic assumptions and its more subjective methods and theories."[6]

In the current models of the writing of the Gospels, Paul's Christian career matches the period of free growth of the stories about Jesus and the teachings attributed to him. The Apostle to the Gentiles was converted soon after the Crucifixion and was an influential leader from about A.D. 38 until his death late in the reign of Nero, who took his own life in 68.[7] So Paul's life spans the three decades when the Jesus of history supposedly evolved into the Christ of faith. But to what else would this Pharisee be converted? No one was more consistent in his Christian career. His first known letters went to converts at

Thessalonica and Corinth. Early in each letter, he reviews how he stood before their synagogues in pure testimony that Jesus was the Christ and that he had determined to know nothing but Christ. Because every letter of Paul afterward repeats this message, the humbled Pharisee certainly made this declaration from the time of his conversion, just as described in Acts 9. If this most visible spokesman had a fixed message of the divinity of Jesus from the first decade of the Christian church, why assume the movement was then in ferment on the subject?

SLANTING THE TEACHINGS OF JESUS?

Most experts claim that literary evidence proves evolving historical accounts of Jesus: "It is evident from the several decades between the times when the texts were written and the times of the events recounted in them that we have to reckon with a period during which sayings and stories were orally transmitted before being written down either in our present texts or in their sources. The principal evidence for this process of oral transmission consists in multiple versions of sayings and stories that cannot well be accounted for by simply attributing them to the use of written sources."[8]

This quotation refers to the frequent individuality of stories and teachings in Matthew and Mark and Luke. Of course chronology and description vary in many episodes reported by more than one Gospel. They were obviously not crafted by modern professionals who worried about minor discrepancies or proofread their quotations. Scholars today struggle with how approximations can be considered history. Yet until recent times history was largely composed from approximations. That does not mean that we fail to have real events and many correct details. Nor are "the very words of Jesus" necessarily absent from the Gospels. Ancient collections preserve several hundred authentic letters from Roman emperors and senators and their correspondents. Many historians of antiquity incorporate well-copied documents in rather poor narrative. Yet today's analysts tend to overstate differences among the Gospels. For instance, a respected linguist downgrades a blending approach to the four Gospels, adding this observation about Jesus: "The one statement written about him during his lifetime, the 'title' on the cross, appears with *different* wording in each gospel (see Mark

15:26; Matt. 27:37; Luke 23:38; John 19:19)."[9] But the effect of this comment is hardly justified by the record. "The king of the Jews" is on the execution placard in every Gospel, with "Jesus" added in Matthew and "Jesus of Nazareth" added in John. The art of history normally reconstructs full events from partial reports, and summaries of course omit details that are rounded out in more complete versions.

When two Gospels differ on the precise wording of a teaching of Jesus, some analysts pronounce the sources unreliable rather than look for their agreement on the thought. Even if there are major differences in context or wording, rather than labeling both records nonhistorical, one could consider the option that one account may contain fuller data whereas the other may be a freer version from an eyewitness or reporter of responsible memories. Different events with loose resemblances in two Gospels are too often labeled variants of the same episode, with an arbitrary claim that one version was radically rewritten. But responsible history interprets its sources without changing them. In the case of differing details in accounts of the same event, one should avoid imposing standards of a technical era on the reasonable integrity of another period.

Although the following criticism pertains to overstating differences between Acts and Paul's letters, the same issues apply to perfectionism in comparing the synoptic Gospels: "In historical sources from other fields such discrepancies are no surprise to the scholar, nor do they make him doubt the historical reliability of the accounts except at a few points where they directly contradict each other. But many New Testament scholars adopt a very stringent attitude when no complete agreement exists among the different accounts, regardless of the fact that perfect agreement would be suspect or proof of artificial construction."[10]

Current theories project a period when stories of Christ evolved in major substance, a process supposedly discovered through form criticism. This procedure first classifies story and teaching patterns, and then similar episodes from different Gospels are compared to determine their direction of development. For instance, Matthew fully reports Peter's testimony of

Christ and also Christ's promise of authority to Peter to lead the Church (Matthew 16:13–20). Then settings and brief summaries are compared in Mark 8 and Luke 9, with the conclusion that the fuller account displays later creative development: "It seems likely that Matthew has followed his custom of adding things, in this case, to the sayings of both Simon Peter and Jesus."[11]

As a documentary historian, I see such analysis as unsupported theory. Differences in synoptic narratives are assumed by the form critics to be evidence for evolution of the narrative, but there are good alternative explanations for synoptic diversity, such as an author's habit of brevity, his particular interests, or his decision that certain events were adequately treated in another Gospel. Because Jesus adapted teachings to different audiences, a shift of emphasis in another setting may have nothing to do with the growth of the "story unit." These double and triple accounts are a main focus for form criticism: "The purpose of NTFC [New Testament Form Criticism] as traditionally defined was to rediscover the origin and history of the individual units and thereby to shed some light on the history of the tradition before it took literary form, that is, to determine whether the various units are traceable to Jesus, to the early Church, or to the redactional (editorial) activity of the Gospel writers."[12]

Redaction has heavy connotations of question-begging. *Editor* in today's practice means compiling, not altering. But *redactor* in New Testament scholarship suggests modifying or shifting the point of the inherited story. Redaction criticism, which now supplements form criticism, is defined as "the evangelist's use, disuse, or alteration of the traditions known to him."[13] It is one thing to say that every writer reveals a personality and point of view—mindprints of the author are clear characteristics of each of the four Gospels. But the intense search for "alteration of the traditions" is regrettable. As just noted, accounts of the same event show commonality and also individuality, both of which can be explained in terms of the writer, his skills, his sources, his personal style. "They can't all be right," is essentially what we hear from form and redaction critics. Many aim for the one original account by peeling off its later developments. But that is a historical version of the either-

or fallacy. Each Gospel may have had independent access to some original details, even when there is literary interdependence in the synoptic trio.

The norm in this reconstructive system is illustrated in a recent survey of scholarship on Jesus by Aramaic expert Joseph A. Fitzmyer, an intellectual of faith who concludes basically that Christ's portrait in the Gospels is severely overstated but early Christians were afterward led to his divinity through the Holy Spirit. Fitzmyer is used here because of his positive stance, and my evaluation is given with respect for his friendship and his lifetime devotion to religious learning. Although he views the Gospels as fictionalizing the life of Jesus, he also thinks that they carry far more authentic information than do their apocryphal imitations, some of which are now touted as having equal validity to the four biblical records: "Despite the contentions of some modern scholars (H. Koester, J. D. Crossan), these apocryphal gospels are scarcely a source of real information about Jesus of Nazareth."[14]

Consistent with one point in this paper, Fitzmyer finds the outline of the death and resurrection of Jesus validated by a dozen major allusions in Paul's letters.[15] So he sees the Gospels rooted in events but with such lush overgrowth, mainly in regard to teachings, that the proportion of fully authentic incidents is small and the proportion of reliably recorded teachings of Jesus even smaller. He reviews this wisdom as the fruit of the twentieth century, which started with form criticism and then advanced to redaction-composition criticism and other types of literary analysis. The result is a "sophisticated mode of gospel interpretation [that] was unknown in earlier centuries of the church."[16]

With other Roman Catholic scholars, Fitzmyer speaks of three stages: Jesus teaching, traditions expanding, and gospel authors freely adapting. Basically the first century is trisected, with story development in the middle third and editorial creativity in the final third. The system breeds a puzzling certainty. One may be sure that "none of the evangelists was an eyewitness of Jesus' ministry."[17] In this view unnamed authors sorted out stage-two folk traditions and created the four Gospels "by redactional modifications and additions."[18] In doing so they relied on

stories produced with a slant by the unknown middle generation: "Yet none of these disciple-preachers ever sought to
reproduce with factual accuracy the words and deeds of Jesus
himself; they understood those words and deeds with hindsight
and adapted them to the needs of those to whom they
preached."[19]

PAUL AND EYEWITNESSES

But the New Testament contains a different information
model about Christ, and Paul is the first one known to state it.
Because he never hints of personal experience with Jesus, the
apostle is clearly at the critics' stage two. In 1 Corinthians he
reviews the conversion of southern Greeks as he carefully
argues for the Resurrection. Paul makes a sharp distinction
between his vision and the first appearances of Christ to the
Galilean apostles and their associates, naming five occasions
when the resurrected Lord was seen by them (1 Corinthians
15:5–7). Here Paul is really defining his mentors for the earthly
Christ, as he stresses the Atonement and Resurrection: "For I
delivered unto you first of all that which I also received" (1
Corinthians 15:3). Information about Christ's appearance to
Peter certainly came from Peter himself, because Paul tells
about spending two weeks with the chief apostle three years
after the conversion vision (Galatians 1:18), and they counseled
together at Jerusalem and Antioch afterward (Acts 15; Galatians
2:11–14). Information about Christ's appearance to James
clearly came from James, because Paul tells about visiting James
not very long after the conversion vision (Galatians 1:19), and
they counseled together at Jerusalem afterward (Acts 15; see
also Acts 21:18–25). Although Paul is an intermediary, he insists
he has relayed firsthand testimony on the resurrection appearances (1 Corinthians 15:11–15).

In 1 Corinthians, Paul refers to his first preaching in Corinth
about A.D. 50, the midpoint of the scholars' second stage, when
disciple-preachers were supposedly expanding the words and
deeds of Jesus. But historical constancy is Paul's message. The
Corinthians are told that Christ appeared to Peter first and afterward to the eleven apostles, James, and "above five hundred
brethren at once, of whom the greater part remain unto this
present" (1 Corinthians 15:6). So Paul corrects current form

critics: the original eyewitness stage existed simultaneously with their stage two. Speaking of the Galilean eleven, Paul insists that the leaders are united on the historical truth of Christ's atonement and resurrection: "Therefore whether it were I or they, so we preach, and so ye believed" (1 Corinthians 15:11). These are not anonymous "disciple-preachers." Anyone speaking or writing at that point, or until the deaths of Peter and Paul nearly two decades later, would have had access to the testimony of those who walked with Christ and also to responsible conduits such as Paul who were scrupulously careful not to modify knowledge that came from the eyewitnesses.

This is exactly the viewpoint of the author Luke, honored in Paul's letters as a trusted companion. To remove his name from the Gospel that has his byline in the earliest manuscripts is equivalent to erasing authorship from the best Roman and Greek histories. Because later apocryphal writings falsely claimed to have been written by leading Christians, the traditional authors of many New Testament books are widely questioned today. But second-century papyrus copies exist of the books of Matthew, Luke, and John with their names in headnotes or afternotes.[20] There is also a major fragment of an important second-century list of approved books, broken at the beginning but naming Luke and John as writing the "third" and "fourth" Gospels. This list sought to clarify which books were historically authentic: "There are also many others which cannot be received in the General Church, for gall cannot be mixed with honey."[21] Luke has low New Testament visibility and is not a likely name for adding prestige to a pseudo-Gospel. Indeed, the books known to be in the latter category have obvious agendas and/or contents that do not integrate with events, topography, geography, and culture in the real world. The four Gospels are impressive for their factual framework accompanying the life and teachings of Christ.

A book on Luke's preface (Luke 1:1–4) would of course do it more justice than the few comments possible here. That preface contradicts redactional theory by subtracting those not knowing Jesus from the source level of the Gospels. First for Luke are the "eyewitnesses," the Galilean Twelve who shared events with Jesus "from the beginning." Luke's second stage is preserving the Christian epic in writing. The following language from the New Revised Standard Version reflects most current translations: Because the eyewitnesses "handed on to us" their knowledge of the founding events, "many have undertaken to set down an orderly account." Luke then writes "after investigating everything carefully from the very first." The result is what the King James Version correctly calls "certainty" that the record of Christ is reliable.

In my view, Luke penned this preface no later than A.D. 63, less than a decade after 1 Corinthians. Even if Luke wrote later, this missionary companion of Paul stood in his shoes as having had contact with important witnesses of the ministry of Jesus, which is a great part of the meaning of "investigating everything carefully from the very first." As Paul's associate, Luke here names Paul's sources of information about Christ—observers and possibly their writings.

Luke's preface leads away from speculative models and straight to basic biography. Paul's letters from Rome mention Luke's being there with him in the early sixties, which verifies the Acts picture of Luke's going to Rome with Paul after two years in Israel.[22] That underlines the critical insight from 1 Corinthians 15 already discussed. Prominent apostles and brothers of the Lord mingled with converts during the middle third of the founding century. Writing 1 Corinthians about A.D. 57, Paul appeals to common knowledge that "other apostles" were travelling with their wives, naming Peter and "the brethren of the Lord," a term that undoubtedly includes James and Jude (1 Corinthians 9:5; Matthew 13:55). Peter was slain about 67; James, the Lord's brother, was slain in 62; his brother Jude wrote his letter perhaps a decade later; the originally prominent James of Zebedee was killed about 44; and responsible Christian sources report his brother John exercising apostolic supervision in Asia Minor at the end of the century.[23]

Besides those documented apostles, other leading Christians, including relatives of the Lord and prominent women, lived to see some or all of the synoptic Gospels written. If one survived childhood in the ancient world, one's longevity would on average trail current levels by ten years or so. Yet the question of sources for the Gospels continues to be discussed in a vacuum.

Handwritten note:

Pelagian
1. created good
2. capable
3. No orig sin
4. free will
5. earn reward
6. grace facilitates given in proportion to merit

es that Mark's Gospel
ts that not all "person-
but muzzles anyone
1 firsthand information

epressing lines. From
iistles have a constant
ppeals to Jesus. As we
ld the Corinthians that
ces that he "received"
15:3–7). History from
erved before our eyes
ittle insensitivity about
Christ established that
very close to those
l's source: "For I have
lelivered unto you" (1
cord is evidently not
tion, but from the Lord
er room—the pattern
observers in the later
3). At a minimum, the
apostle is in contact with other apostles and writing bits of their oral history.

In my judgment Hebrews is from Paul and was definitely written before the destruction of the temple in A.D. 70.[25] Referring to the earthly teachings and trials of Jesus, this book confirms the observer-to-author process in Luke's preface. In Hebrews, the things "spoken by the Lord" came face to face from "them that heard him" (Hebrews 2:3).

Written between A.D. 50 and 63 Paul's messages to churches are a public block against changes. They refer to Christ's Davidic credentials, the Last Supper, Jewish and Roman trials, crucifixion, burial, and resurrection appearances. Because references to Christ's life are spontaneously given throughout the apostle's letters, they indicate that Paul had a working knowledge of the Lord's ministry. Further, the apostle merely refers to events rather than explaining them, expecting his readers to understand incidental references to the career of the Savior.

This point is pivotal in understanding why the apostle does not more often name Jesus as his source. A common body of knowledge makes powerful allusions possible without the clumsy ritual of naming the Lord and designating a given teaching. Today's public writings, for example, are filled with catchphrases on human rights without naming the Constitution or the Fifth or Fourteenth Amendments. Similarly, Paul's direct references to Christ show that there is a constant between-the-lines appeal to Christ's authoritative message when the Savior's words are loosely paraphrased or even condensed as concepts. Mentioning Christ as source could indicate apostolic revelation instead of Jesus' Jewish ministry, but major doctrinal revelations were well known and openly described (Galatians 1–2). So when Paul names the Lord for authority, the apostle alerts modern readers to look for words or precepts possibly given during Christ's preaching in Israel.

PAUL'S DIRECT CITATIONS OF JESUS

Paul's intent to quote or rephrase teachings from Jesus' mortal ministry is clearer in some examples than others. While the more skeptical subtract a half dozen of the traditional fourteen letters, most of Paul's important paraphrases of Jesus are in the earlier books not generally challenged: Romans, 1 Corinthians, and 1 Thessalonians. My approach, however, is documentary, relying on second-century manuscript evidence and second- and third-century writings, and I judge that Paul wrote all of the traditional fourteen letters.

First Corinthians 15:3–7

The microgospel of 1 Corinthians has already been discussed, with Paul's retrospect on first teaching his converts "that which I also received" about Christ's atonement and resurrection. By mentioning the Lord's appearance to Peter, James, and the Galilean eleven, Paul discloses major sources of information, and it is known that he had contact with them. This appeal to firsthand evidence indicates reliable oral history, though Paul might have possessed early lists of resurrection appearances. Luke's Gospel also contains the first appearances on Paul's list—to Peter and then to the Twelve (Luke 24:33–36). Moreover, part of "that which I also received" was "that Christ died for our sins according to the scriptures." This wording is close to Christ's own explanations in Luke on how the suffering and resurrection fulfilled scripture (Luke 24:26–27, 45–46). This also connects with Paul's Corinthian narrative of the Lord's words in the upper room—"my body, which is broken for you" (1 Corinthians 11:24). "Died for our sins" agrees with the synoptic account of the Last Supper (Mark 14:24; Luke 22:20) but is closest to Matthew's wording of the cup representing Christ's blood "shed for many for the remission of sins" (Matthew 26:28). Not only does Paul testify that Church leaders agree on Christ's sacrificial atonement but the apostle may be relaying the Lord's own words.

First Corinthians 11:23–25

As detailed earlier, in 1 Corinthians 11 Paul reviews Christ's actions and words in establishing the sacrament and says, these "I have received of the Lord." Because Paul's account is so particularized, he is likely presenting narration originating from the apostles rather than from personal revelation. He is tapping the synoptic record at an early point, with Christ's words in establishing the sacrament almost identical to those appearing later in Luke's Gospel: "This is my body, which is broken for you: this do in remembrance of me. . . . This cup is the new testament in my blood" (1 Corinthians 11:24–25; see also Luke 22:19–20). This correlation indicates either careful memorization or a document. Luke's preface explains that such words were obtained by his contact with those present at the Last Supper. Yet Paul wrote them down much earlier as common knowledge, "received" in the same process as the apostolic testimony of the Resurrection that Paul relayed in the same letter.

First Corinthians 7:10–11, 25

The frequent possibility that Christ's words are behind Paul's words is shown when the apostle gives his own command but quickly clarifies that it is really the command of the Lord: "Let not the wife depart from her husband . . . and let not the husband put away his wife." Between these two directives there is a caution about remarriage not necessarily from Jesus, because Paul jots ideas within ideas. As he does in the passage on the sacrament, the apostle gives an early form of synoptic teachings. These interrelated Gospels summarize Jesus' direction on divorce, with Luke lacking a context but Matthew and Mark reporting the situation when Jesus answered the Pharisees' question on the subject. Only Matthew gives a permitted divorce initiative for males in cases of adultery, and only Mark gives a generalized rule against divorce for men and also women (Mark 10:11–12). Paul's dual instruction from the Lord resembles the male-female warning in Mark. Finally, Paul drops the question of divorce and addresses the problem of when to marry, about which the apostle remarks, "I have no commandment of the Lord" (1 Corinthians 7:25). The four Gospels are also silent on this point, which underlines Paul's broad knowledge in directly citing Jesus—when the letters directly refer to Christ's teachings, we usually find the equivalent words of Jesus in the Gospels. This practice suggests that the apostle designed his Church messages to remind Christians of a fairly defined body of information about the Lord.[26]

First Corinthians 9:14

The New Testament contains several equivalent command terms. Paul uses one of them in a long answer to faultfinding Corinthians as he insists that he has the right to be supported as a missionary but does not demand it: "Even so hath the Lord ordained that they which preach the gospel should live of the gospel" (1 Corinthians 9:14). Paul first quoted Old Testament scripture on support of the priests and then evidently added the directions of Jesus about missionaries. These words broadly summarize the charge to the Seventy to rely on the people for food (Luke 10:5–7) and the short form of this same instruction to the Twelve in Matthew (10:10), with only a terse suggestion in Mark (6:8). But Paul's main argument is the authority of the apostleship (1 Corinthians 9:1)—he is probably appealing to knowledge that Jesus directed support for the Twelve, as indicated in Matthew, where Christ's missionary instructions close by saying that he "made an end of commanding his twelve disciples" (11:1).

First Thessalonians 4:15–5:2; 2 Thessalonians 2:1–15

"For this we say unto you by the word of the Lord" opens a series of Thessalonian parallels to Jesus' most featured discourse in the Gospels, the prophecy of the Second Coming and of extended events that would precede it. On the Mount of Olives the original Twelve asked about the time of Christ's return. The importance of Jesus' long answer is shown by every synoptic Gospel reporting it in detail, though Matthew's version has more words and components, plus several long parables afterward that were part of the Savior's response.

Paul's first letter to the Thessalonians unwittingly fed expectations of an early second coming in explaining the accompanying resurrection. So Paul wrote again to clarify prior events. Both letters follow distinct blocks of material in Jesus' Olivet discourse. These correlations show that the introductory "by the word of the Lord" really means his known teachings. "By" correctly translates the Greek preposition *en,* usually a simple "in" in the sense of location, but the New Testament very often displays an "instrumental" meaning—here "by means of the word of the Lord." The context of dependence is so strong that the New Jerusalem Bible clarifies the idea: "We can tell you this from the Lord's own teaching" (1 Thessalonians 4:15).

A broad pattern links Matthew 24 to the Thessalonian letters. Paul's first epistle to the Thessalonians counters their confusion on personal immortality by describing what would come: "For the Lord himself shall descend from heaven . . . with the trump of God" (1 Thessalonians 4:16), which follows Matthew's version of the Olivet prophecy: "They shall see the Son of man coming in the clouds of heaven . . . with a great sound of a trumpet" (24:30–31). Although the trumpet is mentioned only in Matthew, it is part of detail shared with Mark on the angels calling forth God's "elect" from heaven and earth when Christ appears (Matthew 24:30–31; Mark 13:26–27). Paul uses this as the essential message: "Then we which are alive and remain shall be caught up together with them in the clouds, to meet the Lord in the air" (1 Thessalonians 4:17). Paul continues by reminding the Thessalonians that discussion of "the times and the seasons" is unnecessary: "For yourselves know perfectly that the day of the Lord so cometh as a thief in the night" (1 Thessalonians 5:1–2). Though Luke has this comparison elsewhere (12:39–40), the Olivet discourse begins with questions on the time of the coming and ends in Matthew with several parables, one of which pictures the thief coming in the most unexpected vigil (24:43–44). In each synoptic Gospel, Jesus closes the prophecy with the warning to stay awake and "watch," adding the counter example of drunkenness in Matthew and Luke. And Paul closes his minidiscourse by these verbal reflections of "watch," adding that drunkenness is for the worldly (1 Thessalonians 5:4–7). The sequence of the synoptic prophecy and Paul's survey is the same. And Paul starts with "the word of the Lord" and reminds them that they already "know perfectly" how the appearance of Christ will surprise the world. It seems the basic Olivet discourse was available to Paul and his converts, probably in written form because of the duplicated detail and order, together with several striking words. Luke's "unawares" (21:34) is the same word in Greek as Paul's "sudden" (1 Thessalonians 5:3), though the idea is vivid in each of the triple Gospels. Significant parallels to Paul's writings appear in more than one Gospel or in Matthew alone.

Second Thessalonians settles the false expectation of Christ's quick return, and evidence of Paul's authorship does not lag far behind that of the first letter. Though Paul's follow-up letter is questioned, that debate has much to do with academic shock at the vivid picture of Satan's approaching power. To correct false enthusiasm for an immediate Second Coming, the apostle again parallels the Olivet prophecy for major events preceding the Lord's return. Thus Paul's second letter to the Thessalonians concentrates on the era of wickedness that Jesus predicted before coming again.

Removing some important misconceptions will highlight the parallels. First, Paul's labels for the coming evil power are too spectacular for mere mortals—the high titles for the ruling "man of sin . . . the son of perdition" (2 Thessalonians 2:3) resemble terminology for Satan at that period, and they should be seen as naming God's chief competitor behind the scenes. Second, Paul's image of the arrogant pretender in God's temple has little to do with the Jerusalem temple, which was destroyed two decades after the apostle wrote. Paul has the temple takeover last until Christ's return, which he insists is not in the near future (2 Thessalonians 2:3–8). Satan aims to possess not one building but all of Christ's church, which is regularly called

God's temple in Paul's letters and early Christian literature (Ephesians 2:21).[27]

As Paul explains what must precede the Second Coming, the parallels are striking, especially in Matthew. Though conservative commentators tend to see a compressed period of evil just before the Second Coming, Christ in Matthew predicts the era of "false prophets" right after the apostles were killed (24:9–11) and restates the point by positioning "false Christs, and false prophets" right after the first-century fall of Jerusalem (24:24). Then "iniquity shall abound" (24:12), and Paul uses the same word for the beginning of fulfillment in his day: "the mystery of iniquity doth already work" (2 Thessalonians 2:7).

So Paul follows the substance and timetable of the Olivet prophecy. With allowance for Paul's imagery, the processes are the same: "Many," Jesus said, would aspire to take his place, "saying, I am Christ; and shall deceive many" (Matthew 24:5; see also Mark 13:6; Luke 21:8); the evil one, Paul said, would aspire to take the place of God, "shewing himself that he is God" (2 Thessalonians 2:4). Paul's forthcoming "signs and lying wonders" (2 Thessalonians 2:9) match Christ's predicted "signs and wonders" from counterfeit prophets in the Olivet prophecy (Matthew 24:24; Mark 13:22).

This does not exhaust the interplay of words and ideas between Matthew 24 and the Thessalonian correspondence. They are full counterparts in event and stage, once it is seen that Paul has extracted the religious future without repeating Christ's extensive commentary on persecution, wars, and signs of His coming. These earliest known letters of the apostle were sent about twenty years after Jesus outlined the stages between the first and the second comings. And Paul quite certainly used a full record of the prophecy corresponding to the present Matthew 24. It is even possible that Matthew's Gospel was already written and carried by certain leaders. Moreover, the Olivet discourse is not dependent on Paul, for he introduced the advent theme by relying on the existing "word of the Lord."

Romans 14:14

Paul appeals for more charity for others among Jewish converts with rigid dietary convictions and then insists, "I know, and am persuaded by the Lord Jesus, that there is nothing unclean of itself." The apostle adds that a thing is unclean if one thinks it is so; on its face his explanation of the idea he attributes to the Lord. "Nothing unclean of itself" is quite close to Mark's report of the Savior's judgments on ritual purity: "There is nothing from without a man, that entering into him can defile him" (7:15). The parallel is closer in Greek, where *defile* is the verb meaning "to make unclean or common." Current translations of Romans 14:14 favor "persuaded in the Lord Jesus," though the Greek preposition *en* ("in") is regularly instrumental, meaning here "through" or "because of the Lord Jesus." In any event, Paul's idea is quite clear—reflection on Jesus' viewpoint, which is learned through Jesus' words, has convinced the apostle that objects do not cause impurity of themselves. Paul could be brief on this sensitive subject only if it was well-known that the Lord took a strong stand on over-done purification. In this central clash of opinion between Paul and defenders of the Mosaic dietary law, one of Paul's weapons was paraphrasing Jesus.

Romans 12:14–19; 14:10

In addition to the Olivet prophecy and John's discourse on the Last Supper, one very significant address should resonate in New Testament letters—the Sermon on the Mount. It has the lead location in Matthew as Jesus' declaration of Christian standards for those who became "disciples" (Matthew 5:1) by repenting and accepting the "gospel of the kingdom" (Matthew 4:23). For this purpose, restatements would be necessary for waves of converts. The teachings in Matthew's chapters 5 through 7 are primarily found in the Sermon on the Plain in Luke 6, but other fragments appear in Luke in different settings. This arrangement leads some to assume that Matthew assembled scattered sayings of Jesus. Yet Luke is a skilled writer by ancient standards that stressed logical as much as chronological order. For the interest of the reader, he perhaps reported a concise version of this important sermon and placed some sections elsewhere by topic. Or did the Master Teacher use repetition so regularly that both views are true—an original broad manifesto of principles followed by systematic segments in various teaching moments? His unsurpassed mind was perfectly capable of organizing an effective moral overview instead of leaving that task to chance. And a unified image of this superb sermon emerges through the lens of the letters, particularly Romans: "The ethical admonitions of this and other New Testament letters, whether Paul's or not, bear a marked resemblance to the ethical teaching of Christ recorded in the Gospels. They are based, in fact, on what Paul calls 'the law of Christ' (Gal. 6:2; cf. 1 Cor. 9:21). In particular, an impressive list of parallels can be drawn up between Romans 12:3–13:14 and the Sermon on the Mount. While none of our canonical Gospels existed at this time, the teaching of Christ recorded in them was current among the churches—certainly in oral form, and perhaps also in the form of written summaries."[28]

Paul closes his epistle to the Romans with several chapters of personal instruction instead of the briefer admonitions found in other church letters. But Romans is the one epistle sent to an important area where Paul had not preached. That explains his obvious drive to review authoritative standards with Saints who had not heard him. The closing chapters of Romans use Christ's teachings and Christ's example in several ways; the strongest of Paul's indirect allusions to Christ's teachings, the summary of the Lord's laws of love, is recorded in Romans 13:8–10.

The last part of Romans 12 corresponds to the last part of Matthew 5 with a series of close relationships on the subject of nonretaliation. Although some content also reflects Luke's Sermon on the Plain, the style of expression follows Jesus' as reported by Matthew. Paul opens the subject with: "Bless them which persecute you: bless, and curse not" (Romans 12:14). In the longer traditional text of Matthew, the parallel is: "Bless them that curse you . . . and pray for them which . . . persecute you" (5:44), which is a bit closer to Paul's key words than Luke's similar report, "Bless them that curse you, and pray for them which despitefully use you" (Luke 6:28). In Romans 12:17 the apostle restates this theme, which is clearer in literal translation: "Returning evil for evil to none, providing good things before all men." "Providing good things" has a close parallel in 1 Thessalonians: "See that none render evil for evil . . . but ever follow that which is good, both among yourselves, and to all men" (5:15). In a word, repay those doing you evil,

not with evil, but with good. Matthew has the close model
for the above negative command: "Resist not evil" (Matthew
5:39); this form is lacking in Luke, though both Gospels give
examples from Jesus on how to return good for evil. And some
key words of Matthew's version are in this section of Romans
following the Sermon on the Mount. Paul's "live peaceably"
(Romans 12:18) could also be translated "bring peace" and definitely correlates with Jesus' beatitude for "peacemakers"
(Matthew 5:9); Paul's warning against anger (Romans 12:19) is
closely related in Greek to Jesus' warning against anger
(Matthew 5:22). This subtle coloring supplements the close
comparisons to a well-defined section of the Sermon on the
Mount.

Luke and Matthew place Jesus' caution against judging near
the end of their versions. Paul uses a similar location and a
form close to Christ's speech: "But why dost thou judge thy
brother? or why dost thou set at nought thy brother? for we
shall all stand before the judgment seat of Christ" (Romans
14:10). As already discussed, these questions are embedded in
a long correction about being overcritical because of Jewish
dietary rules, with Jesus cited on nothing being unclean of itself
(Romans 14:14). In this chapter on attitude, the Sermon on the
Mount parallel is strongly felt: "Judge not, that ye be not
judged. For with what judgment ye judge, ye shall be judged"
(Matthew 7:1–2). This phrasing corresponds to Paul's dual form
just quoted—caution on judging now, as well as a prophecy of
future judgment. But in Luke's pattern, one technically will not
be judged if he does not judge (6:37), a step away from the
coming judgment found in Matthew and Romans. Moreover,
Paul confronts his readers with questions in the same style
as Jesus, who follows "Judge not" with cross-examination on
why we see only the faults of others (Matthew 7:3–5). Paul's
parallels conform in content and wording to two sections of
Matthew's report of the Sermon on the Mount.

Romans 13:8–10

"Love one another: for he that loveth another hath fulfilled
the law. . . . and if there be any other commandment, it is
briefly comprehended in this saying, namely, Thou shalt love
thy neighbour as thyself. Love worketh no ill to his neighbour:

therefore love is the fulfilling of the law" (Romans 13:8–10). Though Paul does not name Christ in this passage, he reasons from the teachings of Jesus that love is the overarching precept. Paul's own evaluation of love begins and ends this pointed passage on charity: "love is the fulfilling of the law." *Fulfilling* in Greek essentially means "completion"—love is the purpose of all revealed laws and the crowning result of obeying them. Then Paul backs up this main concept with two silent citations of Jesus. In full form, Romans 13:8–10 names five of the Ten Commandments, adding that loving one's neighbor permeates the rest.[29] The apostle did not need to identify the Savior's use of this Old Testament imperative. Nor did he need to mention Christ behind his second supporting saying: "Love one another" was given at the Last Supper as a "new commandment" by which all would "know that ye are my disciples" (John 13:34–35).

Although John's Gospel was not yet circulated, the eleven apostles at the Last Supper were morally obligated to share Christ's instruction on this supreme principle. This was done afterward in the letters of Peter (1 Peter 1:22) and John (1 John 3:11). But those faithful stewards no doubt declared Christ's "new commandment" to "love one another" in the churches long before Paul used those phrases in Romans. And the same is true for "love thy neighbour as thyself," Jesus' revitalized injunction from Leviticus 19:18. In Mark's Gospel, Jesus said no commandments were more important than loving God and loving neighbor (12:28–31). But Matthew reported the more profound perspective found Romans. Jesus had concluded: "On these two commandments hang all the law and the prophets" (Matthew 22:40). Jesus did not merely list the two in top position: he said the entire law reflected or expressed them. That is Paul's meaning in explaining the second commandment: his Greek says literally that "every other commandment is summed up" in the saying to love one's neighbor as oneself. The summary of charity in the epistle to the Romans brings together Christ's two main instructions on love.

PAUL AS A HISTORIAN OF JESUS

The preceding eight examples are segments of letters, and some include several instances of Paul referring to Christ's teaching. These verbal-doctrinal parallels are usually accompanied by an express reference to the Lord, but such a reference is not always required for us to be confident that Paul relies on sources from Christ. Today's writer may quote Shakespeare and squarely say so or without much ado quote phrases that the aware will recognize. Thus Paul's pattern of openly quoting the Lord should alert us to many silent references to Jesus' teachings that were commonly known and appear in our Gospels. In fact, Paul's mention of Jesus does not always indicate him as a source. Paul may name the Lord because the apostle speaks with Christ's authority (1 Corinthians 14:37) or because the Lord's life is a model to follow (Romans 15:3–7). The preceding eight examples are impressive partly because they name the Lord or an earlier source and partly because they mirror Jesus' teaching with some complexity. Shared words may reflect only a common culture; however, relationships are shown not by terms alone but by shared phrases, sentence syntax, and sequence and uniqueness of idea. After that, the direction of the relationship must be assessed. And Paul answers that question several times by insisting that knowledge of Jesus has come down to him.

Recent publications show how much this subject interests religious scholars, but I have cut my own path and will simply compare another researcher's conclusions: "We have ascertained over twenty-five instances where Paul certainly or probably makes reference or allusion to a saying of Jesus. In addition, we have tabulated over forty possible echoes of a saying of Jesus. These are distributed throughout all of the Pauline letters, though 1 Corinthians and Romans contain the most. . . . Echoes of Jesus' sayings are discernible in all the major themes of Paul's theology. . . . Paul also provides hints of his knowledge of the narrative tradition of Jesus' passion, his healing ministry, his welcoming sinners, his life of poverty and humble service, his character and other aspects."[30]

In short, there is a "Gospel according to Paul" embedded in his letters. Like Luke's, it stems from contact with the Galilean "eyewitnesses" (Luke 1:2), who answered Jesus' call, marvelled at his miracles, and listened intently to his public sermons and private dialogues. The historic ministry of prominent apostles to Mediterranean lands shows both zeal toward and capability at communication.[31] Were they articulate enough to carry knowledge of Jesus to new areas but lacking in power to write memoirs of him or see that such were written? Paul knew the apostles who knew Jesus. And Paul's presentation of Jesus' life and teachings in his letters has the scope, if not the detail, of the other Gospels. This apostle's comments combine to make up an abstract of Jesus' ministry. It is unedited, but it forms a blueprint of the synoptic Gospels, reflecting their own stress on the final days—the sacrament as the key to the meaning of Christ's suffering, the condemnation and his crucifixion, the reality of his resurrection, with names of witnesses to whom he appeared. Paul's framework includes Christ's comments on Jewish practices of ritual cleanliness and on divorce as well as a fragment of Jesus' missionary instruction to the first Twelve. And there are salient parts of the Sermon on the Mount, the laws of love, and Christ's testimony of his return in power as part of two main segments of the Olivet prophecy. For details one reads the Gospels, but Paul authenticates their overall narrative of Jesus and his basic teachings.[32]

The early "Gospel according to Paul" can be compiled as a document because the apostle occasionally says he is reporting what Jesus said or did, furnishing written evidence that is far stronger than literary inferences behind widely accepted theories like the precise limits of assumed source "Q," the priority of Mark, or the early oral period with highly volatile images of Jesus. The "Gospel according to Paul" is also historically sound because it is datable. Paul's explicit references to Christ's teachings begin as early as his correspondence is preserved—in the Thessalonian letters from about A.D. 50, followed by recurrent references to Jesus' ministry in 1 Corinthians and the attributions and allusions in Romans about A.D. 58. Furthermore, Paul's first inside knowledge of the Jewish Jesus came much earlier than the apostle's first known expressions of that knowledge. It is glibly said that Paul transformed the historic Jesus into the divine Christ, but the problem is in how experts frame the issue rather than in Paul's own records. The apostle's testimony is consistent—he first learned of the resurrected Christ through the vision on the road to Damascus (Acts 9; 1

Corinthians 9:1). This event of about A.D. 35 marked the beginning of a natural education about Jesus for a man of more than usual curiosity. The understanding Paul received next came from the first disciples—they taught Paul about the Last Supper (1 Corinthians 11:23) and about Christ's first appearances as a resurrected being (1 Corinthians 15:3). So Paul's letters document the churchwide spread of the basics of the synoptic Gospels before A.D. 50. Whether the authors of the Gospels wrote soon or long after Paul does not affect the central story or main teachings. In fact, all New Testament Gospels were not necessarily composed after Paul sent the epistles. Paul's letters and the Gospels produce comparable versions of what Jesus said and did. Whether information available to Paul was preserved in manuscript or in shared memory or in both does not matter much for the big picture, but some of Paul's matching patterns seem too intricate for memory alone.

MATTHEW, JAMES, AND THE BOOK OF MORMON

Matthew unexpectedly emerges in my analysis with the greatest number of specific equivalents to Paul's words of the Lord. In the New Testament lists of the apostles, only one appears by profession, "Matthew the publican" (Matthew 10:3). His career in Galilee required multiple languages, as well as practice in accounting and making reports. Such facts are impressive when he is early named as author of a Gospel. Moreover, the writings of the Christian historian Eusebius record an amateurish but guileless investigation of what the Church knew about the writing of the Gospels while John the apostle was still available at the end of the century. Papias, an early second-century bishop, talked to the elders of the previous generation, including John, who seems to have been the apostle, because Papias calls him the Lord's disciple, a known title of the apostle (John 21:24). This bishop's goal was to learn anything handed down from Christ's apostles, and among those attracting his interest, he names Peter, John, and Matthew.[33]

Papias said this about the publican-apostle: "So then, Matthew compiled the oracles in the Hebrew language; but everyone interpreted them as he was able."[34] Commentaries widely discount this early reference because Matthew's Gospel seems to have been written in Greek rather than translated from Hebrew or its cousin language of Aramaic. Details cannot be discussed here, but the early Church went through a Hebrew period before reaching out to the Greek-speaking eastern Mediterranean. These two stages are reflected accurately in the quotation from Papias—"interpreted" is the usual Greek word for "translated," apparently indicating that the many gentile converts had difficulty reading Matthew's original record in Hebrew or Aramaic, which contained the "oracles" (sing., *logion*), a term that in the Greek New Testament means "sayings" in the sense of revealed or sacred words. Paul and Barnabas opened the era of gentile predominance with their mission to Cyprus and central Asia Minor soon after A.D. 44 (Acts 13–14). The publican-apostle may well have kept records of Christ's ministry in a Hebrew dialect before a Greek version was composed for gentile Christians when their needs became intense by midcentury. Someone genuinely bilingual could start fresh and produce a Greek record without obvious Semiticisms. Most current critics discount Matthew as the writer or rewriter but on virtually ideological grounds: "The most powerful reason today for denying even the possibility of apostolic authorship is bound up with an entire array of antecedent judgments about the development of the gospel tradition, about the shape of the history of the church in the first century, about the evidence of redactional changes, and much more."[35]

Evidence of early records of Jesus is not strange to Book of Mormon readers, where the resurrected Savior said on his first appearance: "And I command you that ye shall write these sayings after I am gone" (3 Nephi 16:4). This instruction was repeated throughout his American advent: "Write the things which ye have seen and heard, save it be those which are forbidden" (3 Nephi 27:23). And much as he did in the early ministry recorded in Matthew, the descended Christ first proclaimed his divinity, called for repentance and baptism for entrance to "the kingdom of God," and immediately afterward gave the law of the kingdom, the American counterpart to the Sermon on the Mount. As is well known, the Book of Mormon (3 Nephi 12–14) correlates with Matthew's version (Matthew 5–7), though it is independent in many verses. Sidney B. Sperry long ago warned against assuming one sermon: "The text delivered to the Nephites did not in all respects follow that given in Palestine."[36] Despite this obvious fact, some continue to claim that the Book of Mormon cannot be ancient because it adopts textual errors found in the King James Version. Though Joseph Smith evidently followed his Bible when satisfied that it mirrored Christ's message to the new world, phrase-specific translation is not indicated in Joseph Smith's discourses, where he shows a broad interest in scriptural doctrine instead of textual technicalities. Indeed, many Bible translators today favor idea equivalents over literalism, as consistently illustrated by the New Jerusalem Bible or the Revised English Bible. And as we have already mentioned, Jesus' most important message must have been given in various forms during the Jewish ministry, a significant insight that Joseph Smith added to the Sermon on the Mount in his inspired version of Matthew: "Now these are the words which Jesus taught his disciples that they should say unto the people" (JST Matthew 7:1). Parts rephrased by the Master or his disciples would easily collect slight variations of equal authority. For instance, early Greek manuscripts and early church writers are divided between Jesus commanding no anger, the Book of Mormon reading, or the traditional no anger "without a cause" (Matthew 5:22). Did the Savior give both forms, one a clarification of the other? Because no first-century Greek manuscripts of the Gospels are known, it is intellectual cheating to claim to give Christ's original words by choosing between later manuscript readings in Matthew.

Yet the Book of Mormon supports the structural integrity of this sermon as recorded in Matthew. Stated another way, the Sermon on the Mount in the first Gospel is a significant test of the Nephite record. If a "Matthew-editor" created a late, non-historical speech, as some experts suppose, one might argue that Joseph Smith copied a faulty model. But Paul's letters in the fifties are the test. We have seen Romans 12 reproduce the thoughts and significant vocabulary of a section near the close of Matthew 5; Romans 14 does the same thing with the fault-finding warnings at the beginning of Matthew 7. In addition, the epistle of James paraphrases many more thoughts and lines of the mountainside sermon in Matthew. For authenticity of James, one can choose between the affirmative judgment of ancient Christians who were highly sensitive about forgeries, or modern assumptions that a lack of early quotation by name throws doubt on its authorship. According to the early historian Eusebius, the author of the New Testament epistle is James, the brother of the Lord, and there is very early information on his martyrdom in A.D. 62.[37] A number of scholars accept this identification, are impressed with the absence of Jewish-Gentile problems, and therefore think James composed his letter before the beginning of Paul's gentile missions in about 44. Thus James' extensive use of the Sermon on the Mount shows it was available in some form even before Paul wrote the epistle to the Romans. James shows strong individuality and piety, with constant use of the Old and New Testaments: "There are more parallels in this epistle than in any other New Testament book to the teaching of our Lord in the gospels."[38]

The goal of James is clarifying the righteousness that is the thrust of the Sermon on the Mount. Though not naming Jesus as his source, this quotation-oriented author heavily uses Jesus' teachings found in the synoptic Gospels. About two dozen equivalents impressed W. D. Davies, and about three dozen impressed Peter Davids.[39] Two dozen from their combined lists have survived my judgment, based on correlations of phrasing and distinctive idea, and they follow the trend observed by Davids—James reflects the structure of Matthew's Sermon on the Mount more than Luke's Sermon on the Plain.[40] In my calculations, the distinctive verse-resemblances between James and the Gospels fall into these categories: thirteen are shared by Matthew and Luke; eight unique to Matthew; two shared by Matthew and Mark; one unique to Luke.[41] James does use some striking language found in the short sermon in Luke, but more often he follows Christ's language in Matthew. For instance, there is close quotation by James (5:12) of the Lord's command (Matthew 5:33–37) not to make daily honesty depend on special oaths—not to swear by heaven or by earth but to make promises with a simple yes or no. And James closely reflects Christ's beatitude on the merciful receiving mercy (Matthew 5:7), switching to negative phrasing that those showing no mercy will receive judgment instead of mercy (James 2:13).

What emerges is the early authority of the extensive

discourse in Matthew over Luke's compressed counterpart. In my calculations, twenty verses correlate in James and Matthew's Sermon on the Mount: ten in chapter 5, three in chapter 6, and seven in chapter 7.[42] So James has used representative sections of Christ's full sermon in Matthew. How much of the epistle reflects the sermon? The answer is implicit in Massey Shepherd's conclusion that James depended on Matthew "for the presentation of his themes."[43] But these views should be read with awareness that James cites little else in Matthew but the Sermon on the Mount: "The number and extent of the Matthean parallels to James . . . are impressive; for they relate to every single section of the Epistle, and to almost every major theme."[44]

Though current scholars tend to see only "the unwritten Jesus tradition" behind these correlations,[45] James uses words, distinctive thoughts, and selection from all parts of the longer discourse. More than spontaneous memory is at work here. Scholars favor oral tradition because of the loose nature of many parallels. But casual rephrasing is also consistent with using a well-known record. Structure and particulars in James indicate he is basically following the same version of the Sermon on the Mount used in the Gospel of Matthew. This and the Romans-Matthew correlations make memory alone an unlikely tool for these complex agreements of language, concept, and structure. Because Paul and James independently point to a record of the sermon made before their epistles were written, credibility is added to Papias' information that Matthew kept a Jewish-language record of the "oracles," the "authoritative words" of the Lord. The Savior's thorough explanation of the moral law of his kingdom was preserved in historical systems on both hemispheres. There is great integrity in the literary structures and the doctrines within them in the Book of Mormon.

PAUL'S WITNESS IN SUMMARY

Paul's visions of Christ become an either-or trap for those who claim the apostle paid no attention to the Lord's earthly life. But at every period of writing, the epistles speak of both the mortal ministry and the exalted Jesus. A middle example precedes the Savior's words on the sacrament: "Be ye followers of me, even as I also am of Christ" (1 Corinthians 11:1). Paul has just explained his empathy for others in a context of exempting Greeks from the Jewish dietary code and here makes the point that he is following the doctrinal model of his Master. Christ's example has not faded in the next sentence: "Hold to the traditions, just as I delivered them to you" (1 Corinthians 11:2; literal translation mine). Paul soon repeats "deliver" in restating his earlier public preaching about the Savior's appearances after the Resurrection: "For I delivered unto you . . . that which I also received" (1 Corinthians 15:3). Such language throughout 1 Corinthians calls up both doctrines and deeds of Jesus—in chapter 15, atonement for sin as well as resurrection of the body. And Paul insists on common preaching: "Therefore whether it were I or they, so we preach, and so ye believed" (1 Corinthians 15:11). This fifties headline reveals corporate teaching about the close of Jesus' mortal ministry—Jesus' suffering at the end and his physical return afterwards.

The convert-apostle periodically draws on general knowledge of the man of Galilee: "Now I Paul myself beseech you by the meekness and gentleness of Christ" (2 Corinthians 10:1). Moreover, the apostle's later letters repeat the Corinthian pattern of defending doctrine by the Lord's known earthly words. Nonetheless, any survey of Paul faces modern redefinitions of his writings. As earlier mentioned, there is a heresy-resistant list of the Christian books recognized at about A.D. 170, and its partially preserved text accepts all but one of the New Testament letters attributed to Paul. This early list includes Ephesians, probably written during Paul's Roman imprisonment about 62, and the messages to Timothy but a few years afterward.[46] Like 1 Corinthians, Ephesians reviews what converts first heard, though Paul is more general in what seems to be an area letter. Christians had been called out of the world—they had "learned Christ" with complete directness: "Ye have heard him, and have been taught by him, as the truth is in Jesus" (Ephesians 4:20–21). Paul means they know Christ's teachings, because the apostle follows with standards of putting away lust and anger that correspond to those recorded in Matthew 5 (Ephesians 4:22, 31), and with the message, similar to that in Matthew 6, that Saints should freely forgive because God's forgiveness is freely offered them (Ephesians 4:32). The expressed and unexpressed rule of Paul's ministry is that faithfulness is measured by "wholesome words, even the words of our Lord Jesus Christ" (1 Timothy 6:3). They are always in the background and are readily brought forward when stumbling Saints need explanation or refutation.

The corporate apostleship carried the burden of preserving authentic knowledge of the Lord. Paul is early, accessible, and an example of the teaching methods of his colleagues. He periodically makes Christ the teacher, giving glimpses of the Savior's ministry to inspire or solve problems. This documented process has no time slot for anonymous teachers tinkering with the real Jesus. The New Testament Church operates by administrative and doctrinal authority. Most of the Galilean Twelve lived through Paul's period, and when observed, they are using Christ's earthly ministry as the norm in conversion and correction, though their preserved letters are few. James essentially adapts the Sermon on the Mount. And other apostles stress Christ's ministry, as shown by Peter's challenge to "follow his steps" (1 Peter 2:21) and John's repeated segments of the Last Supper discourse (1 John). While the apostles lived, wandering preachers with wandering stories were not in control. The full origin of proto-Gospels and present ones is not known, but by using facts about Jesus that reliably came to him, Paul has inserted datable history in his letters. These show that the mid-century Church had stable and specific knowledge of Jesus' major teachings—that its testimony that Jesus was the divine Christ was already firm and founded on broad information from witnesses who walked with him.

NOTES

1. My memories of Sidney B. Sperry reach back nearly this far, to his going out of his way to welcome a searching student to Brigham Young University and taking time for counseling and personal Hebrew tutoring in years afterward. He left a legacy of commitment to research and faith in the restored gospel.

2. See the weaving of recollections in Gerald Parshall, "Theirs But to Do and Die," in *U.S. News and World Report,* 23 May 1994, 71–81.

3. Donald Guthrie, *New Testament Introduction,* 4th ed. rev. (Downers Grove, Ill.: InterVarsity Press, 1990), 128–29.

4. See Eusebius, *Ecclesiastical History* 3.24.5–8, for specific earlier information on this point.

5. For the dating of John's Gospel near the end of the first century, see Richard Lloyd Anderson, "The First Presidency of the Early Church: Their Lives and Epistles," *Ensign,* Aug. 1988, 20, and references.

6. Stephen E. Robinson, "Bible Scholarship," in *Encyclopedia of Mormonism,* ed. Daniel Ludlow, 4 vols. (New York: Macmillan, 1992), 1:112.

7. For approximate dates in Paul's life, see Richard Lloyd Anderson, *Understanding Paul* (Salt Lake City: Deseret Book, 1983), 393–97.

8. Norman R. Petersen, "Introduction to the Gospels and Acts," *Harper's Bible Commentary* (San Francisco: Harper and Row, 1988), 948.

9. Joseph A. Fitzmyer, *A Christological Catechism,* 2d ed. (New York City: Paulist Press, 1991), 15.

10. Johannes Munck, *The Acts of the Apostles, The Anchor Bible* (Garden City, N.Y.: Doubleday, 1967), xxxiii–xxxiv.

11. Fitzmyer, *Christological Catechism,* 66.

12. Richard N. Soulen, *Handbook of Biblical Criticism,* 2d ed. (Atlanta: John Knox Press, 1981), 73.

13. Ibid., 165.

14. Fitzmyer, *Christological Catechism,* 21.

15. Ibid., 14.

16. Ibid., 23.

17. Ibid., 25.

18. Ibid.

19. Ibid.

20. "The Gospel according to" is the title formula in the manuscripts noted. For data on Luke and John, see Richard Lloyd Anderson, "The Testimony of Luke," in Kent P. Jackson and Robert L. Millet, *Studies in Scripture, Volume Five: The Gospels* (Salt Lake City: Deseret Book, 1986), 88. For data on Matthew, see Martin Hengel, *Studies in the Gospel of Mark* (Philadelphia: Fortress Press, 1985), 66 n.3.

21. Daniel J. Theron, *Evidence of Tradition* (Grand Rapids, Mich.: Baker Book, 1958), 111. Theron gives the full translation of the Muratorian Canon, which is well dated by reference to second-century individuals and shows Christian hostility to invented books by naming several and criticizing their heretical sources.

22. For specifics on contact with James, the Lord's brother, and others in Israel, see Anderson, "Testimony of Luke," 93–94.

23. Acts 12:1–2 gives the execution of James, John's brother, at just before the death of his persecutor, Herod Agrippa, which is dated at A.D. 44 in Josephus; for the stoning of James, the Lord's brother, soon after the death of the governor Festus at 62, see Eusebius, *Ecclesiastical History* 2.23; for the deaths of Peter and Paul near the end of Nero's

reign at 68, see Anderson, *Understanding Paul,* 362–65; for the historical ministry of John at the end of the century, see Irenaeus, *Against Heresies* 3.1.1, 3.3.4, and Anderson, "First Presidency of the Early Church," 20–21.

24. Obert C. Tanner, Lewis M. Rogers, and Sterling M. McMurrin, *Toward Understanding the New Testament* (Salt Lake City: Signature Books, 1990), 31.

25. See Anderson, *Understanding Paul,* 197–201, including the photograph of the last page of Romans in the earliest manuscript (second century) of Paul's letters, in which Hebrews is copied between Romans and 1 Corinthians.

26. Yet no record was made of all of the Lord's words, as the close of John's Gospel says. "It is more blessed to give than to receive" (Acts 20:35) is directly attributed to the Lord by Paul, though it does not appear in the Gospels. For non-Gospel words of Jesus, early citations are far more reliable than the postapostolic collections of sayings that were compiled and colored to support deviant doctrines.

27. For fuller discussion, see Anderson, *Understanding Paul,* 85–87.

28. F. F. Bruce, *The Letter of Paul to the Romans,* 2d ed. (Grand Rapids, Mich.: William B. Eerdmans Publishing, 1985), 212–13.

29. When the rich young ruler asked about requirements for salvation, Jesus quoted several of the Ten Commandments, those with social obligations. Although the three synoptic Gospels agree thus far, in Matthew Jesus adds the Leviticus 19:18 direction to love neighbor as self (Matthew 19:18–19). Paul does the same thing in the Romans passage under discussion, another of many ties to Matthew's Gospel.

30. Seyoon Kim, "Jesus, Sayings of," in Gerald F. Hawthorn and Ralph P. Martin, eds., *Dictionary of Paul and His Letters* (Downers Grove, Ill.: InterVarsity Press, 1993), 490. For the chart "Possible Echoes of Sayings of Jesus," see 481. The considerable recent bibliography on 491–92 shows that the topic of Paul's historical access to Jesus' ministry is to be taken seriously. For instance, the studies of David Wenham are listed, some of which have intriguing insights.

31. For comments on the writing environment of early Christianity, see Richard Lloyd Anderson, "Types of Christian Revelation," in Neal E. Lambert, ed., *Literature of Belief* (Provo, Utah: Religious Studies Center, Brigham Young University, 1981), 64–65.

32. For the similar judgment of a scholar trained in classical sources, see F. F. Bruce, *The New Testament Documents,* 5th rev. ed. (Grand Rapids, Mich.: William B. Eerdmans Publishing, 1987), chap. 6, "The Importance of Paul's Evidence," 76–79.

33. Eusebius had Papias' writing and quotes the material summarized here in *Ecclesiastical History* 3.39.1–4. Eusebius adds his own theory

that Papias names two Christians named John and could not have known
the apostle. Yet Papias lived in the area and period of the apostle.

34. Eusebius, *Ecclesiastical History* 3.39.16. The translation is literal and
agrees with my interpretation of the meaning of the Greek text; it comes
from the edition of Hugh Jackson Lawlor and John Ernest Oulton,
Eusebius (London: S.P.C.K., 1954), 1:101.

35. D. A. Carson, Douglas J. Moo, and Leon Morris, *An Introduction to the
New Testament* (Grand Rapids, Mich.: Zondervan Publishing, 1992), 73.

36. Sidney B. Sperry, *Our Book of Mormon* (Salt Lake City: Stevens and
Wallis, 1947), 185.

37. For the identification of Eusebius and his quotation of the much earlier
accounts of James' martyrdom, see Anderson, "First Presidency of the
Early Church," 18, 21.

38. Guthrie, *New Testament Introduction*, 729.

39. For lists of verses in James modeled on Jesus' teachings in the synoptic
Gospels, see W. D. Davies, *The Setting of the Sermon on the Mount*
(Cambridge: University Press, 1964), 402–3; and Peter H. Davids, *The
Epistle of James, New International Greek Testament Commentary* (Grand
Rapids, Mich.: William B. Eerdmans Publishing, 1982), 47–48.

40. See Davids, *Epistle of James*, 48: "Of the 36 parallels listed, 25 are with
the Sermon on the Mount and 3 others with the Sermon on the Plain."

41. *Matthew-Luke parallels:* James 1:2 with Matthew 5:11–12 and Luke 6:23;
James 1:5 with Matthew 7:7 and Luke 11:9; James 1:17 with Matthew 7:11
and Luke 11:13; James 1:22 with Matthew 7:24 and Luke 6:46–47; James
1:23 with Matthew 7:26 and Luke 6:49; James 2:5 with Matthew 5:3, 5
and Luke 6:20; James 3:12 with Matthew 7:16 and Luke 6:44–45; James
4:2 with Matthew 7:7 and Luke 11:9; James 4:9 with Matthew 5:4 and
Luke 6:25; James 4:10 with Matthew 23:12 and Luke 14:11 and 18:14;
James 4:11–12 with Matthew 7:1 and Luke 6:37; James 5:2 with Matthew
6:19–20 and Luke 12:33; James 5:10 with Matthew 5:11–12 and Luke 6:23.
Unique Matthew parallels: James 1:4 with Matthew 5:48; James 2:10 with
Matthew 5:19; James 2:13 with Matthew 5:7; James 3:18 with Matthew
5:9; James 4:8 with Matthew 5:8; James 4:13–14 with Matthew 6:34; James
5:9 with Matthew 5:22; James 5:12 with Matthew 5:34–37.
Matthew-Mark parallels: James 1:6 with Matthew 21:21 and Mark
11:23–24; James 2:8 with Matthew 22:39 and Mark 12:31.
Unique Luke parallel: James 5:1 with Luke 6:24–25.

42. See previous note for chapter numbers in Matthew.

43. Massey H. Shepherd Jr., "The Epistle of James and the Gospel of
Matthew," *Journal of Biblical Literature* 75 (1956): 47.

44. Ibid.

45. Davids, *Epistle of James*, 49.

46. See Theron, *Evidence of Tradition*, 111, and note 21 above.

CHAPTER TWO

PAUL'S EARNEST PURSUIT OF SPIRITUAL GIFTS

ROBERT C. FREEMAN

True disciples of the Lord in both former and latter days proclaim in a united voice that the gifts of the Spirit are among the chief distinguishing features of the true and living gospel of the Lord Jesus Christ. Through his teachings and the example of his life the ancient apostle Paul demonstrated the powerful influence of such endowments. Latter-day Saints desiring to enjoy a similar influence of spiritual gifts will be blessed by following the pattern set by this great disciple.

The doctrine of spiritual gifts constitutes an important theme of Paul's New Testament teachings. His writings relative to spiritual gifts are principally contained in 1 Corinthians. In chapter 12, Paul enumerated several of the chief gifts and outlined the principles associated with their use in Christ's church. In chapter 13, the apostle taught that all gifts must be exercised in concert with the preeminent gift of charity. Finally, in chapter 14, Paul explained the proper application of the gifts as he defined and compared certain gifts, primarily those of prophecy and of tongues.

Paul's enumeration of the spiritual gifts was meant to be illustrative, not comprehensive. Indeed, as Elder Bruce R. McConkie affirmed, "In the fullest sense, they [spiritual gifts] are infinite in number and endless in their manifestations."[1]

Paul's instruction to the Saints at Corinth corresponds with teachings conveyed to Latter-day Saints in Doctrine and Covenants 46:8–33 and in Moroni 10:8–18. It is noteworthy that Moroni's discourse on spiritual gifts was included among the

□ □ □ □ □

Robert C. Freeman is a teacher in the Church Educational System and resides in Gilbert, Arizona.

ancient American prophet's final words, effectively punctuating his mighty discourse.

"I WOULD NOT HAVE YOU IGNORANT"

The Corinthians were plagued by ignorance stemming from their preoccupation with material and immoral attractions and from their obeisance to false gods and idols (1 Corinthians 8:1–5). One measure of the importance of the Corinthian epistles is that they make up approximately 25 percent of Paul's New Testament writings.

Scholars have noted the difficulties Paul faced in broadcasting his message to the Saints in Corinth. As one writer observed, "Corinth was depraved. Going beyond the licentiousness of other trading cities and ports it lent its own name as the symbol of debauchery and corruption."[2] Paul indicated his frustration over the conditions in Corinth: "And I, brethren, could not speak unto you as unto spiritual, but as unto carnal, even as unto babes in Christ" (1 Corinthians 3:1).

Paul knew that a correct understanding of spiritual gifts would anchor the Saints as they sought to establish a stronghold of Christianity among the spiritually divided and morally malignant citizens of Corinth. Paul encouraged the Saints, "Even so ye, forasmuch as ye are zealous of spiritual gifts, seek that ye may excel to the edifying of the church" (1 Corinthians 14:12). By inviting all Saints to anxiously pursue such gifts, Paul rejected the theology of "spiritual elitism" as God's method of allocating spiritual gifts. Instead, Paul sought to educate the Saints about the need for each to petition God for the various gifts promised to all worthy Saints.

A key to Paul's instruction is the principle that unity in the Church actually springs from a diversity of gifts among the Saints. Paul taught of the need for diverse gifts by comparing the Church to the body: "For as the body is one, and hath many members, and all the members of that one body, being many, are one body: so also is Christ. . . . Now ye are the body of Christ, and members in particular" (1 Corinthians 12:12, 27).

Paul supported the concept of unity through diversity by likening it to the workings of the Godhead. In 1 Corinthians 12 Paul's reference to "the same Spirit" (v. 4) acknowledges the Holy Ghost as the conduit through which all gifts are received from God, his term "the same Lord" (v. 5) refers to Christ's universal role in administering the gifts, and his phrase "the same God" (v. 6) identifies Heavenly Father as the origin from which all gifts derive their existence. The Godhead, made up of three distinct individuals with separate functions, are one in purpose. Similarly, wise Saints of God, notwithstanding their diverse gifts, seek for unity with Christ's church. Teaching the Saints in Corinth to qualify for endowments from on high, Paul acknowledged that it is God who determines to whom each gift is entrusted "as it hath pleased him" (v. 18).

"TRULY THE SIGNS OF AN APOSTLE WERE WROUGHT AMONG YOU"

The divine dispensation and appropriate use of spiritual gifts in the life of Paul illustrate a characteristic of special witnesses both ancient and modern. Enjoyment of a wide array of spiritual gifts is one defining attribute of a true apostle of Christ. Latter-day revelation declares, "That unto some it may be given to have all those gifts, that there may be a head" (D&C 46:29). The title of apostle, meaning "one sent forth,"[3] is used to denote those divinely called servants who possess all those gifts which in the economy of Deity are deemed necessary to fulfill their sacred calling.

Paul's several missions, as recorded in the last half of the book of Acts, document the generous outpouring of spiritual gifts in the life of this chosen servant of God. Throughout his apostolic life, Paul qualified himself to be entrusted with those divine allocations of heavenly treasures.

Paul's masterful sermon on spiritual gifts seems as much a personal reflection as it does a doctrinal discourse. Indeed, from the very beginning of his personal ministry until his martyrdom in Rome, Paul was showered with extraordinary gifts from God. Moreover, the gifts he enumerated are exemplified during his ministry as a special witness of Christ.

"NO MAN CAN SAY THAT JESUS IS THE LORD, BUT BY THE HOLY GHOST"

Paul taught that true disciples do not repudiate the Savior; indeed, all who deny the Savior are "Anathema"[4] (1 Corinthians 16:22). He further indicated that "no man can say that Jesus is the Lord, but by the Holy Ghost" (1 Corinthians 12:3). Joseph Smith's substitution of the word *know*[5] for the word *say* enhances this New Testament teaching as it confirms the quality of testimonies borne through the Holy Ghost.

From the earliest moments of his conversion as a disciple of Christ (Acts 9:1–8), Paul learned of the power and grace-filled nature of spiritual endowments. Paul's testimony of the risen Christ was made sure through the witnessing power of the Holy Ghost during his vision on the road to Damascus.[6]

The reader of the book of Acts is left to ponder why Paul, who earlier had sought "to do many things contrary to the name of Jesus" (Acts 26:9), received so great a blessing in a seemingly unsolicited way. Paul's experience can reasonably be seen as an outgrowth of his premortal life. Elder Bruce R. McConkie explained: "Truly, as the scripture saith, 'the gifts and calling of God are without repentance' (Romans 11:29), meaning the Lord takes a Paul, an Alma, or a Matthew, as he chooses, because that called servant was prepared and foreordained from the premortal eternities to perform the labors to which the call extends. Manifestly all such do repent and make themselves worthy in all respects for the divine labor that is then theirs."[7]

Concerning the connection between the premortal existence and the divine allocation of spiritual gifts, Elder Neal A. Maxwell wrote, "Each mortal is 'endowed' genetically, environmentally, but also premortally."[8] In this respect, Paul joined other valiant sons and daughters of God as a beneficiary, in the mortal sphere, of righteous choices made in the premortal councils.

Paul's vision of the Savior on the road to Damascus was not an isolated event: Paul later received visions of Christ in consequence of his apostolic calling (Acts 18:9; 23:11).

"BUT WE SPEAK THE WISDOM OF GOD IN A MYSTERY"

Paul's early training as a Pharisee at the feet of Gamaliel, the renowned doctor of laws, furnished him with an abundant supply of man's knowledge and wisdom. Nevertheless, the spiritual gifts of wisdom and knowledge that Paul enjoyed sprang not from such earthly fountains but rather from the well of God. Paul taught his fellow Saints to lean upon the word of

God "because the foolishness of God is wiser than men" (1 Corinthians 1:25).

Paul expended much of his energy during his mortal ministry preaching "so that all they which dwelt in Asia heard the word of the Lord Jesus, both Jews and Greeks" (Acts 19:10). In Thessalonica, Paul and Silas went into a synagogue where for three Sabbaths they "reasoned with them out of the scriptures" (Acts 17:2). They taught of the Atonement and the saving power of the risen Christ. "A great multitude" believed the message of the two disciples (Acts 17:4).

Each of Paul's epistles bears witness of this great apostle's gift of teaching. Teaching the things of God to a people choked by the wisdom of man was an arduous and sometimes perilous challenge. Despite the often angry response to his message, the faithful apostle persevered. He wrote, "And my speech and my preaching was not with enticing words of man's wisdom, but in demonstration of the Spirit and of power" (1 Corinthians 2:4).

"STAND FAST IN THE FAITH"

At the conclusion of his vision of the resurrected Savior, Paul's faith was tested. Christ directed Paul to "arise, and go into the city [Damascus], and it shall be told thee what thou must do"; the newly converted disciple then "arose from the earth; and when his eyes were opened, he saw no man" (Acts 9:6, 8). After Paul fasted and prayed for three days, the Lord sent Ananias to heal him. Paul exercised his young faith, and his vision was restored. It is not improbable that the Lord's words came to Paul at this moment as he recognized that Christ had come into his life "to open [his] eyes, and to turn [him] from darkness to light, and from the power of Satan unto God, that [he] may receive forgiveness of sins, and inheritance among them which are sanctified by faith" (Acts 26:18).

Certainly, the faith of Paul accounts for much of the success he reaped in his labors. During his first mission the apostle acknowledged the value of faith when he expressed "how he [God] had opened the door of faith unto the Gentiles" (Acts 14:27). Over the course of his ministry, Paul truly learned to "walk by faith, not by sight" (2 Corinthians 5:7).

"OTHERS ALSO . . . CAME, AND WERE HEALED"

A marvelous witness to this great apostle's enjoyment of gifts was his ability to heal. During Paul's first mission and on his visit to Lystra, the people expressed astonishment over Paul and Barnabas' healing of a man crippled from birth. Those observers erroneously identified the gift of healing as proof that "the gods are come down to us in the likeness of men" (Acts 14:11). Paul, much disturbed by that assertion, chastened the people and commanded them to "turn from these vanities unto the living God" (v. 15).

Another remarkable demonstration of healing occurred while Paul was in Ephesus. He sent "handkerchiefs or aprons" to the sick, who were then cured of diseases of both mind and spirit (Acts 19:12). The circumstances of this healing are similar to an experience in the life of Joseph Smith. The Prophet, unable personally to administer to a pair of ailing infant twins, sent his handkerchief with Wilford Woodruff. Following the Prophet's instructions, Brother Woodruff wiped the children's faces when he administered to them, and they were restored to health.[9]

Paul's healing power was also manifested at a meeting where "the disciples came together to break bread" (Acts 20:7). The meeting went late into the night, and a young man, Eutychus, fell into a deep sleep. He subsequently "fell down from the third loft, and was taken up dead," but "Paul went down, and fell on him, and embracing him said, Trouble not yourselves; for his life is in him" (vv. 9–10).[10]

Yet another miracle is documented in the closing chapter of Acts, which records Paul's stop on the island of Melita. Paul was received there with what he declared to be "no little kindness," though the inhabitants of the island were described as "barbarous people" (Acts 28:2).[11] Paul administered to a man stricken with dysentery, whereupon he was healed. Reports of the miracle spread throughout the island, prompting others to seek the apostle for his gift of healing.

"AND GOD WROUGHT SPECIAL MIRACLES BY THE HANDS OF PAUL"

The use of spiritual gifts by Paul and his missionary companion Barnabas caused the people in Jerusalem to declare "what miracles and wonders God had wrought among the

Gentiles by them" (Acts 15:12). Indeed, Paul's whole ministry was filled with "special miracles" (Acts 19:11).

The miracles in the lives of sincere disciples strengthened already existent stirrings within their souls. In some instances, miracles destroyed barriers to building up the kingdom. For example, a sorcerer named Elymas confronted Paul, "seeking to turn away the deputy [Sergius Paulus] from the faith" (Acts 13:8). Filled with the Holy Ghost, Paul cursed Elymas: "Behold, the hand of the Lord is upon thee, and thou shalt be blind, not seeing the sun for a season." Immediately a "mist and a darkness" fell upon the sorcerer, and "he went about seeking some to lead him by the hand" (Acts 13:11). This miracle resulted not only in the cursing of an unbeliever but also in the convincing of Paulus, a prudent man.

Another miracle occurred when Paul and Silas were unjustly incarcerated at Philippi for alleged heretical preaching. The prisoners prayed and sang praises, "and suddenly there was a great earthquake, so that the foundations of the prison were shaken: and immediately all the doors were opened, and every one's bands were loosed" (Acts 16:26). Not only did this miracle hasten the release of the prisoners but it also resulted in the conversion of the keeper of the prison and his house.

Miraculous too was the protection that safeguarded Paul in his several missionary journeys. While preaching during his enforced three-month stay on the island of Melita, Paul was bitten by a venomous snake (Acts 28:3–6). The expected symptoms of swelling and death did not eventuate, much to the people's astonishment. Paul became the vicarious beneficiary of the promise of immunity that Christ pronounced upon his disciples just before his ascension: "They shall take up serpents; and if they drink any deadly thing, it shall not hurt them" (Mark 16:18).

"FOR YE MAY ALL PROPHESY"

No endowment better demonstrates Paul's standing as a recipient of generous outpourings of heavenly gifts than that of prophecy. Writing of the imperative nature of that gift, Hugh Nibley observed: "And when the gift of prophecy departs, we witness at the same time the cessation of the other heavenly gifts, and with that the church changes its views of the other world, becoming perplexed and uncertain about things which it once knew so well."[12]

A most perilous experience in Paul's ministry occurred when, as a prisoner, he traveled by ship to Rome. At the outset of this journey Paul prophesied, "Sirs, I perceive that this voyage will be with hurt and much damage, not only of the lading and ship, but also of our lives" (Acts 27:10). His prophecy was disregarded, for "the centurion believed the master . . . more than those things which were spoken by Paul" (v. 11). Paul's prophecies were fulfilled, and the stormy seas "ran the ship aground" (v. 41). Paul, knowing that the Lord was protecting him, did not experience the feelings of despair that overcame the rest of the sailors. Indeed, the apostle challenged them to "be of good cheer" (v. 25) and instructed all aboard how to ensure their safety. Despite the soldiers' plan to kill the prisoners, "it came to pass, that they escaped all safe to land" (v. 44), and thus was Paul's prophecy fulfilled.

Perhaps the most clear evidences of Paul's prophetic gifts are in his prophecies of the great apostasy and the latter-day restoration of the fulness of the gospel. Paul used the imagery of grievous wolves that would prey upon the flock at a future time and warned of perverse doctrines that would seek to lure away followers (Acts 20:28–32). The chilling prophecies of false teachers and apostasy are not Paul's last words on the subject. Speaking of a restoration of the gospel in the latter days, Paul wrote to the Ephesians, "In the dispensation of the fulness of times he might gather together in one all things in Christ, both which are in heaven, and which are on earth; even in him" (Ephesians 1:10). In a direct prophecy of things to come, Paul was able at once to evoke feelings of great concern and of great hope among the believers.

"BUT HE THAT IS SPIRITUAL JUDGETH ALL THINGS"

Paul knew the power of gifts from the Spirit, and he also recognized the perfidious manipulations of false spirits. In fulfilling his calling as a special witness, Paul expended much energy seeking to awaken in the ancient Saints a desire to draw upon the power to distinguish between the genuine workings of the Spirit and the counterfeits of the adversary. Joseph Smith taught that Paul and other ancient apostles had control over the "agency, power and influence of spirits; for they could control them at pleasure, bid them depart in the name of Jesus, and detect their mischievous and mysterious operations when trying to palm themselves upon the Church in a religious garb, and militate against the interest of the Church and spread of truth."[13]

While traveling in Macedonia, Paul and Silas were followed for many days by a woman soothsayer, who cried, "These men are the servants of the most high God, which shew unto us the way of salvation" (Acts 16:17). Paul detected the spirit and commanded it to depart from the woman. Of that event Joseph Smith declared, "Although she spake favorably of them, Paul commanded the spirit to come out of her, and saved themselves from the opprobrium that might have been heaped upon their heads, through an alliance with her, in the development of her wicked principles, which they certainly would have been charged with, if they had not rebuked the evil spirit."[14]

On another occasion Paul awakened the people to the workings of evil spirits. The sons of Sceva, who were exorcists, attempted to cast out evil spirits, saying, "We adjure you by Jesus whom Paul preacheth" (Acts 19:13). The evil spirit answered, "Jesus I know, and Paul I know; but who are ye?" (v. 14). The spirit recognized the authority of Christ and Paul and knew that the sons of Sceva did not possess it. "And the man in whom the evil spirit was leaped on them, and overcame them, and prevailed against them, so that they fled out of that house naked and wounded" (v. 16). Word of this episode spread throughout the land, and the name of the Lord was glorified. Many people "which used curious arts brought their books together, and burned them before all men" (v. 19).

The Prophet Joseph taught, "No man nor sect of men without the regular constituted authorities, the Priesthood and discerning of spirits, can tell true from false spirits."[15] In the latter days, the gift of discernment acts as a sentry at the gospel doors to warn against any who might endeavor to turn back the progress of the Lord's kingdom.

"I THANK MY GOD, I SPEAK
WITH TONGUES MORE THAN YE ALL"

In his discourse on spiritual gifts, Paul referred to the gift of

tongues in approximately one-third of the verses.[16] This gift is
one of the so-called charismatic gifts and was subject to much
misuse, owing to its strange and wonderful elements. Such
abuse provoked Paul to liken the indiscriminate exercise of
tongues to instruments with "uncertain sound" (1 Corinthians
14:7–9). Paul understood that the common misuse of tongues
was largely an effort of some to satisfy appetites for self-
enlargement: "He that speaketh in an unknown tongue edifieth
himself; but he that prophesieth edifieth the church" (v. 4).[17]
Paul urged the Saints to "let all things be done decently and in
order" (v. 40). He taught, "If any man speak in an unknown
tongue . . . let one interpret. But if there be no interpreter, let
him keep silence in the church; and let him speak to himself,
and to God" (vv. 27–28).

Concerns about manipulation of this divine gift for purposes
of deceit or spiritual boasting have also been confronted by
prophets of this dispensation. Joseph Smith echoed Paul's
instructions when he taught: "If you have a matter to reveal, let
it be in your own tongue; do not indulge too much in the exercise of the gift of tongues, or the devil will take advantage of
the innocent and unwary. . . . I lay this down for a rule, that if
anything is taught by the gift of tongues, it is not to be received
for doctrine."[18]

Although Paul repeatedly warned against the misuse of
tongues, he specifically endorsed the proper use of the gift. He
provided clear direction when he admonished the Saints to
"forbid not to speak with tongues" (1 Corinthians 14:39).
Furthermore, Paul himself exercised the gift of tongues in his
ministry. Rejoicing in his use of the gift he expressed, "I thank
my God, I speak with tongues more than ye all" (1 Corinthians
14:18). Paul also was the conduit through which the gift of
tongues was conferred upon newly baptized converts (Acts
19:6).

"COVET EARNESTLY THE BEST GIFTS"

Paul plainly admonished Christ's Saints to "covet earnestly
the best gifts" (1 Corinthians 12:31). The word *covet* is used to
translate the Greek word *zēlŏŏ,* meaning "to have warmth of
feeling for" or "to desire earnestly."[19] In all dispensations of
time, the abundant bestowal of spiritual gifts among men has

indicated the vitality of gospel blessings among the Saints of God. Father Adam himself inaugurated the enjoyment of these gifts among men (Moses 5:9–10; D&C 107:56). In latter days, through the reemergence of the divine bestowal of gifts, Latter-day Saints are invited to actively and appropriately seek those "best gifts" known of old (D&C 46:8).

Scholars have remarked about the abundance of gifts in what is termed "the apostolic age" as well as the gradual cessation of those gifts, reflecting the loss of authority on earth. The departure of such endowments was one of the casualties of the great apostasy. One biblical scholar noted: "Concerning these [spiritual gifts], our whole information must be derived from Scripture, because they appear to have vanished with the disappearance of the Apostles themselves, and there is no authentic account of their existence in the Church in any writings of a later date than the books of the New Testament."[20]

The latter-day return of the Lord's gospel to the earth included the revival of spiritual gifts, which for centuries had remained dormant. Indeed, the characterization of the latter days as the dispensation of the fulness of times hinges in great part upon the reemergence of the full array of spiritual gifts among mankind. The life of the Prophet Joseph Smith exemplifies this truth. Not only was he endowed with such outpourings of the Spirit but he acknowledged the role of such gifts in the lives of his fellow Saints: "I preached in Chester, Sparta and Bellville. From thence returned home, and again visited Ottawa, La Salle county. Spent two weeks, and baptized seven. I found the Church there in good spirits and in the enjoyment of the spiritual gifts."[21]

"NEGLECT NOT THE GIFT THAT IS IN THEE"

Not unlike the child whose Christmas gifts are at first cherished but soon neglected, the Saints of God may likewise lose their inheritance owing to disregard or apathy or both. Chief among the indictments that might be leveled against an unwise steward is that of rejecting the very gifts conferred according to the design of the Lord. Teaching the Saints of the divine assignment of gifts, Paul asserted, "But all these worketh that one and the selfsame Spirit, dividing to every man severally as he will" (1 Corinthians 12:11).

Further complaint may be lodged against one whose efforts are squandered seeking spiritual gifts not ordained while ignoring those divinely bestowed. "For all have not every gift given unto them; for there are many gifts, and to every man is given a gift by the Spirit of God" (D&C 46:11). In this respect, Latter-day Saints would do well to heed the words of the ancient writer Flavius Magnus Aurelius Cassiodorus: "He is invited to great things who receives small things greatly."[22] No matter what the gift of God, valiant Latter-day Saints will accept humbly, with arms outstretched in thanks, the things of God. Such gratitude signals that the recipient of unmerited prizes contemplates that the value of any good gift is without bounds if carefully nurtured and magnified.

With voices reaching heavenward, imperfect Saints petition a perfect God for the divine dispensation of perfect gifts. Righteous and humble Saints qualify themselves for service in the Lord's kingdom through earnestly pursuing those gifts. By so doing, God's elect stand to reap the blessings promised by Paul to those who zealously seek "a more excellent way" (1 Corinthians 12:31).

N O T E S

1. Bruce R. McConkie, *Mormon Doctrine,* 2d ed. (Salt Lake City: Bookcraft, 1966), 315.

2. Paul W. Marsh, "To the Corinthians," in *A New Testament Commentary,* ed. G. C. D. Howley (Grand Rapids, Mich.: Zondervan Publishing, 1969), 373.

3. Bible Dictionary, LDS edition of the King James Version of the Bible, s.v. "apostle."

4. *Anathema* ("an accursed thing") is a transliteration from the Greek. Paul's use of the term refers to the accursed state of all who preach any other salvation but through Christ. For a discussion of its usage, see W. E. Vine, *The Expanded Vine's Expository Dictionary of New Testament Words* (Minneapolis: Bethany House Publishers, 1984), 254.

5. Joseph Smith, *Teachings of the Prophet Joseph Smith,* sel. Joseph Fielding Smith (Salt Lake City: Deseret Book, 1976), 243.

6. Richard Lloyd Anderson, *Understanding Paul* (Salt Lake City: Deseret Book, 1983), 26–27.

7. Bruce R. McConkie, *The Mortal Messiah,* 4 vols. (Salt Lake City: Deseret Book, 1980), 2:57.

8. Neal A. Maxwell, *Deposition of a Disciple* (Salt Lake City: Deseret Book, 1976), 36.

9. Wilford Woodruff, *Leaves from My Journal,* in *Three Mormon Classics,* comp. Preston Nibley (Salt Lake City: Bookcraft, 1988), 78–79.

10. A similar experience is recorded in 1 Kings 17:17–23, in which the Old Testament prophet Elijah restored life to a widow's son.

11. *Webster's New World Dictionary of the American Language,* 2d college ed. (New York: Simon and Schuster, 1982), 112, s. v. "barbarous." Webster indicates that in the ancient world the term applied especially to non-Greeks, non-Romans, or non-Christians.

12. Hugh Nibley, *The World and the Prophets,* vol. 3 in The Collected Works of Hugh Nibley (Salt Lake City: Deseret Book, 1987), 165.

13. Smith, *Teachings of the Prophet Joseph Smith,* 206.

14. Ibid., 206–7.

15. Ibid., 213.

16. There are eighty-four verses in 1 Corinthians 12–14, of which approximately twenty-three, or 30 percent, discuss "tongues" at some length. Most of the discussion warns about misuse of this gift.

17. 1 Corinthians 14:2, fn. *a,* in the LDS edition of the King James Bible, shows that the Joseph Smith Translation uses the word *another* in place of the phrase "an unknown" in every instance in this chapter.

18. Smith, *Teachings of the Prophet Joseph Smith,* 229.

19. James Strong, *The Exhaustive Concordance of the Bible* (McLean, Va.: McDonald Publishing, 1989), 34.

20. William J. Conybeare and J. S. Howson, *The Life and Epistles of Saint Paul* (Hartford, Conn.: S. S. Scranton, 1900), 372. Further acknowledgment of the departure of spiritual gifts that preceded the great apostasy was made by John Wesley, who lamented: "'It does not appear that these extraordinary gifts of the Holy Spirit were common in the church for more than two or three centuries. We seldom hear of them after that fatal period when the emperor Constantine called himself a Christian.' *Wesley's Works,* vol. 7, 89: 26, 27." As cited in James E. Talmage, *Articles of Faith,* Classics in Mormon Literature ed. (Salt Lake City: Deseret Book, 1984), Appendix 12, 445.

21. Joseph Smith, *History of The Church of Jesus Christ of Latter-day Saints,* ed. B. H. Roberts, 2d ed. rev., 7 vols. (Salt Lake City: The Church of Jesus Christ of Latter-day Saints, 1932–51), 5:395.

22. Flavius Magnus Aurelius Cassiodorus, *Institutiones,* in John Bartlett, *Familiar Quotations,* 15th ed. (Boston: Little, Brown and Co., 1980), 130.

CHAPTER THREE

"AN HEBREW OF THE HEBREWS": PAUL'S LANGUAGE AND THOUGHT

C. WILFRED GRIGGS

A discussion of the language and thought of the apostle Paul would seem to be a rather straightforward matter. One of the few things upon which scholars of the New Testament agree is that Paul wrote or dictated his letters in Greek to audiences which were able to communicate in the same language. Most scholars, though not all, also believe that Paul is responsible for placing the teachings and practices of Jesus and the first disciples into a basic system of theology or doctrine upon which the later Christian Fathers built.

If we were to ask how Paul's background prepared him to accomplish these tasks, the answer would be simple for the question of language and only somewhat problematic with regard to his thought. His having been born and raised in Tarsus, a major center of Greek culture, accounted for his training in the Greek language, and his later study in Jerusalem under the great Jewish teacher and sage Gamaliel instilled in him the philosophical foundation which he later used in formulating Christian theology. Those beliefs seem so reasonable and have been published for so long that questioning them might at first appear presumptuous or at least unnecessarily contentious.

We live in a time, however, in which change is occurring in all fields of study, including ancient history. Biblical manuscripts written in various languages and sometimes dating to early in

□ □ □ □ □

C. Wilfred Griggs is professor of ancient studies at Brigham Young University.

the Christian era, the Dead Sea Scrolls and other Jewish documents from ancient Palestine and nearby areas, Christian and other religious writings from the same era and general geography, and ongoing archaeological work at many sites in the eastern Mediterranean all combine to necessitate a revaluation of such questions as the background and training of Paul. As every student of the past knows, such reconsideration in all areas of history is a continuing activity, and our understanding of the New Testament will be enhanced by increased awareness of the setting in which Jesus and the apostles lived and fulfilled their sacred callings to preach the gospel. Recent studies of the written sources, coupled with the results of archaeological work in the eastern Mediterranean, particularly in Israel, have demonstrated that perhaps the traditional views concerning Paul's background and training have been misunderstood and misrepresented.

A brief review of the trends of scholarship concerning Paul during the past century or so will not necessarily increase our faith, but it will be instructive to show how training and scholarly bias can influence one's perspective. We can also appreciate how scholarship that is not tempered by prophetic guidance and insight can wander off into nonproductive and meaningless trivia. If we have a knowledge of eternal gospel principles and practices as restored in modern times and believe that Paul knew and preached the same gospel, a study from that perspective of the same written and archaeological materials can provide insights into that apostle's life which will enhance our understanding of and appreciation for his ministry in the New Testament Church.

In considering the relationship of Paul to the Judaism of his day, some major tendencies have emerged during the past century or so.[1] One of the most dominant views, characterized by H. St. John Thackeray,[2] considers Paul to have been antithetical to Judaism, although originally dependent upon it. Still early in the twentieth century, C. G. Montefiore attempted to minimize the differences between Paul and rabbinic Judaism by arguing that the Judaism against which Paul objected was not traditional rabbinical Judaism but rather a Judaism weakened by the influences of Hellenistic syncretism.[3] Although the distinction between Palestinian Judaism and Hellenistic Judaism (or Diaspora Judaism, as some identify it) has been appealing to some commentators, others, such as George Foot Moore, contend that Paul's criticism of Judaism was not directed at Jews to refute them, because his position was inexplicable to a Jew. Rather, as Moore puts it, Paul was writing to gentile converts to protect them from the influence of Jewish propagandists, who would try to persuade them that "observance of the law was necessary along with allegiance to Christ."[4]

In a work considered by many to be a turning point in the scholarship on Paul and Judaism, W. D. Davies denied the neat division of Judaism into separate Palestinian and Hellenistic or Diaspora components, showing the interpenetration of both without regard to geographical considerations.[5] Despite Davies's arguments that many motifs in Paul, which were often viewed as being the most Hellenistic, can in reality be paralleled in or derived from Palestinian Judaism, Sanders claims that his mentor Davies "did not, however, deal with the essential element which Montefiore found in Rabbinic literature but which is not taken into account in Paul's critique of Judaism: the doctrine of repentance and forgiveness." Sanders faults Davies for using Judaism "to identify Paul's *background,* not compare *religions.*"[6] Sanders's own work, also perceived by many to represent a watershed in Pauline scholarship, goes beyond a comparison of Pauline motifs with rabbinic statements to describe and define the religion of Paul and the religion of Judaism, which can then be contrasted with each other.

Sanders takes positions different from those of Davies, both in many of his perceptions of what constitutes first-century Judaism in Palestine and in how Paul differed from the Judaism of his day. Two of his conclusions that emphasize Paul's differences with Palestinian Judaism would be expected because of Paul's encounter with the resurrected Christ on the road to Damascus and the subsequent reordering of his religious beliefs according to the gospel which was revealed to him (Galatians 1:12–16). Whereas Davies had stated that "Paul carried over into his interpretation of the Christian Dispensation the covenantal conceptions of Judaism,"[7] Sanders takes an opposite position: "Paul's 'pattern of religion' cannot be described as 'covenantal nomism', and therefore Paul presents an *essentially different type of religiousness from any found in Palestinian Jewish literature.*"[8]

Despite that negative assertion, Sanders states that in many ways Paul reflects Palestinian Judaism more than Hellenistic Judaism. One example relates to defining righteousness: "The righteousness terminology is related to the righteousness terminology of Palestinian Judaism. One does not find in Paul any trace of the Greek and Hellenistic Jewish distinction between being righteous (man/man) and pious (man/God); nor is righteousness in Paul one virtue among others. Here, however, there is also a major shift; for to be righteous in Jewish literature means to obey the Torah and to repent of transgression, but in Paul it means to be saved by Christ."[9]

Is it really possible to draw such distinctions between Judaism and Hellenistic culture in the first century? "The works of E. Bickerman, D. Daube, S. Lieberman, and M. Smith have abundantly established the interpenetration between Hellenism and Judaism by the first century, so that Pharisaism itself can be regarded as a hybrid."[10] Even Sanders, whose cited book focuses on Paul and Palestinian Judaism, admits the problem of identifying to what extent Hellenistic culture may have influenced the thought and language of Paul: "Paul does not have simply a 'Jewish' or a 'Hellenistic' or a 'Hellenistic Jewish' conception of man's plight. It appears that Paul's thought was not simply taken over from any one scheme pre-existing in the ancient world.

"In claiming a measure of uniqueness for Paul we should be cautious on two points. One is that we must agree with the common observation that nothing is totally unique. Indeed, with respect to man's plight, one can see relationships between what Paul thought and various other conceptions in the ancient world. What is lacking is a precise parallel which accounts exhaustively for Paul's thought, and this has partly to do with Paul's making use of so many different schemes of thought."[11]

Although some commentators drew sharp distinctions between Judaism, Hellenism, and Christianity and thus had Paul move through some version of the first two on his way to becoming the first Christian theologian, Krister Stendahl de-emphasizes the formality of religion in the first century. Admitting that the vision on the road to Damascus resulted in a great change in Paul's life, Stendahl characterizes the change as more like a "call" than a "conversion" from one religion to another, for "it is obvious that Paul remains a Jew as he fulfills his role as an Apostle to the Gentiles."[12] The question Stendahl raises is not mere pedantry, for Christian missionaries of every age have had to distinguish between cultural mores that must be abandoned at conversion and those that can be retained. Furthermore, given the increasingly anti-Semitic position of many Christian churches in late antiquity, it is of more than idle interest to see whether the noted Apostle to the Gentiles himself exhibited any tendencies to turn away from or renounce Judaism.

Establishing Paul's relationship to the Judaism of his day and also establishing the relationship of Judaism to the Hellenistic world of the first century, therefore, continues to be of interest to students of the early Church. Even the confrontations between Paul and the so-called Judaizers are seen by some to be problems with other Christians rather than with Jews. Lloyd Gaston represents that position when he notes that "the opponents seem to be in every case rival Christian missionaries, and it is not at all sure either that they represent a united front, or that all of them are Jewish Christians." He further asserts: "Even if some of Paul's argumentation should be directed against individual (Christian) Jews, Judaism as such is never attacked. Paul's letters cannot be used either to derive information about Judaism or as evidence that he opposes Judaism as such."[13]

The difficulty of trying to fit Paul into one or another category of Judaism, such as Palestinian or Hellenistic (if they really are discrete and identifiable entities), is increased by statements found both in the apostle's letters and in Luke's Acts of the Apostles. Luke quoted Paul's telling the military tribune in Jerusalem that he is "a man, a Jew of Tarsus in Cilicia, a citizen of no insignificant city" (Acts 21:39),[14] supposedly placing him squarely in the context of Diaspora Judaism. Nevertheless, Luke recorded Paul's telling the audience in the temple courtyard: "I am a Jew, and though I was born at Tarsus in Cilicia I was brought up in this city and was educated at the feet of Gamaliel according to the strict manner of our ancestral law, being zealous for God as all of you are this day" (Acts 22:3).

Paul declared the strictness of his Jewish upbringing. In beginning his speech before Agrippa II and Berenice, he said: "My manner of life from my youth, which was from the beginning among my own nation and in Jerusalem, is known by all the Jews. They have known me for a long time, and should they wish to testify, that according to the strictest party of our religion I lived as a Pharisee" (Acts 26:4–5). When Paul addressed the Jewish council of Pharisees and Sadducees, he declared that he was "a Pharisee, the son of a Pharisee" (Acts 23:6), and that he had lived in good conscience before God up to that time (Acts 23:1), making a claim of such strict obedience to Jewish law that the high priest had someone strike (backhand) him on the mouth.

Paul did not refer to his origins outside of Palestine, and his own statements emphasized his strict adherence to Jewish law and practices before his encounter with the resurrected Christ. In Galatians, to give an example, Paul summarized his pre-Christian life: "For you have heard of my former way of life in Judaism, . . . and I progressed in Judaism beyond many of those of my same age in my race, because I was far more zealous for the traditions of my fathers" (Galatians 1:13–14).

Later, when writing to the Philippians from Rome where he was awaiting trial, Paul again declared his earlier strict adherence to Jewish law: " . . . although I have confidence in the flesh. If someone else thinks he has confidence in the flesh, I have more: circumcised on the eighth day; a member of the race of Israel; of the tribe of Benjamin; an Hebrew of the Hebrews; as to the law, a Pharisee, as for zeal, one who persecuted the church; and as to uprightness according to the law, I was blameless" (Philippians 3:4–6).

Even conversion to Christianity did not cause Paul to denigrate or repudiate his Jewish origins: "Therefore, I say, has God rejected his people? Far from it! For I am also an Israelite, of the seed of Abraham, of the tribe of Benjamin. God has not cast aside his people whom he knew beforehand" (Romans 11:1–2).

If one agrees with Davies that the distinction between

Palestinian, or rabbinic, and Diaspora, or Hellenistic, Judaism is not easily defended, Paul's birth in Tarsus and his education in Jerusalem would not necessarily represent a significant shift in religious orientation or training. Such an observation does not by itself clarify or explain how much exposure to Greek culture Paul experienced in his pre-Christian years or whether he was likely to have had more of such exposure in Tarsus before moving to Jerusalem than he would have encountered in Palestine. Behind that question is an even larger one for students of the New Testament: how likely was any Jew in Palestine, either from Jerusalem or the Galilee, to have significant and continuing interaction with the Hellenistic culture? We might add, parenthetically, that to answer the question for Paul brings us closer to having to answer it as well for Jesus and his apostles in the early Church.

It must be obvious by now that despite claims in both Luke's Acts and Paul's letters that Paul was raised in the strictest form of Judaism of his day, commentators have not arrived at a consensus about his relationship to the Judaism they encounter in the documentary evidence. In a very recent assessment of the problem, Victor Furnish stated in his presidential address to the Society of Biblical Literature: "In short, the more that historical research has been able to uncover about the varieties and complexities of first-century Judaism, the more difficult it has become to put Paul in his place as a Jew." Furnish further stated that the same difficulties exist when evaluating Paul's relationship to early Christianity or the Hellenistic world in general: "As research has taught us more about the diversity and complexity of nascent Christianity, it has become harder to put Paul in his place within it.

"The same is true of attempts to situate Paul more generally within the Hellenistic world. It is no longer necessary, or even plausible, to attribute the Hellenistic characteristics of Paul's letters and thought to his direct and deliberate borrowing from the philosophical schools and mystery religions. Research has shown that one must first reckon with his background in Hellenistic Judaism, and also with the time that he spent in the mixed community of Antioch. . . .

"Considering all of this, must one conclude that the historical

Paul is still on the loose, successfully evading every effort to put him in his place in history?"[15]

Given a common scholarly compulsion to identify and explain everyone and everything in terms of previously defined categories, the problem of a century of scholarship may be an attempt to force Paul into a Jewish, ecclesiastical, or Hellenistic mold established by the research of the period. It is certain that Paul did not see the gospel of Christ as fitting into such limiting categories, and as an emissary of the Lord he must, as he said, transcend the very classifications into which modern scholars have tried to place him:

"For while I am free from all men, I made myself a servant to all, in order that I might gain more of them. And I became as a Jew to the Jews, in order that I might gain Jews; as one under the law to those under the law, although I am not under the law, in order that I might gain those under the law; as one without the law to those without the law, although I am not without the law of God but am subject to the law of Christ, in order that I might gain those without the law. I became weak to those who are weak, in order that I might gain the weak; I became all things to all men, in order that I might at least save some. Now I do all things on account of the Gospel, in order that I might become a fellow participant in it" (1 Corinthians 9:19–23).

If indeed Paul was taught the strictest (generally understood to be synonymous with the narrowest, or most parochial) form of Judaism in Jerusalem as a student of Gamaliel from his youth, how are we to explain his developed ability to express himself in the Greek language? Even though Davies makes a strong case for not making great distinctions between rabbinic, or Palestinian, Judaism and Hellenistic, or Diaspora, Judaism, few in the scholarship of the past would go so far as to argue for Greek-teaching synagogues in Jerusalem or chief rabbis whose mother tongue was Greek rather than Aramaic and whose primary scriptural source was a revised Septuagint translation rather than a Hebrew text.

Before proceeding with the question of Paul's language and education, an explanation of the rabbinate in the first half of the first century is in order. Martin Hengel trenchantly observes that "in fact before [A.D.] 70 there was still no rabbinate and no ordination of scholars who then were given the right to bear the title 'rabbi'."[16] There were numerous synagogues in Jerusalem with schools and houses of learning attached to them, however (one later rabbinic text states there were four hundred eighty before the Roman War[17]), and they were likely less institutionalized and more free than in the second century when the victorious Tannaites were producing the Mishnah.[18] So little is known of Gamaliel I, under whom Paul studied, that were it not for mention made of him in Josephus[19], confusion with his famous grandson, Gamaliel II, might have caused scholars to dismiss him as a Lucan invention. Jacob Neusner collected the traditions relating to Gamaliel I, and he notes that his task was "complicated by the existence of traditions of Gamaliel II of Yavneh, by the absence of references to Gamaliel in accounts of the debates of the contemporary Houses of Shammai and Hillel, by the end of the system of listing pairs, and most of all, by the failure of the tradents everywhere to distinguish carefully among the Gamaliels." Neusner further states that his account of this great teacher, the first of the Pharisees before A.D. 70 to be honored with the title Rabban and probably the most famous instructor in the Judaism of his day, "can by no means be so comprehensive and reliable as those of earlier masters."[20]

If so little can be stated with certainty regarding Gamaliel, and if the Jewish rabbinate was so ill-defined and unstructured before A.D. 70 as Hengel observes, what evidence can be produced to clarify the language of the biblical texts to which the young Saul would have been exposed in Jerusalem? The student of Hellenistic history will know that in the three centuries following the death of Alexander the Great, Greek culture penetrated deeply into Egyptian society, as vividly brought to light through the tens of thousands of papyri discovered in Egypt during the last century. Eastward toward India, though the evidence is less well preserved, Tarn could note that "to parts of India, perhaps to large parts, [the Greeks] came, not as conquerors, but as friends and 'saviors'."[21] Greeks ruled in India "until well into the first century" and Greek culture is described as being firmly established in India by the second century before Christ.[22] If those regions were significantly Hellenized before the first century, should one expect less in Palestine, which is both between Egypt and India and closer to Greece? Has far too much been made through the centuries between the supposed, and perhaps erroneous, dichotomy between Judaism and Hellenism? (The later church fathers labeled it the dichotomy between Athens and Jerusalem for somewhat different reasons).

The primary meanings given in Liddell and Scott for *Hellenizein* are "to speak Greek, write or read correct Greek," and so forth.[23] A large body of material relating to Hellenistic culture in Palestine is the inscriptional evidence. For there "the triumphal progress of Greek makes an impressive showing in *inscriptions*," and "if we disregard later Nabaatean inscriptions in Transjordania and the typically Jewish tomb, ossuary and synagogue inscriptions . . . from the third century B.C., we find almost exclusively Greek inscriptions in Palestine."[24] More recently, Hengel stated that about 33 percent of the nearly two hundred fifty inscriptions found in or around Jerusalem from the Second Temple period are in Greek.[25]

For a non-Jew in Hellenistic Palestine, "the principle could probably very soon be applied that anyone who could read and write also had a command of Greek."[26] Further, within Judaism, Hengel asserts, "The high priest and the financial administrator of the temple will also have had impeccable Greek-speaking and Greek-writing secretaries for their correspondence with Ptolemaic offices and the court. If one goes on to include members of the Ptolemaic garrison, officials and merchants, even the Jerusalem of the third century B.C. may be assumed to have had a considerable Greek-speaking minority."[27]

By the time of the Roman conquest (in the first century before Christ), we must add an influx of hundreds of thousands of Jews to Jerusalem for various festivals, most Greek-speaking, and the need for the local inhabitants to know Greek to accommodate their needs. Josephus claims that on the basis of a count taken of Passover sacrificial lambs, greater Jerusalem contained more than 2.5 million people during that celebration.[28]

Not only did the visitors to Jerusalem speak and write Greek, but in the second century before Christ, Jerusalem itself was becoming a Greek polis. According to Hengel, "the process of Hellenization in the *Jewish upper class* then entered an acute phase, the aim of which was the complete assimilation of Judaism to the Hellenistic environment. . . . Presumably Greek 'education' in Jerusalem not only led to training the ephebes in sports but also had intellectual and literary elements."[29]

All of this presupposes the existence of a Greek school in Jerusalem, with some evidence that a knowledge of Homer was part of the curriculum.[30] Some remnants of Jewish literature written in Greek in Palestine can be found in Josephus (the romance concerning the Tobiad Joseph and his sons, composed in Egypt, but perpetuated in Palestine[31]) and Eusebius (fragments of the Jewish historian Alexander Polyhistor and fragments of an anonymous Samaritan[32]). That anonymous Samaritan writer quoted in Eusebius wrote in the second century before Christ, determined to glorify Abraham and substantiate the truth of the Old Testament. In the quotations from Alexander Polyhistor in Eusebius are statements from another Jewish historian, Eupolemus, who appears to have been a Greek-educated Palestinian Jew.[33] Second Maccabees contains a summary of yet another Jewish writer, Jason of Cyrene, and, though he was trained in rhetoric outside of Palestine, it is assumed by its detail and historical vividness to have been written in Palestine soon after the Maccabean Revolt.[34]

The countermovement to the Hellenizing forces in Jerusalem that was victorious after A.D. 70 both gave rise to the rabbinate and resulted in the suppression of the explicit Hellenization of the earlier era.[35] Once Judaism lost two of the key elements of its identity after A.D. 70, through the destruction of the temple and the dispossession of the Jews from their land, new identifying elements had to be found. The establishment of the Jewish canon of scripture near the end of the first century and the rise of rabbinic Judaism in the first centuries of the Christian era, as expressed in the Mishnah, the two Talmuds, and related literatures, have provided a Jewish identity that has persisted through the centuries. It has been difficult until very recently to penetrate the historical barriers resulting from the

Jewish-Roman war of A.D. 66–70 to see the diversity and pluralism in Judaism of the first half of the first century. Rabbinic
Judaism, which defined itself at the end of the first century and
suppressed the pluralism and Hellenization that characterized
prewar Palestine, was the normative Judaism which scholars
used in their analysis of Paul's background. With the recent
archaeological discoveries in the region and the resulting studies relating to Judaism in the prewar period before the destruction of the temple, the cosmopolitan nature of Palestine in general and of Jerusalem in particular during the New Testament
era is much more evident that it was previously.

Because Paul is from the earlier period, there is no reason to
deny that he could have received a good education in the
Greek language and culture in Jerusalem. Remembering that
the primary meaning of *Hellenizein* is to speak, read, and write
Greek, and not necessarily to embrace Greek history or litera-
ture, we need not assume that Paul studied Homer, Euripides,
Plato, or any other authors in the traditional curriculum of the
Greeks. In point of fact, awareness of those sources in Paul is
usually denied.[36] Yet, given the subject matter of Paul's epistles
and the epistolary style in general, any argument relating to the
substance of Paul's education based on his writings in the New
Testament would be like reconstructing Elder Bruce R.
McConkie's law school curriculum from his book *Mormon
Doctrine*. Paul's awareness of Greek literature, as suggested
above, may have been considerably greater than would be dis-
played in his letters to Christian congregations and close
friends.

To say that Paul spoke and wrote Greek as a native tongue
in no way argues against his also knowing Aramaic and
Hebrew. Indeed, he stated that the resurrected Lord spoke
Aramaic to him in the vision he had while traveling to
Damascus (Acts 26:14), and Paul spoke in Aramaic to the
crowd in the temple courtyard after his first arrest (Acts 21:40;
22:2). There can be no doubt that he knew some Hebrew text
of Old Testament writings, even if in his speeches and letters
he favors a revised version of the Septuagint. One should not
underestimate Paul with regard either to his Judaism or to the
influence of Hellenism in his life.

Some passages in Paul's letters might be understood to acknowledge his lack of familiarity with Greek literary sources or training in rhetoric. The most famous of these are found in the Corinthian correspondence, in which Paul testified of the superiority of God's wisdom to that of man: "And when I came to you, Brethren, I came not with excellency of speech or of wisdom, because I was declaring to you the mystery of God. . . . And my speech and my preaching were not given in persuasive words of wisdom, but in demonstration of the Spirit and power, in order that your faith might not be in the wisdom of men, but in the power of God" (1 Corinthians 2:1–5). In 2 Corinthians Paul strongly defended his apostolic calling, quoting his critics who spoke condescendingly of him: "For his letters, they say, are weighty and powerful; but his bodily presence is weak and his manner of speech is contemptible" (2 Corinthians 10:10). Paul acknowledged that he was a layman in the matter of public speaking, but he denied that he was deficient in knowledge: "But although I might be unskilled in speaking, I am not unskilled in knowledge, for in every way we have made knowledge known to you in the presence of all men" (2 Corinthians 11:6). Elsewhere Paul warned against being led captive by the learning of the world, although he did not devalue the acquisition of such knowledge: "Beware lest there be one who will lead you captive through philosophy and the vain deceit according to the tradition of men, according to the rudiments of the world and not according to Christ" (Colossians 2:8).

Such disclaimers of his rhetorical skills and of the value of philosophy are not the same as saying he was ignorant of such matters. In their commentary on 1 Corinthians, William Orr and James Walther argue that Paul must have received a good Greek education, even if he didn't parade under its banner: "It may be significant that Paul never felt moved to mention any Greek education he may have received. But the thoroughness of his instruction in contemporary Koine Greek is demonstrated by the fact that he could occasionally rise to true eloquence while using this language to express warm religious conviction and subtle points of doctrine and morals (e.g. I Cor 13,15; Rom 8,12; II Cor 3). It is hard to believe he could have mastered an alien language to this degree without having received considerable instruction in its literature, particularly that of the Hellenistic Greek communities, such as Alexandria or Tarsus. His description of his early life and instruction appears to include him among those Jews of the intellectual ghetto who had extensive knowledge of their own history and culture, but had completely cut themselves off from any knowledge of Greek or Roman paganism. However, the quality of the letters themselves leads us to believe that his experience somewhere and somehow enabled him to break out of this insularity."[37]

Hans Dieter Betz placed 2 Corinthians 10 through 13 in the Socratic tradition, stating that these chapters compose an apology, or defense, written in letter form.[38] It is not necessary to assume that Paul read a Socratic apology (though he very well may have done so) to express some of the sentiments found there, for it was common for philosophers in the Socratic tradition to disavow the pretentiousness of the rhetoricians and sophists.[39] Plato has Socrates tell the jury in his trial that he will not try to emulate the professional orators: "Now they, as I say, have said little or nothing true; but you shall hear from me nothing but the truth. Not, however, men of Athens, speeches finely tricked out with words and phrases . . . for surely it would not be fitting for one of my age to come before you like a youngster making up speeches."[40]

Socrates was seventy years old at his trial, and he had held interviews with the leading intellects of Athens,[41] which certainly exposed him to the best speakers of the day. He nevertheless denies having any knowledge of their rhetorical skills in his jury trial, a setting in which orators were famous for showing off their skills. Just as Paul will later tell the Corinthians to concentrate on truth more than on language, so Socrates speaks in his defense: "This is the first time I have come before the court, although I am seventy years old; I am therefore an utter foreigner to the manner of speech here. Hence, just as you would, of course, if I were really a foreigner, pardon me if I spoke in that dialect and that manner in which I had been brought up, so now I make this request of you, a fair one, as it seems to me, that you disregard the manner of my speech—for perhaps it might be worse and perhaps better—and observe and pay attention merely to this, whether what I say is just or not."[42]

One could debate endlessly—and uselessly—whether the obvious echoes from the Apology of Socrates on the theme of content over form found in Paul's Corinthian letters demonstrate his familiarity with the Greek literary tradition. Even if training in and exposure to the Greek literary tradition were part of Paul's educational background, he makes it abundantly clear that his apostolic calling does not require him to refer to such materials in testifying of the Savior and His gospel or in counseling Christians on how to improve their lives. Most of Paul's writings in the New Testament are composed to give advice and correction in response to specific problems. There would be little need or opportunity for the apostle to draw upon the poetry, philosophy, or history he might have learned as a student.

As a sidelight to this discussion and with reference to the larger question of Hellenism and the New Testament, let me note that if Jerusalem had become a Hellenistic city where the common language of general discourse was Greek, the situation in the Galilee was perhaps even more likely to have been Hellenized. There was a large gentile population in the Galilee, and Matthew, quoting Isaiah (9:1–2), referred to a large part of the region as "Galilee of the Gentiles" (Matthew 4:15). Eric Meyers, in an article strongly critical of the degree of Hellenization claimed for Palestine by Hengel, still admitted that "there is no doubt that Greek language was widely used in Palestine by the first century, especially in daily commercial settings and in simple forms of communication."[43] Meyers does not define "simple forms of communication," except, perhaps, to note that one should not believe that a high degree of Greek literacy (presumably of Greek literature) dominated a society in which most of the people were Jews. For some time, the belief prevailed that Galilee was simply a rural region populated by farmers, fishermen, and others who were tied too closely to the land or the lake to be interested in or aware of the Hellenistic world around them. Recent and continuing excavations, however, at such sites as Caesarea Philippi, Beth-Shean, and Sepphoris (where Meyers is one of the codirectors) demonstrate a thriving Hellenistic presence in these Galilean cities. Can we truly agree with Stuart Miller and others that Jesus and his disciples avoided going into Sepphoris, some three miles from Nazareth, or Caesarea Philippi, or any of the other Hellenized cities?[44] If Jerusalem were as Hellenized as even Meyers is willing to suggest,[45] and if Jesus spent as much time in Jerusalem as the Gospels suggest, surely it was not to avoid contact with non-Jewish culture that kept Jesus from entering Galilean cities that had a strong Hellenistic influence. The argument from silence in the scriptures about visits to those cities is inadequate, because the scriptures certainly do not attempt to provide a complete list of places Jesus visited. Even Jesus' statement that he was to minister only among the house of Israel (Matthew 15:24) does not preclude his finding Israelites throughout Palestine, including places where Gentiles and Hellenized Jews might be found.

The chief purpose of this presentation is not to assert categorically that Paul studied in a Greek school or a Greek-speaking synagogue in Jerusalem, though he may well have done either or both. Neither can we assert with confidence that Jesus actually gave the Sermon on the Mount (or on the Plain) in Greek, even though he may have done that very thing, or perhaps he gave it in Aramaic on one occasion and Greek on another. The main point is that our understanding of the past is changing rapidly, and, therefore, we should distinguish between what is spiritually enduring and unchanging and what is subject to modification with new discoveries. The New Testament and early Christian landscapes appear quite different now from how they appeared half a century ago, and the dynamic forces of intercultural contacts were greater than we previously understood. That Jesus and his apostles, including Paul, ushered in and spread abroad a dispensation of the eternal gospel in such a world should be both exciting to study and encouraging to the members of the restored Church in a rather similar contemporary setting.

NOTES

1. See Ed Sanders, *Paul and Palestinian Judaism: A Comparison of Patterns of Religion* (Philadelphia: Fortress Press, 1977), 2–13.

2. Henry St. John Thackeray, *The Relation of St. Paul to Contemporary Jewish Thought* (London: Macmillan, 1900).

3. C. G. Montefiore, *Judaism and St. Paul: Two Essays* (London: Max Goschen Ltd., 1914).

4. Sanders, *Paul and Palestinian Judaism,* 6, referring to George Foot

Moore, *Judaism in the First Centuries of the Christian Era: The Age of the Tannaim,* 3 vols. (Cambridge: Harvard University Press, 1927–30, 3:151.

5. W. D. Davies, *Paul and Rabbinic Judaism* (New York: Harper and Row, 1958), 1–16.

6. Sanders, *Paul and Palestinian Judaism,* 7, 10.

7. Davies, *Paul and Rabbinic Judaism,* 259–60.

8. Sanders, *Paul and Palestinian Judaism,* 543.

9. Ibid., 544.

10. W. D. Davies, "From Schweitzer to Scholem: Reflections on Sabbatai Svi," *Journal of Biblical Literature,* vol. 95, no. 4 (December 1976): 532, n. 14.

11. Sanders, *Paul and Palestinian Judaism,* 555.

12. Krister Stendahl, *Paul among Jews and Gentiles* (Philadelphia: Fortress Press, 1976), 11.

13. Lloyd Gaston, *Paul and the Torah* (Vancouver, B.C.: University of British Columbia Press, 1987), 3, 4.

14. This and all other quotations from the New Testament are translations by the author unless otherwise noted.

15. "On Putting Paul in His Place," *Journal of Biblical Literature,* vol. 113, no. 1 (Spring 1994): 9, 10–11.

16. Martin Hengel, *The Pre-Christian Paul* (London: SCM Press, 1991), 28.

17. Ibid., 119, n. 160.

18. Ibid., 29.

19. Josephus, *The Life,* trans. H. St. J. Thackeray (Cambridge: Harvard University Press, 1926), lines 190, 309; *The Jewish War* (trans. Thackeray), bk. 4, line 159; *Jewish Antiquities* (trans. Thackeray), bk. 20, lines 213, 223.

20. Jacob Neusner, *The Rabbinic Traditions about the Pharisees Before 70* (Leiden: E. J. Brill, 1971), 341; see also 341–76.

21. W. W. Tarn, *The Greeks in Bactria and India,* 3d ed. rev. (Chicago: Ares Publishers, 1984), 180.

22. G. W. Walbank, *The Hellenistic World* (Cambridge, Mass.: Harvard University Press, 1981), 140, 66.

23. Henry George Liddell and Robert Scott, comps., *A Greek-English Lexicon,* 9th ed. (Oxford: Oxford University Press, 1940), 536.

24. Martin Hengel, *Judaism and Hellenism: Studies in Their Encounter in Palestine During the Early Hellenistic Period,* trans. John Bowden, 1 vol. ed. (Philadelphia: Fortress Press, 1974), 58.

25. Hengel, *Pre-Christian Paul,* 55.

26. Hengel, *Judaism and Hellenism,* 59.

27. Ibid.

28. Josephus, *Jewish War,* bk. 6, lines 422ff.

29. Hengel, *Judaism and Hellenism,* 103.

30. Ibid.
31. See Josephus, *Antiquities,* bk. 12, lines 157–85, 224.
32. Eusebius, *Praeparatio Evangelica* 9.17–18.
33. J. Freudenthal, *Hellenistiche Studien* (Breslau: Verlag von H. Skutsch, 1875), 82–129.
34. 2 Maccabees, passim; Hengel, *Judaism and Hellenism,* 95–99.
35. Ibid., 103.
36. Hengel, *Pre-Christian Paul,* 38.
37. William F. Orr and James Arthur Walther, *I Corinthians,* in *The Anchor Bible* (Garden City, N.Y.: Doubleday, 1976), 5–6.
38. H. D. Betz, *Der Apostel Paulus und die sokratische Tradition* (Tübingen: J. C. B. Mohr, 1972), 14.
39. Ibid., 66.
40. Plato, *Apology* 17b-c, trans. Harold North Fowler (Cambridge, Mass.: Harvard University Press, 1971), 69, 71.
41. Plato, *Apology* 21e-22a.
42. Plato, *Apology* 17d-18a.
43. Eric M. Meyers, "The Challenge of Hellenism for Early Judaism and Christianity," *Biblical Archaeologist,* vol. 55, no. 2 (June 1992): 87.
44. Stuart S. Miller, "Sepphoris, the Well Remembered City," *Biblical Archaeologist,* vol. 55, no. 2 (June 1992): 74–81.
45. Meyers, "The Challenge of Hellenism for Early Judaism and Christianity," 86.

CHAPTER FOUR

PAUL AMONG THE RHETORICIANS: A MODEL FOR PROCLAIMING CHRIST

GARY LAYNE HATCH

In his essay from the 1987 Sperry Symposium, Richard P. Anderson set up an exclusive opposition between rhetoric, the art of persuasion, and revelation. He took as his text Paul's speech at the Areopagus (Acts 17:15–34) to show how Paul the apostle addressed himself to the people of Athens, the city that was the center of ancient rhetorical education. Anderson admitted Paul's training and skill as a rhetorician and suggested that Paul's Roman education made it possible for him to speak at the Areopagus in the first place. But, Anderson concluded, when Paul spoke as an apostle, he had to cease speaking as a rhetorician so that he could speak as a witness and so that the Spirit could confirm the truth of his words.[1]

Other Latter-day Saint speakers have made the same opposition between rhetoric and revelation, some even more forcefully than Anderson. In his general conference address of 1914, Elder James E. Talmage distinguished between "oratory" and "eloquence": "We do not come to be impressed by pulpit oratory. There is none of the attractiveness of oratorical display about the addresses that are delivered from this stand. I have rejoiced many times and do now rejoice, that our public speaking in the Church of Jesus Christ is devoid of those characteristics usually classed under the name of oratory. Oratory too often means little more than the sounding of brass and the tinkling of cymbals to tickle the ears. I do rejoice, however, in the

◻ ◻ ◻ ◻ ◻

Gary Layne Hatch is assistant professor of English at Brigham Young University.

eloquence of those who speak under the influence of the Spirit of God. Oratory is addressed to the ears; eloquence given of God, to the heart."[2] President Brigham Young said: "Let one go forth who is careful to logically prove all he says . . . and let another travel with him who can say, by the power of the Holy Ghost, Thus saith the Lord, . . . though he may tremble under a sense of his weakness, cleaving to the Lord for strength, as such men generally do, you will invariably find that the man who testifies by the power of the Holy Ghost will convince and gather many more of the honest and upright than will the merely logical reasoner."[3]

The harshest of all Latter-day Saint critics of rhetoric has been Hugh Nibley. His most famous article on the subject is called "Victoriosa Loquacitas: The Rise of Rhetoric and the Decline of Everything Else." (I have been told that Nibley considers this essay one of his favorites.) The ostensible subject of this essay was the corruption and decadence of the Roman empire during the period in the history of rhetoric known as the "Second Sophistic," a period extending roughly from the death of Cicero in 43 B.C. and the great civil war that ended the Republic through the reigns of the Caesars to the fall of the empire in A.D. 410. According to Nibley, this period was so corrupt that even the teachers of rhetoric had some concerns about the subject: "Everywhere the ancients give us to understand that rhetoric is their poison, that it is ruining their capacity to work and think, that it disgusts and wearies them, and that they cannot let it alone, because it pays too well and, having destroyed everything else, it is all they have left of remembered grandeur."[4]

Despite this uneasiness, many of the ancients argued in defense of rhetoric, indicating to Nibley "the awareness that there is something basically wrong about the thing. No one denied, of course, that rhetoric could be abused . . . but the question was whether it was bad as such, by nature. That was a disturbing question which could hardly be asked of an honest trade."[5] Even if rhetoric has a good side (which he denied), Nibley maintained that there exists a "fatal Gresham's Law by which bad rhetoric, art, and education, like bad money, will always force the better product out of circulation."[6] After describing how rhetoric ruined the Roman empire and the early Christian church, Nibley gave a brief but impressive survey of rhetoric in the Near East to show how rhetoric contributed to the decline of that civilization as well. Indeed, Nibley suggested that the rise of rhetoric will lead to the decline of *any* civilization: "Like the passions and appetites it feeds on, rhetoric is one of the great constants in human history. Because it is a constant, nothing can tell us better the direction in which a civilization is moving or how far it is along the way. Like the residue of certain radioactive substances, rhetoric, leaving an unmistakable mark on all that it touches, may yet prove to be the surest guide to the history of our own times."[7] As is typical of Nibley in many of his historical studies, he wrote with an eye to contemporary problems: he saw parallels between the Second Sophistic and our own time and hoped that his readers would recognize those he considered to be the intellectual descendants of the Sophists.

What then is the status of rhetoric? Is it, as Anderson argued, a potentially useful worldly skill but a poor substitute for revelation? As with Dante's Virgil, can rhetoric guide us through the Inferno but take us only to the outside of the gates of Paradise? Or, as Nibley contended, is rhetoric the language of the Inferno itself, Satan's best chance for destroying the work of God? If, as Nibley claimed, rhetoric is inherently evil, that it cannot be used without corrupting the person who uses it, then it must certainly be avoided, particularly by those who desire to follow Christ. If, however, not all forms of rhetoric are incompatible with revelation, then by our universal damning of the study of rhetoric, we may be neglecting a valuable tool for doing God's work.

The period in the history of rhetoric known as the Second Sophistic takes its name from the revival of Greek rhetoric in the manner of the Older Sophists, such as Gorgias and Protagoras. This period, as we have said, began around the time of the death of Cicero and the fall of the Roman republic and extended through the reign of the Caesars to the fall of imperial Rome in A.D. 410. It was known as "a period of oratorical excess in which subject matter became less important than the interest in safer matters like the externals of speech,

especially style and delivery."[8] Part of the emphasis on appearances and externals stemmed from the oppressiveness of the
Roman emperors, whose iron-fisted control of the body politic
prevented any serious debate about public affairs. The historian
Tacitus, in his *Dialogue Concerning Oratory,* a review of oratorical practices in the first century of the empire, addressed the
question "What are the causes of the decay of eloquence?" He
mentioned the focus on unimportant issues, the lack of any real
forum for public debate, the tight control of the government,
and the "introversion of the rhetorical schools."[9] Seneca complained, "We train for the school, not for life."[10] Nibley, who
measured all of rhetoric by the Second Sophistic, wrote that
"issues gave way to personalities, the most popular speaker
being the best entertainer. The Second Sophistic aimed at nothing but selling the public exactly what it wanted."[11]

The period of the Second Sophistic covered about the same
period as another major movement in the Roman empire: the
spread of Christianity. Paul, more than any other figure in the
early Christian church, drew upon the two movements.
Because he was a Roman citizen and spoke the languages of
the empire, Paul probably had some familiarity with rhetoric,
which was the core of Roman education. He may have learned
the techniques of legal oratory at the law school in Troas, an
important Greek city in Asia Minor,[12] or possibly at a school in
Tarsus.[13] If he had no formal rhetorical training, he may have
learned about rhetoric from his own participation in the life of
the empire, of which rhetoric was an important part.

At any rate, however he learned it, Paul was familiar with the
rhetoric of the Second Sophistic. Anderson summarized the evidences of Paul's rhetorical technique in his analysis of Paul's
speech at the Areopagus (Acts 17:16–34).[14] Anderson found that
Paul built on concepts familiar to the Stoics and Epicureans,
such as the Stoic belief that all things were created by God or
that "God does not live in man-made temples." Paul used two
lines from Greek authors: "In him we live and move and have
our being," which comes from a poem by Epimenides, and "for
we also are his offspring," which comes from the *Phenomena,*
by Aratus. Both those authors were Stoics, so by quoting them,
Paul established common ground with his audience and

demonstrated his knowledge of Greek literature, establishing his credibility.[15] He drew very little upon Jewish history or doctrine. Even his choosing a local monument as his text was a rhetorical commonplace for many religious teachers of the time. Paul began his speech with a conventional *exordium,* an orator's call to attention: "Men of Athens."[16] Paul's knowledge of Greek learning and rhetorical conventions allowed him to make what Kennedy considered "a remarkable effort to carry the gospel to the gentiles in terms they might have understood."[17]

Paul also showed an awareness of rhetorical techniques in his speech before Felix, when he stood accused by the Roman rhetorician Tertullus. Ananias and the elders of the Jews who accused Paul brought with them before Felix "a certain orator named Tertullus" (Acts 24:1). Tertullus delivered his speech to Felix, and then Paul followed with his account of the events. The word used in the Greek New Testament for *orator* is *rhetor*—a rhetorician. The Jews knew that to argue their case before the Roman judges they needed someone trained in Roman rhetoric.

Little is known about him, but Tertullus was probably a typical product of rhetorical education during the Second Sophistic. He seems to have been a professional public speaker who argued legal cases for a fee. He knew the conventions and manner of speaking at the Roman court. His Latin name indicates that he may have spoken Latin and was probably a Roman citizen. In his speech, Tertullus aligned himself with the leaders of the Jews and claimed to be an eyewitness to the events, but that was probably a rhetorical strategy. Speaking as an eyewitness would give more credibility to him as a speaker and more immediacy to the events he narrated.[18] In other words, Tertullus was a rhetorical "hired gun," as Paul implied in his response.

Although brief, Tertullus' speech to Felix followed the conventions of a Roman legal oration. Such a judicial speech usually began with a *proem,* or *exordium,* which sought to obtain the attention of the audience and goodwill or sympathy toward the speaker. Then came a *narration* of the facts, or background information, and the *proposition* that the speaker wished to prove, often with a *partition* of it into separate headings. The speaker then presented his arguments in the *proof,* followed by a *refutation* of opposing views; here he might incorporate a *digression,* often a relevant examination of motivations or attendant circumstances. Finally came an *epilogue,* or *peroration,* which summarized the argument and sought to arouse the emotions of the audience to take action or make judgment.[19]

Tertullus' speech contained many of those features. He began with a *proem,* in which he attempted to win the goodwill and approval of Felix by flattering him in conventional terms. Felix must have heard many similar introductions from such speakers as Tertullus. Such flattery was the Roman equivalent of clearing one's throat before beginning to speak (see Acts 24:2–4). Tertullus praised Felix for his "worthy deeds" and apologized for troubling one who is so busy keeping the peace, with such a matter. He thanked Felix for his "clemency" in allowing him to speak. Tertullus emphasized that Paul had violated the very values that Felix was supposed to preserve, particularly the "great quietness" so important to Roman governors in the provinces. The first sentence in the speech is a well-crafted, elaborate periodic sentence. The main clause was delayed to the end of the sentence so that Tertullus could build rhetorically to a climax to demonstrate his linguistic skill, further adding to his credibility with Felix.

The next section of the legal oration is the narration of the facts and the proposition. Tertullus reported the evidence against Paul (see Acts 24:5–8) and ended by inviting Felix to examine Lysias to establish the truth of what he said. Tertullus chose arguments that would be particularly effective for his audience. He implied that Lysias was wasting Felix's time in bringing Paul before him and that Felix should return Paul to the Jews, who "would have judged [him] according to [their] law" (Acts 24:6). The leaders of the Jews were not really concerned about Paul's being "a mover of sedition among all the Jews throughout the world," but Tertullus knew that as a Roman governor charged with keeping the peace, Felix, like Pontius Pilate, would be moved by this claim.

Paul showed his awareness of Greek rhetoric in his response. He avoided the flattery and stylistic flourishes of Tertullus, but he followed the same rhetorical form. Paul began his speech with a proem addressed to Felix but without the flattery (see Acts 24:10). Paul acknowledged Felix's position as judge but also pointed out that his accusers had hired someone to speak for them rather than speaking for themselves. If Paul spoke well, that would help his own credibility while damaging that of Tertullus and the leaders of the Jews. Moreover, Paul used a simple but elegant periodic sentence in contrast to Tertullus' elaborate periodic sentence.

Paul then related the facts of the case as they occurred, answering the charges made against him. Kennedy analyzed the rhetorical qualities of Paul's defense: "Paul denies that he has engaged in disputation or stirred up a crowd (12) or that he has profaned the temple (18). He begins with a short and respectful proem, couched in a good classical Greek periodic sentence (10), which he follows with an equally short narration (11) and proposition (12). Some use is made of Greek proverbs (14, 26). The rest of the speech is devoted to proof, with no epilogue. Paul admits belonging to 'the way' (14), which was not known to be illegal, and claims that he had purified himself before entering the temple (18), that the accusation is not being made by those who witnessed the incident (19), and that it is not specific (20), but he admits that he did speak of the resurrection of the dead." Kennedy further noted that because Paul offered no proof, he must have been relying on his "confident candor" and a presumption of innocence to convince Felix.[20] It may also be that the author of Acts recorded a summary, or precis, of the two speeches without the particular proofs.

Acts 24:14–16 may be a digression, for Paul related his faith in what is written in the Jewish scriptures and described his own pure motives. As is true of most digressions in classical oratory, this digression only seems irrelevant or unrelated. Paul made a concession to Felix by admitting that he did belong to "the way" but also established his belief in the traditional Jewish scriptures and in a resurrection. He was careful to point out that his accusers held the same belief. Finally, he declared his pure motives and clear conscience. When he ended his speech by saying that all he did was state his belief in the resurrection of the dead (a fact that could be confirmed by Lysias or other eyewitnesses), he trivialized the case brought against him by the Jews and made them appear to be wasting Felix's time, thus turning one of Tertullus' arguments upon itself. It appears that Paul's argument prevailed, for though he was held for further questioning, he was not imprisoned or punished in any way and was not released to the Jews.

Despite his familiarity with rhetorical conventions and his success as a speaker, Paul was highly critical of the practices of the Second Sophistic. He distinguished between his preaching and the "enticing words of man's wisdom" (1 Corinthians 2:4). Paul encouraged his readers to seek God and Christ "in whom are hid all the treasures of wisdom and knowledge. . . . lest any man should beguile you with enticing words" (Colossians 2:3–4). He then wrote, "Beware lest any man spoil you through philosophy and vain deceit, after the tradition of men, after the rudiments of the world, and not after Christ" (Colossians 2:8). But those comments must be understood in the context of Paul's time. What he knew as rhetoric, or oratory, was the rhetoric of the Second Sophistic, a rhetoric characterized by manipulation, deceit, stylistic excess, and elaborate performance, a rhetoric that has now come to be called "sophistry." Statements by Brigham Young, Hugh Nibley, and James E. Talmage must also be understood according to what they would have considered rhetoric.

The scriptures give a clear warning against sophistry, the intentional deceit and manipulation of others through specious reasoning and hypocritical emotional appeals. But the scriptures do not indict rhetoric altogether, if by rhetoric we mean influencing "thinking and behavior through the strategic use of symbols."[21] For Sherem, there is Jacob; for Nehor, Gideon; for Korihor and Zeezrom, Alma; for Tertullus, Paul. Those men of God also used the power of language to respond to sophistry and to promote the gospel of Christ. Indeed, the scriptures abound in examples of those who use the power of language for good. In other words, I believe one should not judge all rhetoric, all persuasive discourse, by the practice of the Second Sophistic.

What then is the difference between the rhetoric of Paul and the rhetoric of Tertullus? Part of Paul's persuasive ability came from the power of his message and his calling as an apostle. There is a power in truth that conveys power to the speaker, and Heavenly Father often confers such power on those he has called to do his work. The scriptures attest to the power of that kind of rhetoric. Mormon observed that "the preaching of the word had a great tendency to lead the people to do that which was just—yea, it had had more powerful effect upon the minds of the people than the sword, or anything else, which had happened unto them" (Alma 31:5). An event in the life of the prophet Enoch provides another great example of the power of the word of God. When Enoch was chosen by the Lord to speak to the people, he complained that he was "slow of speech" and hated by the people. The Lord responded, "Open thy mouth, and it shall be filled, and I will give thee utterance" (Moses 6:31–32). Enoch obeyed, and the Lord's promise was fulfilled: "And so great was the faith of Enoch that he led the people of God, and their enemies came to battle against them; and he spake the word of the Lord, and the earth trembled, and the mountains fled, even according to his command; and the rivers of water were turned out of their course; and the roar of the lions was heard out of the wilderness; and all nations feared greatly, so powerful was the word of Enoch, and so great was the power of the language which God had given him" (Moses 7:13).

Another difference between the rhetoric of Paul and the rhetoric of Tertullus lies in the manner in which language was used. Tertullus and other Roman rhetoricians were trained to use language as power without regard to the purposes of that power. The scriptures teach that the power of language should be governed by the principles of priesthood power. Section 121 of the Doctrine and Covenants was given to Joseph Smith in Liberty Jail at a time when the Church was using rhetorical means to seek redress for what the Saints had suffered in Missouri. Their petitions to the government had failed, so Joseph pleaded with the Lord for help. The Lord comforted his prophet and revealed the true nature of priesthood power: "No power or influence can or ought to be maintained by virtue of the priesthood, only by persuasion, by long-suffering, by gentleness and meekness, and by love unfeigned; by kindness, and pure knowledge, which shall greatly enlarge the soul without hypocrisy, and without guile" (D&C 121:41–42). The Lord thus outlined a pattern for godly persuasion, a rhetoric based on love, gentleness, knowledge, and sincerity.

Another essential difference between the rhetoric of Paul and the rhetoric of Tertullus lies in the role each created for the speaker and the audience. Prophets and other effective teachers of the gospel pay close attention to their audience, adapting their message to the needs of their listeners. Enos indicated that he chose his examples and arguments to match the telestial nature of those he was addressing: "And there was nothing save it was exceeding harshness, preaching and prophesying of wars, and contentions, and destructions, and continually reminding them of death, and the duration of eternity, and the judgments and the power of God, and all these things— stirring them up continually to keep them in the fear of the Lord. I say there was nothing short of these things, and exceedingly great plainness of speech, would keep them from going down speedily to destruction" (Enos 1:23).

Missionaries are familiar with the way in which Ammon and Aaron adapted their preaching to the needs of the Lamanites (Alma 17–18; 22). Jacob, who had hoped to preach "the pleasing word of God, yea, the word which healeth the wounded soul," instead spoke harsh words that enlarged "the wounds of those who are already wounded" (Jacob 2:8–9). Isaiah was instructed to "make the heart of this people fat, and make their ears heavy, and shut their eyes—lest they see with their eyes, and hear with their ears, and understand with their heart, and be converted and be healed" (2 Nephi 16:10). Christ also adapted his messages to the needs of his audience, drawing upon commonplace examples for his parables and addressing his disciples and apostles in a more direct manner than he addressed the world. Our Father in Heaven adjusts the language he uses to suit the occasion, his purpose, and the needs of his audience. For example, in his preface to the Doctrine and Covenants, the Lord stated: "Behold, I am God and have spoken it; these commandments are of me, and were given unto my servants in their weakness, after the manner of their language, that they might come to understanding" (D&C 1:24).

Nephi said that the Lord "speaketh unto men according to their language, unto their understanding" (2 Nephi 31:3).

But teachers of the gospel ought to limit the appeals they are willing to make to gain the ear of an audience. They should refrain from creating a role for themselves or others that is inconsistent with the example of Jesus Christ. The *ethos,* the speaker or writer's representation of himself, is in a sense always a fiction, a creation of the writer's language; similarly, the speaker or writer creates with language a role for the audience to take. If the role the teacher creates for himself and for his audience truly is consistent with the gospel, then the Spirit can testify to the truth of the message. If the audience assumes the role created for them by the teacher, a role that is consistent with the example of Christ, then the teacher and the audience identify with each other and emulate Christ. Perhaps that is one way of understanding Doctrine and Covenants 50:11–12, 17–22:

"Let us reason even as a man reasoneth one with another face to face.

"Now, when a man reasoneth he is understood of man, because he reasoneth as a man; even so will I, the Lord, reason with you that you may understand. . . .

"Verily I say unto you, he that is ordained of me and sent forth to preach the word of truth by the Comforter, in the Spirit of truth, doth he preach it by the Spirit of truth or some other way?

"And if it be by some other way it is not of God.

"And again, he that receiveth the word of truth, doth he receive it by the Spirit of truth or some other way?

"If it be some other way it is not of God. Therefore, why is it that ye cannot understand and know, that he that receiveth the word by the Spirit of truth receiveth it as it is preached by the Spirit of truth?

"Wherefore, he that preacheth and he that receiveth, understand one another, and both are edified and rejoice together."

Even though Paul used some of the techniques from his training as a Roman rhetorician, he did not flatter Felix in the same way that Tertullus did for the same reason that he could not deny the facts of what happened in the riot at the temple:

Paul could not create a role for himself or for Felix that was out of harmony with his mission as an apostle.

That the scriptures may seem to support the practice of certain types of rhetoric does not necessarily justify the study of an art of rhetoric. Few of the prophets and apostles received any type of formal rhetorical education: their eloquence came from their testimony of Christ and the power of the Spirit. Yet the scriptures do not necessarily exclude an art of rhetoric either. In fact, the formal study of rhetoric can be not only useful but even beneficial to the followers of Christ, as long as we remember that "there is no substitute for revelation."[22]

We can all become better teachers, speakers, and writers by learning some of the arts of rhetoric. Even though the Spirit ultimately changes a person's heart, knowing how to analyze an audience and adapt language to the needs of that audience can create an environment in which the Spirit can be felt. In addition, although the Spirit ultimately bears witness, the arts of rhetoric may help us to make the best presentation we possibly can, allowing the Spirit to affirm what we have said. Certainly, no formal training is required to be a missionary or a teacher. All that is required is a testimony of Christ, worthiness, a desire to serve, and a call. But in the presentation of the gospel message—in creating roles for ourselves and our audiences that are consistent with the example of Christ—there is still a lot of room for making different types of appeals and presentations in adapting the message to the values and knowledge of the particular audience. The Church recognizes that missionaries will be more effective if they learn to make the best presentation possible. As a result, missionary training centers have been established, in part, to teach the arts of language and rhetoric. And without doubt, the spirituality of our sacrament meetings would increase and the efficacy of our teaching would improve if members of the Church understood more about the principles of effective public speaking.

Understanding something about rhetoric can also help us interpret and evaluate the rhetoric of others. Rhetorical criticism may help us detect the abuses of rhetoric. If the Nephites had been better rhetorical critics, they might not have been so easily deceived by Sherem, Nehor, Zeezrom, and Korihor. If we ourselves were better rhetorical critics, we might not be as susceptible to con artists or false teachers and prophets. Rhetorical criticism can help us to understand the words of the prophets and can make us better readers of the scriptures. I know from my own experience as a teacher at the Missionary Training Center that missionaries become better students of the scriptures by asking questions related to the rhetorical situation of a passage: Who is speaking? Who is being addressed? What is the speaker's purpose? What is the historical context? They might have benefited even further by asking one additional question: How does the speaker use language to achieve his or her purpose? George Kennedy's book *New Testament Interpretations through Rhetorical Criticism* is an excellent study of the scriptures using the principles of classical rhetoric and would be a valuable tool for Latter-day Saint students of the scriptures. Kennedy used rhetoric to build faith and understand the sacred writings. E. W. Bullinger's *Figures of Speech Used in the Bible*[23] used categories from classical rhetoric as a guide to understanding scripture in much the same way that Arthur Henry King used classical rhetoric to read and understand Shakespeare. Burton L. Mack, professor of New Testament studies at the Claremont School of Theology, also provides an excellent introduction to rhetorical criticism of the Bible in his book *Rhetoric and the New Testament*.[24]

A final justification for learning the arts of rhetoric is that much of the communication we encounter each day is not explicitly religious: letters to the editor, business letters, memos, job interviews, town meetings, business transactions, motivational speeches, television programs, advertisements, and so on. Rhetoric can help us communicate effectively with one another in all types of situations in which we are not called upon to teach and testify of Christ. In many such instances, God leaves us to our own abilities, expecting us to develop our talents.

When we follow a divine model for persuasion—gentleness, meekness, love unfeigned, without hypocrisy or guile—then we grow closer to God: we emulate him and, in the process, worship him. Following that divine model gives us the freedom to place the art of rhetoric within the context of the gospel of Christ, adding an ethical dimension to rhetoric, without which rhetoric is a dangerous tool indeed.

NOTES

1. Richard P. Anderson, "Rhetoric versus Revelation: A Consideration of Acts 17:16–34," in *The New Testament and the Latter-day Saints: The Proceedings of the 15th Annual Sidney B. Sperry Symposium,* ed. John K. Carmack (Orem, Utah: Randall Books, 1987), 36–37.
2. James E. Talmage, in Conference Report, Apr. 1914, 93.
3. Brigham Young, in *Journal of Discourses,* 26 vols. (London: Latter-day Saints' Book Depot, 1854–86), 8:53.
4. Hugh Nibley, "Victoriosa Loquacitas: The Rise of Rhetoric and the Decline of Everything Else," *Western Speech* 20 (1956): 57; see also Hugh Nibley, *The Ancient State,* vol. 10 of The Collected Works of Hugh Nibley (Salt Lake City: Deseret Book and F.A.R.M.S., 1991), 243–86.
5. Nibley, "Victoriosa Loquacitas," 62.
6. Ibid., 66.
7. Ibid., 76.
8. James J. Murphy, "The End of the Ancient World: The Second Sophistic and Saint Augustine," *A Synoptic History of Classical Rhetoric,* ed. James J. Murphy (Davis, Calif.: Hermagoras, 1983), 177.
9. Tacitus, as cited in Murphy, "The End of the Ancient World," 178–79; see also Tacitus, *Dialogues, Agricola, Germania,* trans. William Peterson (Cambridge, Mass.: Loeb Classical Library, 1956), 19–129.
10. Seneca, as cited in Murphy, "The End of the Ancient World," 179; see also Seneca the Elder, *Suasoriae,* trans. W. A. Edward (Cambridge: Cambridge University Press, 1928).
11. Nibley, "Victoriosa Loquacitas," 59.
12. Robert Brownrigg, *Who's Who in the New Testament* (Oxford: Oxford University Press, 1993), 268.
13. Anderson, "Rhetoric versus Revelation," 31.
14. Although many take "Areopagus" to refer to "Mars Hill," the word may refer to the Royal Stoa in the northwest corner of the market-place *(agora),* where a "Council of the Areopagus" judged religious crimes. George A. Kennedy, *New Testament Interpretation through Rhetorical Criticism* (Chapel Hill: University of North Carolina Press, 1984), 129. For the mythic origins of the Council of the Areopagus, see Aeschylus' *Eumenides,* the third play in the *Oresteia.*
15. Anderson, "Rhetoric versus Revelation," 32–33.
16. Compare William Shakespeare's imitation of the classical oration in Mark Antony's speech from *Julius Caesar.* The exordium begins, "Friends, Romans, countrymen," act 3, scene 2, line 73. See *The Riverside Shakespeare,* ed. G. Blakemore Evans (Boston: Houghton Mifflin, 1974), 1100–34.
17. Kennedy, *New Testament Interpretation through Rhetorical Criticism,* 131.

18. The Codex Brezae, the important "Western Text" of Acts, suggests that Tertullus was Jewish and that the Romans were preventing Paul from receiving the punishment that Tertullus believed he deserved (Acts 24:6–7). This identification of Tertullus with the Jews does not appear in any of the other New Testament texts. *Harper's Bible Dictionary,* ed. Paul J. Achtemeier (New York: Harper and Row, 1985), 1036.

19. Kennedy, *New Testament Interpretation through Rhetorical Criticism,* 23–24.

20. Ibid., 136.

21. Douglas Ehninger, *Contemporary Rhetoric: A Reader's Coursebook* (Glenview, Ill.: Scott, Foresman, 1972), 3.

22. Hugh Nibley, *The World and the Prophets,* vol. 3 of The Collected Works of Hugh Nibley (Salt Lake City: Deseret Book and F.A.R.M.S., 1987), 116.

23. E. W. Bullinger, *Figures of Speech Used in the Bible* (1893; reprint, Grand Rapids, Mich.: Baker Book House, 1968).

24. Burton L. Mack, *Rhetoric and the New Testament* (Minneapolis: Fortress Press, 1990).

CHAPTER FIVE

HEBREW CONCEPTS OF ADOPTION AND REDEMPTION IN THE WRITINGS OF PAUL

JENNIFER CLARK LANE

For Latter-day Saints, Paul's statement that "the Spirit itself beareth witness with our spirit, that we are the children of God" (Romans 8:16) seems perfectly natural. In jumping to that phrase we pass over the preceding verse, in which Paul declares that "ye have not received the spirit of bondage again to fear; but ye have received the Spirit of adoption" (Romans 8:15). His use of the Greek term for adoption, *huiothesia,* has long been a subject of scholarly debate. The term is found five times in his epistles (Romans 8:15; 8:23; 9:4; Galatians 4:5; Ephesians 1:5). Neither that term nor a Hebrew equivalent exists in the Septuagint or the Old Testament, and many scholars have argued that Paul was referring to a Greek or Roman concept of adoption. There is some merit to that claim, but it does not fully explain the Israelite context in which Paul's statements about adoption are found. Other scholars note incidents of adoption in the Old Testament and the use of adoption imagery to express the relationship between the Lord and his people to argue for an Israelite conception of adoption in the writings of Paul. Between them, these biblical models explain many aspects of Paul's use of *huiothesia,* but none fully explains the repeated association of adoption with redemption. The Roman model does have some associations with redemption but does not fit the Israelite context.

A model that does connect adoption with redemption,

□ □ □ □ □

Jennifer Clark Lane has received a master's degree in ancient Near Eastern studies from Brigham Young University.

however, can be found in the Israelite world of ideas. In ancient Israel a redeemer *(gō'ēl)* was a close family member who had the responsibility to buy his kinsmen out of bondage. In the text of the Old Testament the Lord is described as the redeemer *(gō'ēl)* of Israel. Israel's covenants form an adoptive relationship with the Lord. This new relationship is also indicated by the giving of a new name, a characteristic means of indicating a change in status, nature, or relationship. The adoptive-redemption model fits with other research on biblical adoptive metaphors and could also have been used concurrently with a Roman model of adoption. It explains the context of and connection with redemption better than do the other models by themselves.

REDEMPTION AND ADOPTION IN THE OLD TESTAMENT

In the Old Testament two words, *gā'āl* and *pādāh*, are primarily translated as *redeem* in English and *lutron* in the Greek of the Septuagint. Both incorporate the idea of "buying back" or "release by the payment of a price."[1] The term for a redeemer, *gō'ēl,* derives from *gā'āl. Gā'āl* refers to redemption being made out of family obligation or responsibility. The person who carries this responsibility is known as the *gō'ēl,* the present participle of *gā'āl.* One excellent translation of *gō'ēl* captures both the family relationship and the action: "kinsman-redeemer."[2] The five essential duties of the *gō'ēl* were to buy back sold property, to buy back a man who had sold himself to a foreigner as a slave, to avenge blood and kill a relative's murderer, to receive atonement money, and, figuratively, to be a helper in a lawsuit.[3] The *gō'ēl* was the "cultural gyroscope" of Israel whose purpose was to restore equilibrium in the society.[4]

Throughout the Old Testament Yahweh is described as the *gō'ēl* of Israel. The idea of intimate kinship, essential to the role of the *gō'ēl,* is connected with the Lord in Isaiah 63:16, in which Isaiah cries out, "Doubtless thou art our father, though Abraham be ignorant of us, and Israel acknowledge us not: thou, O Lord, art our father, our redeemer; thy name is from everlasting." An understanding of the Israelite concept of the *gō'ēl* as a redeemer-kinsman explains the significance of the Lord's being called both the redeemer and the father of Israel. This familial relationship between the Lord and Israel can be understood as having been created by covenants that were seen as an adoption.

Adoption is an important metaphor to explain the relationship between the Lord and Israel. Biblical texts include parallels to other ancient Near Eastern expressions of metaphorical adoption in the use of adoption formulas, father-son covenant terminology, and the grant formula. These parallels help to explain how the description of the Lord as father and Israel as son can be understood as covenantal terms and how adoption of Israel is the basis for the inheritance of land.

Israelite practices of making covenants and renaming further explain how the relationship between the Lord and his people can be understood as adoptive. The biblical concept of covenant was to create a new relationship. The Hebrew word *bĕrît* is translated *covenant,* but the range of the concept of covenant in the Old Testament extends the meaning of the term to include the action of creating a relationship.[5] A covenantal relationship could be formed in a variety of ways, including exchanging gifts, shaking hands, eating something together, oath-making, and even performing ceremonies with oil.[6]

The Israelites saw covenant making as a way of creating family relationships. Families were the basis of society, but strangers could enter into households by covenants that implied "an adoption into the household, an extension of kinship, the making of a brother."[7] The covenant meal "means admission into the family circle of another, since only the kinsmen will eat together."[8] Exodus 24:9–11 records a covenant meal that signifies adoption as Moses and the elders of Israel partook of a ritual meal with the Lord as part of the covenant at Sinai (Exodus 24:9–11). McCarthy comments: "To see a great chief and eat in his place is to join his family . . . the whole group related by blood or not which stood under the authority and protection of the father. One is united to him as a client to his patron who protects him and whom he serves.) . . . *Covenant is something one makes by a rite, not something one is born to or forced into, and it can be described in family terms.* God is patron and father, Israel servant and son."[9] By covenanting with the Lord at Sinai the people of Israel entered into his family and his protection. That relationship was explicitly expressed in terms of adoption: "I will take you to me for a people, and I will be to you a God" (Exodus 6:7).

Likewise, renaming in both the ancient Near East and in Israelite culture indicated receiving a new status, nature, and relationship. To understand the significance of renaming in the Old Testament, it is essential to appreciate the importance of names to the Israelites.[10] The Hebrew word *šem,* usually translated *name,* can also be rendered *remembrance* or *memorial,* indicating that the name acts as a reminder to its bearers and others. The name both shows the true nature of its bearer and indicates the relationship that exists between entities.

Several instances of name-changing occur in the Old Testament. These changes indicate a corresponding change in character and conduct and illustrate the Hebrew belief that names represent something of the essence of a person. A new name shows a new status or the establishment of a new relationship. Sometimes symbolic new names were given not to replace the old but to give information about the character of the recipient. Andersen notes that "in these cases an element of the meaning of the name seems to be indicating ownership or belonging—a common function of naming (cf. Isa 44,5)."[11]

The function of new names to indicate ownership and belonging can also be seen in their covenantal use.[12] In the Old Testament, naming is a way of declaring power over the person or object named. Hawthorne notes that the phrase "'to call *[qara']* one's name over' a people or a place is an idiom that does not mean that these will henceforth bear the name of the person whose name was 'called over' them." Rather, the phrase indicates that they are now his possession and are under his authority and protection. He suggests that this idiom is particularly important when used to describe the relationship of the Lord and the people of Israel. When the Lord says that he calls them by name, he is saying that "they are His peculiar possession, subject to His rule and under His protection and care."[13]

The use of renaming to express the covenant relationship can be seen not only in the relationship between the Lord and the people of Israel but also in the relationship between the Lord and individuals. In the ancient Near East, renaming was a significant part of the connection between suzerains and their vassal kings. Their relationship was established by covenant and the renaming of the vassal king at the time of his coronation indicated the authority of the suzerain as well as the kingship of the new vassal king.[14] Andersen notes that "in so far as the covenant between Yahweh and Israel was similar to ancient suzerainty treaties, there may be a link between this and the giving of throne-names." He claims that this similarity can be seen in the examples of the renaming of Abram (Genesis 17:5) and Sarai (Genesis 17:15) and points out that "the meaning of the new names, Abraham and Sarah, are directly connected to the covenant promises." Thus the new names can "be seen as a sign and guarantee of the covenant." Andersen sees the same connection of renaming and covenant where Jacob receives the name "Israel" (Genesis 32:28; 35:10). Here again "the renaming is accompanied by a recitation of covenant promises."[15]

This use of renaming to indicate a covenant relationship may have been a reference point to help Israelites understand their relationship to the Lord. The new name reflected the creation of a new relationship by covenant. Because of that creation of the adoptive relationship, the Lord could act as the *gō'ēl,* the redeemer-kinsman, of his covenant people.

COVENANT MAKING IN NEW TESTAMENT TIMES

To evaluate the concept of adoptive redemption in the writings of Paul, it is necessary to understand the use of *covenant* in an early Christian context. The translators of the Septuagint consistently chose *diathēkē,* meaning "covenant," to translate *běrît,* rather than the Greek term *synthēkē,* meaning "treaty." This usage was followed by the New Testament writers, and *diathēkē* is usually translated as *covenant* in English. Although *diathēkē* occurs in only one of the Pauline verses that use *huiothesia* (meaning "adoption"), several references to adoption occur in a context of Paul's explaining covenants to Christians.

The early Christians often referred to Old Testament images of covenant making to explain baptism. They looked at scripture through Christian eyes "but that did not mean that their Jewish tradition of interpretation was altogether destroyed. On the contrary, it was given reinterpretation and made to point forward in a new way to Christ."[16] The parallels between Jewish tradition and scripture and Christian descriptions of baptism show how baptism was seen as a covenant-making act that created a relationship with God and allowed participants to become the people of God.

In the Septuagint the Greek term *proselutos,* meaning "proselyte," describes those who join the covenant people.[17] Gentile proselytes who sought to become part of the covenant people went through a covenant-making process, just as did those who had been born to Jewish parents.[18] The proselyte baptism to become Jewish included circumcision of males, sprinkling of sin-offering water on the third and seventh days after circumcision, and ablution in water.[19] Although the Christian rites of covenant making clearly differed from Jewish rites, Jewish practices and understanding of those rites would have been clear to many of the early Christians.

Jewish contemporaries of Paul understood Jewish proselyte baptism as adoption into the covenant "in the same way that Israel itself was adopted by Yahweh."[20] The rite of proselyte baptism was understood not only as covenant making but also as adoption by the Lord into the covenant people. The tradition of interpretation connected this rite with participation in the redemption from Egypt, "the crossing of the Red Sea, and of sanctificatory cleansing in the establishment of the Covenant at Mount Sinai."[21]

The Israelite exodus led to the Israelites' covenant with the Lord in which they as a people received his name and became his people. This interpretation may have been preserved in a Jewish proselyte baptismal formula in which the name of the Lord was named over them as it had been named over Israel after the Exodus.[22] The same idea can be found in the Christian baptismal rite, in which people are baptized "in" or "into" the name of Christ. That formula recalls biblical concepts of renaming in which a new name can indicate a new nature and also reflect to whom one belongs.

The association of redemption, covenant making, and adoption with the practice of proselyte circumcision and baptism would have taken on new meaning for early Christians who interpreted the biblical promises and practices in terms of Christ. Understanding the tradition of Jewish biblical interpretation reveals what powerful meaning the ideas of covenant, adoption, and redemption would have had for early Christians who were familiar with the Old Testament either as Jews, proselytes, or "half-converts," who accepted Jewish monotheism and morality without being circumcised.[23]

The terminology and use of covenants in the New Testament and among the early Christians follow the biblical tradition. The term *diathēkē*, meaning "covenant" in both the Septuagint and the New Testament, parallels the idea of the Hebrew term *bĕrît*, which describes the creation of a relationship. Even if the New Testament concept of covenant is understood as a "new" covenant in the sense that it is in the heart, it is still the creation of a relationship with God, which is formalized by ritual action.

The ritual of baptism contains strong covenantal elements and is closely associated with Jewish covenantal practices. This understanding of the creation of a covenantal relationship between God and the believers through the rite of baptism demonstrates the close connection between the early Christian understanding of covenant and the Jewish understanding of covenant in the Old Testament. Recognizing the role of baptism to create a covenant with God whereby the believer is being baptized "into the name" of Christ and adopted by God helps us to understand the meaning of adoption in the writings of Paul. The adoptive nature of the baptismal covenant explains the connection between adoption and redemption in Paul's writings. As in the Old Testament, those who covenant with God enter into an adoptive relationship whereby he can act as their kinsman-redeemer.

ADOPTIVE COVENANT AND REDEMPTION
IN THE WRITINGS OF PAUL

Both the Greco-Roman and the biblical meanings of adoption illuminate part of the meaning of *huiothesia* ("adoption") in Paul's writings. In a Greco-Roman context an adopted son took the name of his father and had all the rights and obligations of a natural son. Similarly, just as if he were a natural son, his life and property were under the control of his new father. The biblical metaphor of adoption, as traditionally viewed, expressed the covenant relationship between the Lord and the house of Israel, as well as between the Lord and individuals, as a father-son relationship.

It is likely that Paul was familiar with both the Greco-Roman practice and the biblical metaphor, and so when using the term *huiothesia* ("adoption") he may have drawn upon all the connotations of both backgrounds. But neither the Greco-Roman nor the biblical model, as traditionally viewed, addresses the connection between adoption and redemption in Paul's writings. A further examination of the Israelite concept of the *gō'ēl* and biblical accounts of redemption demonstrate a connection between the covenantal adoption of Israel and the Lord's acts of redemption. Through their covenantal adoption, Israel be-comes the people of the Lord and he becomes their kinsman-redeemer, responsible for their redemption. The adoptive relationship was established by covenant making and is characterized by the giving of a new name. This process can be seen clearly in Abram and Jacob's covenant making, but it also characterized the adoption of the house of Israel: "Fear not: for I have redeemed thee, I have called thee by thy name; thou art mine" (Isaiah 43:1). When Israel became the people of the Lord, they were called by his name, indicating both adoption and possession (2 Chronicles 7:14).

The adoptive-redemption model can help us understand the emphasis on adoption in Paul's writings. For him baptism in Christ replaces circumcision as the covenantal rite whereby believers are adopted into the people of God. The covenantal rite of baptism makes them God's children and makes their redemption possible. Paul also uses adoption and redemption in an eschatological sense, in which a fuller adoption and redemption are foreseen when the believers return to the presence of God and receive their full inheritance in Christ. This usage is not a contradiction of the adoption and redemption provided by the covenant of baptism but a fulfillment of the promise of baptism.

The following textual analysis attempts to show how understanding the covenant of baptism as the signifying of an adoptive relationship helps to explain the relation of *huiothesia* ("adoption") to redemption.

Ephesians

The first two chapters of Ephesians focus on how even "before the foundation of the world" Christ was the source of adoption, redemption, and inheritance. In those chapters adoption and redemption are not directly linked, but both are connected with Christ. Repetition of how it is "in him" that these and other blessings are possible is reminiscent of baptism in which a person is baptized "into Christ" or "in Christ." God "blessed us with all spiritual blessings in heavenly places *in Christ*" and "hath chosen us *in him* before the foundation of the world" (Ephesians 1:3–4). He "made us accepted *in the beloved. In whom* we have redemption through his blood, the forgiveness of sins" (Ephesians 1:6–7) and "*in whom* also we have obtained an inheritance" (Ephesians 1:11). This emphasis on how "in Christ" redemption and inheritance are available can be understood by seeing baptism "in Christ" as an adoptive covenant whereby a person is baptized in the name of Christ and thus becomes part of his covenant people, able to be redeemed and to receive an inheritance. Paul states that the Gentiles were once "without Christ, being aliens from the commonwealth of Israel, and strangers from the covenants of promise" (Ephesians 2:12), but "now in Christ Jesus ye who sometimes were far off are made nigh by the blood of Christ" (Ephesians 2:13) and are "no more strangers and foreigners" but "of the household of God" (Ephesians 2:19).

This discussion of the blessings that are available "in Christ" is set in a general discussion of how these blessings were given "in heavenly places" where the saints were "chosen . . . in him before the foundation of the world" (Ephesians 1:3–4). In these passages adoption is described not as having taken place before the world but as God foreordaining "us *unto* the adoption *[huiothesia]* of children by Jesus Christ to himself" (Ephesians 1:5). Although this preparation was made "before the foundation of the world," because of the word *unto,* the adoption itself can be understood to take place at a later time, as at baptism, or in an eschatological sense. Those who believe in Christ will receive the "earnest of their inheritance" by being sealed with the Holy Spirit of Promise. The connection of belief and inheritance correlates with baptism as an expression of faith in Christ that makes those who are baptized the "purchased possession," sons and heirs of God. "In whom ye also trusted, after that ye heard the word of truth, the gospel of your salvation: in whom also after that ye believed, ye were sealed with that holy Spirit of promise. Which is the earnest of our inheritance until the redemption of the purchased possession, unto the praise of his glory" (Ephesians 1:13–14). Those who trust and believe in Christ then receive the "holy Spirit of promise," who acts as "the earnest of our inheritance," an assurance that the inheritance awaits even though it cannot be seen, until "the redemption of the purchased possession." *Redemption* here seems to have an eschatological sense that differs from the earlier equation of redemption with the forgiveness of sins (Ephesians 1:7), but in both cases redemption can be understood as being made possible by the ransom price of Christ's blood.

Both the baptismal and eschatological senses of redemption in Ephesians 1 can be seen as developments of the biblical concept of "adoptive" redemption. Through the covenant of baptism, an individual is forgiven of sins and thus redeemed from the bondage of sin. By using the phrase "redemption of the purchased possession," Paul refers to the covenant people of Israel, the "purchased possession" of the Lord, who were redeemed from bondage and brought into the land of promise (Ephesians 1:14; Exodus 15:16; Psalm 74:2). Even so will the people who have entered into the new covenant at baptism be redeemed from the bondage of this world and receive their inheritance. Both the explicit allusion to the Lord's redemption of his covenant people in the Old Testament and the use of the baptismal phrase "in Christ" to describe adoption and redemption support an interpretation of Paul's using an Old Testament adoptive-redemptive model.

Romans

The discussion of adoption in Romans 8 is closely related to redemption in ways explained by the Old Testament adoptive-redemptive model. *Adoption* and *redemption* are used in Romans 8 in both immediate and eschatological senses. Paul tells the Saints that "as many as are led by the Spirit of God, they are the sons of God. For ye have not received the spirit of bondage again to fear; but ye have received the Spirit of adoption [*huiothesia*], whereby we cry, Abba, Father. The Spirit itself beareth witness with our spirit, that we are the children of God:

and if children, then heirs; heirs of God, and joint-heirs with Christ" (Romans 8:14–17).

The spirit of adoption is contrasted to the spirit of bondage, suggesting that adoption is the redemption from bondage to the carnal state in which we are "sold under sin" (Romans 7:14). Earlier in his discussion of justification through Christ, Paul states that "so many of us as were baptized into Jesus Christ were baptized into his death" (Romans 6:3), so that "our old man is crucified with him, that the body of sin might be destroyed, that henceforth we should not serve sin" (Romans 6:6). Here baptism is the means of partaking of redemption from slavery to sin and the carnal state.

The baptismal concept of being one with Christ is used in Romans 8 to explain how the Spirit is in the believers to give them life and make them the sons of God. "If Christ be in you, the body is dead because of sin; but the Spirit is life because of righteousness. But if the Spirit of him that raised up Jesus from the dead dwell in you, he that raised up Christ from the dead shall also quicken your mortal bodies by his Spirit that dwelleth in you" (Romans 8:10–11). Paul had earlier explained that baptism is the source of "newness of life" (Romans 6:4) and that this "newness of spirit" (Romans 7:6) is a deliverance from sin. Here in Romans 8 this "Spirit that dwelleth in you" is also described as the source of adoption, "whereby we cry, Abba, Father" (Romans 8:15). It is the presence of the "Spirit of adoption" in the believers that "beareth witness with our spirit, that we are the children of God" (Romans 8:16).

This use of adoption in a present sense is connected with redemption from sin and the carnal nature, but a later usage extends redemption and adoption to a final deliverance for which those who have the Spirit await: "Because the creature itself also shall be delivered from the bondage of corruption into the glorious liberty of the children of God. For we know that the whole creation groaneth and travaileth in pain together until now. And not only they, but ourselves also, which have the firstfruits of the Spirit, even we ourselves groan within ourselves, waiting for the adoption [huiothesia], to wit, the redemption of our body" (Romans 8:21–23). Although the covenant of baptism provides a witness of adoption, those who are joint-heirs with Christ must also suffer with him "that we may be also glorified together" (Romans 8:17). This future glory is equated with "the manifestation of the sons of God" (Romans 8:19) and a deliverance "from the bondage of corruption into the glorious liberty of the children of God" (Romans 8:21). In this sense, resurrection completes the adoption and redemption provided by baptism, for even those "which have the firstfruits of the Spirit . . . groan within ourselves, waiting for the adoption, to wit, the redemption of our body" (Romans 8:23).

The biblical background to this concept of adoption is emphasized in the beginning of the next chapter, in which *huiothesia* is listed among the privileges of Israel: "Who are Israelites; to whom pertaineth the adoption [*huiothesia*], and the glory, and the covenants [*diathēkai*], and the giving of the law, and the service of God, and the promises; whose are the fathers, and of whom as concerning the flesh Christ came, who is over all, God blessed for ever. Amen" (Romans 9:4–5).

The Old Testament setting of *huiothesia* shows that Paul understands adoption as the relationship between Israel and God and supports an understanding of baptism as a new covenant relationship, allowing the Gentiles to participate in the adoption through Christ. Paul takes the Old Testament adoptive-covenant imagery that makes Israel the son of God through covenant and applies it to Christian baptism. He explains how it is the Spirit received at baptism that "witnesses to our spirit, that we are the children of God" (Romans 8:16).

Galatians

In Galatians *huiothesia* appears in a discussion of covenant, the law of Moses, and Christ. Paul explains the importance of adoptive redemption by showing that God promised inheritances to Abraham and his seed but that the curse of the law placed the seed of Abraham in bondage. The curse of the law exists because "cursed is every one that continueth not in all things which are written in the book of the law to do them" (Galatians 3:10). That inability to perfectly keep the law brings all that are under the law under the curse, but "Christ hath redeemed us from the curse of the law, being made a curse for us" (Galatians 3:13). His "being made a curse" by hanging on a tree paid the ransom price so that "the blessing of Abraham might come on the Gentiles through Jesus Christ" (Galatians 3:14). The covenant of Abraham gave the blessing, or promise, of inheritance, and the law "cannot disannul" it (Galatians 3:17).

Paul explains that the Gentiles can become Abraham's seed and heirs to the promise through their covenantal adoptive relationship with Christ. "For ye are all the children of God by faith in Christ Jesus. For as many of you as have been baptized into Christ have put on Christ. . . . And if ye be Christ's, then are ye Abraham's seed, and heirs according to the promise" (Galatians 3:26–27, 29). The covenant of baptism is an expression of faith in Christ that makes one a child of God, just as biblical covenants act to create family ties. Those who are baptized "into Christ" have "put on Christ," suggesting the change of nature that a new name indicates. Formerly "Abraham's seed" were those who had covenanted by circumcision, but, Paul explains, those who are Christ's through this new covenant relationship are also partakers in the covenant of Abraham and are "heirs according to the promise."

Paul in Galatians 4 then returns to the discussion of how the law is a bondage from which Christ came to redeem us, "that we might receive the adoption of sons." The covenant people under the law are compared to an heir as a child under tutors and governors, who "differeth nothing from a servant." Christ came "to redeem them that were under the law, that we might receive the adoption of sons." The redemption of Christ made the new covenant of baptism possible that thereby those who were in bondage to the law as servants might become adopted as sons under a new covenant. Thus those who have "put on Christ" through baptism and received his Spirit can call on the Father as he did, crying "Abba, Father," an expression which may have become part of the baptism liturgy. Through the adoptive covenant of baptism they are no longer servants but sons and heirs of God through Christ.

CONCLUSION

The adoptive-redemption model explains why Paul connected adoption and redemption. Those who are adopted are redeemed "in Christ" and as "the purchased possession" await their inheritance (Ephesians 1). Their adoption is contrasted with the "spirit of bondage," because through their baptism they are redeemed from slavery to sin (Romans 8). That adoption was formerly one of the privileges of Israel (Romans 9:4–5), but through Christ all can "put on Christ" through baptism and thus become the adopted children of God, redeemed from the curse of the law and made "heirs according to the promise" (Galatians 3–4).

This striking connection of covenant, adoption, and redemption can best be explained by the biblical adoptive-redemption model. Although other views may help us understand some facets of how Paul understood adoption, they fail to recognize the Hebrew practice of a redeemer being a kinsman. With an understanding of the adoptive-covenant relationship of God and Israel as the source of redemption, the relationship between adoption and redemption in Paul's writings becomes clear. Just as in the Old Testament the Lord becomes a redeemer-kinsman through adoptive covenants, so in the writings of Paul the baptismal covenant creates an adoptive relationship whereby Christians can look to Christ as their redeemer.

As members of God's covenant people, we also have the assurance that our baptismal covenant has brought us into a new relationship with the Lord. As King Benjamin says, "Because of the covenant which ye have made ye shall be called the children of Christ, his sons, and his daughters" (Mosiah 5:7). Through our covenants Christ has become our spiritual father and we have been adopted as his children. We are baptized in his name and thereby take his name upon us, a new name that indicates our covenantal adoptive relationship. This adoptive relationship allows the Lord to act as our redeemer and deliver us from the bondage of sin and our carnal state with the price of his blood. By making and keeping our adoptive covenants we can have a firm hope that as the children of Christ we will be redeemed. "For [we] have not received the spirit of bondage again to fear; but [we] have received the Spirit of adoption, whereby we cry, Abba, Father" (Romans 8:15).

NOTES

1. J. Murray, "Redeemer; Redemption," in *The International Standard*

Bible Encyclopedia, ed. Geoffrey W. Bromiley, 4 vols. (Grand Rapids, Mich.: William B. Eerdmans Publishing, 1979), 4:61.

2. Robert L. Hubbard, "The *Gō'ēl* in Ancient Israel: Theological Reflections on an Israelite Institution," *Bulletin for Biblical Research* 1 (1991): 3.

3. *Theological Dictionary of the Old Testament*, ed. G. Johannes Botterweck and Helmer Ringgren (Grand Rapids, Mich.: William B. Eerdmans Publishing, 1975), 2:351–52, s.v. *"gā'āl."*

4. Michael S. Moore, *"Hagō'ēl:* The Cultural Gyroscope of Ancient Hebrew Society," *Restoration Quarterly*, vol. 23, no. 1 (1988): 31.

5. Dennis J. McCarthy, *Treaty and Covenant: A Study in Form in the Ancient Oriental Documents and in the Old Testament,* Analecta Biblica (Rome: Biblical Institute Press, 1978), comments that the relationship is more important than the word; and even though the word might not be there, the relationship can still exist (16). He also notes different suggestions for translation of *bĕrît* but cautions against a rigid definition (22 n. 42).

6. Dennis J. McCarthy, "Covenant in the Old Testament: The Present State of Inquiry," *Catholic Biblical Quarterly* 27 (January 1965): 239.

7. Paul Kalluveettil, *Declaration and Covenant: A Comprehensive Review of Covenant Formulae from the Old Testament and the Ancient Near East,* Analecta Biblica (Rome: Biblical Institute Press, 1982), 204–5.

8. Ibid., 205.

9. McCarthy, *Treaty and Covenant,* 266; emphasis added.

10. The material on the significance of names is from G. F. Hawthorne, "Name," *International Standard Bible Encyclopedia,* 3:481–83, and D. Stuart, "Names, Proper," *International Standard Bible Encyclopedia,* 3:483–88.

11. T. David Andersen, "Renaming and Wedding Imagery in Isaiah 62," *Biblica,* vol. 67, no. 1 (1986): 76.

12. For a discussion of the relationship of new ownership and new names in the Hebrew Bible, see Otto Eissfeldt, "Renaming in the Old Testament," in *Words and Meanings: Essays Presented to David Winton Thomas,* ed. Peter R. Ackroyd and Barnabas Lindars (Cambridge: Cambridge University Press, 1968), 71–74.

13. Hawthorne, "Name," 3:481.

14. Andersen, "Renaming and Wedding Imagery," 75. He indicates that examples of this practice can be found in the Hebrew Bible in 2 Kings 23:24 and 24:17.

15. Ibid., 76.

16. Thomas F. Torrance, "The Origins of Baptism," *Scottish Journal of Theology* 11 (1958): 159.

17. *The Jewish Encyclopedia,* ed. Isidore Singer (New York: Funk and Wagnalls, 1905), s.v. "proselyte," 220.

18. The origins of proselyte baptism are not certain. Clear evidence for it does not appear until the second century after Christ, but it is believed to have existed long before that. Torrance, "The Origins of Baptism," 161. Lars Hartman claims that it developed in the first century after Christ. "Baptism," *Anchor Bible Dictionary*, ed. David Noel Freedman (New York: Doubleday, 1992), 1:583. The practice of circumcising proselytes is well documented in the Hebrew Bible.

19. Torrance, "Origins of Baptism," 161.

20. Ibid., 159.

21. Ibid., 161.

22. See Hawthorne, "Name," 3:483, and A. J. M. Wedderburn, *Baptism and Resurrection: Studies in Pauline Theology against Its Graeco-Roman Background* (Tübingen: J. C. B. Mohr, 1987), 60.

23. A discussion of the "half-converts," or "proselytes of the gate" *[ger ha-sha'ar]*, can be found in *Jewish Encyclopedia*, s.v. "proselyte," 221.

CHAPTER SIX

THE JERUSALEM COUNCIL

ROBERT J. MATTHEWS

The fifteenth chapter of the book of Acts in the New Testament tells of a high-level council meeting in Jerusalem of the leaders of the Church. The date is not recorded, but the events leading up to the council indicate that the meeting was held in approximately A.D. 49 or 50. Within the short space of those sixteen or seventeen years after the death of Christ, the preaching of the gospel of Jesus Christ among non-Jewish people raised questions of doctrine and procedure that the young Church had not encountered when missionary work was done among the Jews only. Those questions made a top-level discussion necessary, for the decision would affect the Church in matters of doctrine, in missionary procedure, and in family religious observances. The council was not held in a vacuum nor was it just an academic exercise. It was the result of, and was attended by, persons having strong opinions, religious convictions, traditions, and biases. In effect, a crisis was forming in the Church.

THE NEW TESTAMENT RECORD

The complete title of the New Testament book of Acts is "The Acts of the Apostles." It is generally understood to have been written by Luke and is in reality a sequel to the book of Luke. Both the book of Luke and the book of Acts are addressed to an acquaintance named "Theophilus" (Luke 1:3; Acts 1:1). Acts refers to the book of Luke as the "former treatise" of "all that Jesus began both to do and teach" (Acts 1:1), whereas the book of Acts itself deals with the work, growth, and development of the Church after the ascension of Christ.

□ □ □ □ □

Robert J. Matthews is professor emeritus of ancient scripture at Brigham Young University.

Although each member of the Twelve is mentioned at least once in Acts, the book deals initially with the ministry of Peter, James, and John and records at great length the conversion and ministry of Paul. It is a record of the "acts" not of all the apostles but of only a few and especially of Paul. Acts is in truth a short account of the missionary outreach of the Church to the Jews in Judea, then to the Samaritans, and finally to the Gentiles throughout the Mediterranean world. Because Paul is the dominant personality in the extension of the Church among gentile people, he becomes the dominant personality in the book of Acts from chapters 13 through 28. Likewise, fourteen of the twenty-one epistles in the New Testament were written by Paul.

Even though our present New Testament does not contain a record of it, there can be no doubt that many, if not all, of the Twelve traveled extensively in giving missionary service. Jesus commanded the Twelve to go unto all nations, teaching and baptizing them (Matthew 28:19–20). Tradition and apocryphal sources suggest that the original apostles were true to their commission and traveled throughout Africa, India, Mesopotamia, the Near East, and so forth, and preached the gospel of Jesus Christ.[1] Yet the New Testament that has been among Christians for the past eighteen hundred years focuses primarily on the area immediately surrounding the northern shores of the Mediterranean Sea: Greece, Turkey, and Italy with only slight mention of Spain. It contains no record of the ministry of the Twelve in such other parts of the world as Egypt and India.

I believe there is a reasonable explanation for that narrow focus. The New Testament is a record of the work and preaching of living prophets and apostles who went forth with priesthood authority to build up and regulate the Church of Jesus Christ in their day, the first century after Christ. Most of the writings and records of travel of those early authorized brethren have not been preserved for later generations, yet the missionary records of Paul, Peter, and John have been. Could it be that those records in particular were preserved for the benefit of the Restoration? Perhaps the Lord, knowing among what people the restoration in the latter days would need to begin, preserved the sacred records that dealt with the establishment of the Church in southern Europe, from where it moved throughout Europe, the British Isles, and Scandinavia. There would thus be among them a scriptural base for the restoration of the fulness of the gospel by the Prophet Joseph Smith.

Most of the settlers in early North America came from the countries of Europe, and they brought a Bible with them. The Protestant Reformation of the sixteenth century based most of its philosophy on the writings of Paul. The Reformation was absolutely necessary as prologue to the Restoration. The Joseph Smith family, the Richards family, the Youngs, the Kimballs, Whitmers, Taylors, and other early families in the Church were of European Protestant stock. Furthermore, when missionaries of the Church went forth in the late 1830s and immediately thereafter, most of the converts came from Europe—from England, Wales, Scotland, Scandinavia, Germany, and Holland.

I believe the Lord preserved what he did in the New Testament because it was that part of the history and doctrine of the early Church that would be most usable and serviceable in establishing The Church of Jesus Christ of Latter-day Saints in the dispensation of the fulness of times. The Lord knew and designed that it should be among those people in America who were of European extraction that the restoration in the latter days should first take root and sprout. It would then be nourished by converts from Europe. From that beginning the gospel in the latter days would spread to all other nations. It would have been a great deal more difficult than it was for The Church of Jesus Christ of Latter-day Saints to be established among people who did not have a New Testament or who had a New Testament that had not produced the Protestant reformation.

EVENTS LEADING UP TO THE JERUSALEM COUNCIL

As noted earlier, the causes that produced the Jerusalem Council did not develop in a vacuum. The need for such a council was the consequence of several doctrinal and cultural factors that had been at work among both Jews and Gentiles for centuries. It will be necessary to review the activities of the Church as recorded in Acts 1 through 15 to understand the thrust and direction of the early Church and see what led to the council itself. Following is a summation of significant events.

Jesus ascends into heaven from the Mount of Olives, having told the Twelve not to extend their ministry beyond Judea until after they receive the Holy Ghost. They will then be empowered to go to Jews, Samaritans, and the "uttermost part of the earth" (Gentiles) in that order (Acts 1:1–12). Because of the vacancy in the Quorum of the Twelve, Peter calls the eleven remaining apostles together, and Matthias is chosen (Acts 1:13–26).

One week after the ascension of Jesus to heaven, at the annual feast of Pentecost, the Holy Ghost descends on the Twelve, and they speak in tongues to people of many nations. Gathered at Jerusalem for the feast are thousands of Jews from at least fifteen nations throughout the Near and Middle East, including Rome, Greece, Turkey, Crete, Arabia, Egypt, Libya, Parthia, and Mesopotamia. These are people of the Jews' religion who have come to Jerusalem for the annual feast of Pentecost, which is held fifty days after the feast of Passover. Many thousands are present, for from among the visitors the apostles baptize three thousand in one day (Acts 2:41).

It is of particular importance that the record states that those who came from those fifteen nations were Jews and proselytes, which means that not all were Jewish by lineage but some were gentile converts to Judaism (Acts 2:10). The term *proselytes* in the New Testament always means gentile converts to Judaism. Certainly some of the three thousand converted to the Church on the day of Pentecost would have been from among the proselytes and thus the first persons of gentile lineage to join the Church in the meridian dispensation. Jesus had instructed the Twelve, when they were starting on their first missions more than two years before, not to go among the Gentiles or the Samaritans at that time (Matthew 10:5). Hence, Church members up till then were exclusively Jewish. But note this important fact: even though individuals of gentile lineage now came into the Church, they had all previously converted to Judaism, which meant complying with the practice of circumcision, eating kosher food, offering sacrifice, and honoring the Sabbath day in proper Jewish style. Although Greek, Galatian, or Roman in lineage, they were Jews in religion.

Acts 3 through 6 deals with the ministry of the Twelve among the Jews in and around Judea. The Church grows rapidly with Jewish converts. Persecution comes from the Jewish leaders. Church growth necessitates administrative adjustments, so seven men are selected to assist the Twelve, primarily in welfare duties. Among those seven are some with such gentile-sounding names as Stephen, Parmenas, and Nicolas. Nicolas is further identified as a proselyte from Antioch (Acts 6:5), thus affirming that he is a Gentile by lineage who first joined the Jews' religion and then was converted to Christ and the Church. Thus at least Nicolas, and possibly others among the seven, is actually of gentile lineage but has been circumcised and practices all that pertains to the Jews' religion and the law of Moses.

Stephen, one of the seven, is accused of having taught that Jesus would destroy Jerusalem and the temple and "change the customs which Moses delivered" unto Israel (Acts 6:14). He is taken before the Sanhedrin and permitted to speak. Found guilty of blasphemy, he is stoned to death. Saul (later known as Paul) witnesses his death (Acts 7). Stephen is the earliest on record who is reported to have said that Jesus will change the Mosaic customs.

Philip, another of the seven, baptizes many men and women in Samaria (Acts 8). That is another extension for the Church, which to this point has not done missionary work there. Peter and John come from Jerusalem to lay their hands on the new converts and confer the Holy Ghost. The Church is thus officially established among the Samaritans but is only a half step away from teaching the Jews. Even though the Samaritans were genealogically Israelite mixed with other nations and thus technically not Jews, they practiced the law of Moses and hence were circumcised, ate kosher food, offered sacrifice, and so forth. In this respect they were similar to the Jews, and the conversion of Samaritans did not challenge allegiance to the law of Moses.

Saul is converted to Jesus Christ by a personal visit in which he sees, hears, and converses with the resurrected Lord (Acts

9). Paul proclaims his testimony of Christ in the synagogues of Damascus. For Paul to have become a follower of Jesus Christ was a great change in his life, but his conversion did not mark a doctrinal or cultural change in the Church because he was already circumcised, ate kosher food, and so forth.

Peter, having been directed by a vision and the voice of the Spirit, baptizes Cornelius and his family at Caesarea (Acts 10–11). Peter is shown in vision animals forbidden to be eaten under the law of Moses, and he is told to eat them. This is a sign to him from the Lord that the dietary restrictions of the law of Moses are about to end. It takes Peter a little time to get used to the idea. Cornelius is a good man, an Italian, a soldier, but he is not a proselyte to Judaism. An angel directed him to send for Peter. Peter, having already been prepared by the Lord, is willing to baptize Cornelius.

This is the first clear case of a Gentile's coming into the Church without having first complied with the law of Moses through circumcision and so forth. The conversion and baptism of Cornelius in this manner is thus a major step—a full step—in extending the Church missionary system. It is very significant that the Lord brought about this new procedure through Peter, who as the senior apostle of the Church can exercise all the priesthood keys and holds the proper office through which such direction from the Lord should come.

Many Jewish brethren in the Church complained to Peter about that direct process for gaining membership in the Church, but he answered their criticism with a recital of the vision, the angel, the voice of the Spirit to him, and the mani-festation of the Holy Ghost to Cornelius and his family before their baptism (Acts 11). Cornelius did not receive the gift of the Holy Ghost before baptism, for such is contrary to the order of the kingdom. What he did receive before baptism was the wit-ness of the Holy Ghost, as the Prophet Joseph Smith explained: "There is a difference between the Holy Ghost and the gift of the Holy Ghost. Cornelius received the Holy Ghost before he was baptized, which was the convincing power of God unto him of the truth of the Gospel, but he could not receive the gift of the Holy Ghost until after he was baptized. Had he not taken this sign or ordinance upon him, the Holy Ghost which convinced him of the truth of God, would have left him. Until he obeyed these ordinances and received the gift of the Holy Ghost, by the laying on of hands, according to the order of God, he could not have healed the sick or commanded an evil spirit to come out of a man, and it obey him."[2]

Even after the landmark conversion of Cornelius, with Peter, the Lord's anointed, directing this phase of the missionary outreach, some Jewish members of the Church refused to accept the change, and they preached the gospel to "none but unto the Jews only" (Acts 11:19). Nonetheless the way was opened for Gentiles to come into the Church without becoming Jews first. At Antioch of Syria, a great gentile city about three hundred miles north of Jerusalem, so many Gentiles joined the Church that the Brethren in Jerusalem sent Barnabas to Antioch to oversee the change that was taking place. Barnabas was a good diplomatic choice: he was a Levite by lineage, was reared in Cyprus, a gentile environment, and converted to the gospel, being "a good man, and full of the Holy Ghost and of faith" (Acts 11:24; 4:36). Upon seeing the magnitude of the gentile conversion in Antioch, Barnabas was pleased with the direction in which the missionary work was going and sent for Saul (Paul) to assist him. Barnabas had known of Saul earlier and had introduced him to the apostles (Acts 9:27).

Acts 12 deals with the martyrdom of James, one of the three most senior apostles and the brother of John. Administrative activities are also discussed in this chapter.

Saul, Barnabas, and John Mark at Antioch are called and set apart to missionary service. They go to Cyprus, Barnabas's native country, and then to many cities in what is now central Turkey. While at Cyprus, Saul changes his Hebrew name Saul to the Latin Paul (Acts 13:9). This name change is very significant and decisive doctrinally and presages some cultural changes. The Brethren preach first to the Jews and then to the proselytes who come to the synagogues. They teach that the gospel of Jesus Christ is greater than the law of Moses and that the law of Moses cannot save them (Acts 13:38–39). The Jews are furious, but many of the gentile proselytes join the Church. Paul and Barnabas thereafter direct their chief attention to the Gentiles (Acts 13:45–49).

Paul and Barnabas establish branches of the Church, ordain elders in each of the cities they visit, and then return to Antioch with glowing reports of their success among the Gentiles. And of course, they have baptized many Gentiles directly into the Church without benefit of the law of Moses—that is, without circumcision and so forth.

When word of the success of Paul and Barnabas reaches certain Church members in and around Jerusalem, these Judean brethren, much concerned, go to Antioch on their own, without authorization from the Twelve or any of the presiding Brethren of the Church, and declare to the gentile Church members at Antioch that "except ye be circumcised after the manner of Moses, ye cannot be saved" (Acts 15:1). Thus the problem is clearly stated: Is obedience to the law of Moses with all its attendant performances required for salvation, now that Jesus Christ has made the Atonement?

Let me digress a moment to explain the great emphasis on circumcision, for it may seem to us today an odd matter for early Church members to have been fighting about. Circumcision is a very old practice among mankind, even among non-Jewish peoples, but the Lord Jehovah appointed it the token of the covenant he made with Abraham (Genesis 17). This covenant was to extend throughout Abraham's posterity, and through this covenant the blessings and promises of God's favor were to be realized throughout time and eternity. Circumcision was the badge, the sign of identification, showing that one was a believer in the true God and in the covenant. That token was continued in the law of Moses. The manner in which the word *circumcised* is used throughout the book of Acts and the epistles is generally as a one-word representation for the entire law of Moses; hence when the Jewish members of the Church insisted that Gentiles be circumcised, they meant that the Gentiles should obey all of the law of Moses. But back to the events at Antioch.

Paul and Barnabas are contending with the brethren from Judea on this important matter, which is not simply a topic about tradition or custom but a fundamental doctrinal issue regarding the atonement of Jesus Christ. The dissension becomes so great that it is decided such a matter can be settled officially only by the Twelve at Jerusalem.

The question is threefold:

1. Did Jesus Christ by his earthly ministry and atonement fulfill the law of Moses with its multitudinous ordinances and performances? and if so,

2. Do converts from among non-Israelite peoples have to obey the law of Moses to become baptized members of the Church of Jesus Christ? and

3. Should Church members, Jew and Gentile, have their sons circumcised as a requirement for salvation?

The settlement of this threefold question would affect how believers regarded Christ's mission, what missionary procedures were implemented, and what would be the practice of every family in the Church with respect to their sons for generations yet unborn.

THE JERUSALEM COUNCIL CONVENES

When Paul and Barnabas arrived in Jerusalem to see the Brethren, they were respectfully received, and they conveyed an account of their success among the Gentiles. There were in Jerusalem, however, many Jewish members of the Church who had been Pharisees before their conversion to Jesus Christ. They would not give up the law of Moses and insisted "that it was needful to circumcise [the Gentiles], and to command them to keep the law of Moses" (Acts 15:5). Therefore the apostles and the elders at Jerusalem "came together for to consider this matter" (Acts 15:6).

After much disputing in the council, Peter declared the baptism of Cornelius and others by his hand. He reminded the congregation that the conversion of the Gentiles was the work of God and that God "put no difference between us and them, purifying their hearts by faith." He also stated that the "grace of the Lord Jesus Christ" (Acts 15:7–11) would save both "us and them," affirming the truth that our works are insufficient without God's grace.

After Peter's testimony, the "multitude" in the council listened as Barnabas and Paul told of the "miracles and wonders God had wrought among the Gentiles by them" (Acts 15:12). Then James, who may have replaced the James who was slain as recounted in Acts 12 and who apparently conducted the meeting, stated as a type of official pronouncement that no greater burden than the necessary things of purity and refraining from idol worship and from eating blood should be placed on the Gentiles who wished to come into the Church. James did not specifically mention the law of Moses, and it is conspicuous by its absence, though the context of the council implies it. The council decreed that Paul and Barnabas should return to Antioch, accompanied by two men from Jerusalem, "chief men among the brethren," named Barsabas and Silas. These two could testify with Barnabas and Paul of the decision of the council. The Brethren prepared an epistle to be carried to Antioch and the surrounding area, stating the decision of the council:

"The apostles and elders and brethren send greeting unto the brethren which are of the Gentiles in Antioch and Syria and Cicilia:

"Forasmuch as we have heard, that certain which went out from us have troubled you with words, subverting your souls, saying, Ye must be circumcised, and keep the law: to whom we gave no such commandment:

"It seemed good unto us, being assembled with one accord, to send chosen men unto you with our beloved Barnabas and Paul,

"Men that have hazarded their lives for the name of our Lord Jesus Christ.

"We have sent therefore Judas and Silas, who shall also tell you the same things by mouth.

"For it seemeth good to the Holy Ghost, and to us, to lay upon you no greater burden than these necessary things;

"That ye abstain from meats offered to idols, and from blood, and from things strangled, and from fornication: from which if ye keep yourselves, ye shall do well. Fare ye well" (Acts 15:23–29).

Upon arriving in Antioch of Syria, the Brethren assembled a multitude of Church members, read the epistle, and exhorted the people, who "rejoiced" at the news (Acts 15:30–33).

Such is the report of the proceedings of the council recorded in Acts 15. We learn from Paul's later epistle to the Galatians the significant information we would not otherwise have that Paul went up early to Jerusalem to confer privately with the Brethren to learn of their views and to make certain they agreed with what he and Barnabas had done in receiving the Gentiles, "lest by any means I should run, or had run, in vain" (Galatians 2:2). This private meeting is probably the one referred to in Acts 15:4–5, but Paul's epistle gives it a clearer focus by expressing his motive for speaking with the Brethren in private.

Another important factor we learn from this Galatian epistle is that Paul and Barnabas took Titus, a young gentile convert probably from Antioch (Titus 1:4), to the council. Paul may have seen in him a kind of "exhibit A," for Titus was an uncircumcised Greek who was a model of faith and virtue, strong in the Spirit. Paul could show the Jewish members of the Church in Jerusalem a living, breathing example of the grace of God given to the Gentiles without the encumbrance of the law of Moses. Paul was apparently successful in his purpose, for he declares, "But neither Titus, who was with me, being a Greek, was compelled to be circumcised" (Galatians 2:3).

The Galatian epistle also helps us determine the date of the council. In chapter 1 Paul tells of his conversion to Jesus Christ; in chapter 2 he tells of going to Jerusalem with Barnabas and Titus to the council fourteen years later. We do not know when Paul joined the Church, but it could not have been less than a year or two after the ascension of Christ. Assuming that is so and that he was baptized in about the year A.D. 35 or 36 (Galatians 1:15–19), fourteen years later would be A.D. 49 or 50. Paul mentions an event "three years" after his conversion, but a close reading of Galatians 1 shows that the three years were within the scope of the fourteen, not in addition to them.

THE JERUSALEM COUNCIL WAS ONLY A HALF STEP

As forward reaching and beneficial as the decision by the Jerusalem Council was, it was only a half step forward in the progress of the Church. For one thing, the council did not decisively declare an end to the law of Moses. The announcement part of the epistle sent from the council does not use the words "law of Moses" nor declare its fulfillment or its final and absolute end as a practice in the Church. Furthermore, the epistle was addressed not to all members of the Church but only to the gentile members in Antioch, Syria, and Cicilia. The council settled the matter of observing the law of Moses with respect to the Gentiles; it did not address the subject with respect to Jewish Church members. So far as the epistle is concerned, the Jewish members of the Church could continue to observe the ordinances of the law of Moses as a supposed requirement for salvation.

Why would the Brethren have been so ambiguous and non-declarative? They seem to have said as little as they could about the matter. Perhaps they hoped to avoid dividing the Church and alienating the strict Jewish members. Likewise, they would not have wanted to invite persecution from nonmember Jews. James seems to have had that in mind when, after announcing the moderate decision, he said to the council: "For Moses of old time hath in every city them that preach him, being read in the synagogues every sabbath day" (Acts 15:21).

The decision of the council was favorable to Paul, Barnabas, Titus, and the Gentiles who were already in the Church and who would yet join, but it also left the Jewish members free to continue the practice of the law of Moses if they cared to do so. The council did not say that the Gentiles could not or must not practice the law of Moses, but only that they need not do so for salvation. By wording the decision in the way they did, the Brethren probably avoided a schism in the Church and no doubt also avoided the ire that would have come from the Jews had the decision been stronger. There must have been many who would have preferred a stronger declaration, but the Brethren acted in the wisdom requisite for their situation.

Not long after the council adjourned, when Paul was on his second mission, he wanted Timothy, a Greek convert at Lystra, to accompany him. Because Timothy's mother was a Jew and his father a Greek, he had not been circumcised. Paul therefore circumcised him so that he would be more acceptable to the Jews among whom he would do missionary work. That may seem contradictory to Paul's standards, but it is fairly simple: the action was expedient because of Jewish tradition and culture but it was not necessary for Timothy's salvation.

The effects of the moderate decision of the council were

far-reaching and long lasting. Ten years later, when Paul returned to Jerusalem at the end of his third mission among the Gentiles of Greece and Turkey (Galatia and Asia), he was greeted by the Brethren, who rejoiced at his great success among the Gentiles of the Roman empire but cautioned him about preaching strong doctrine, especially about the law of Moses, in Jerusalem. Even a decade after the council, Jewish members of the Church in Judea were still observing the law of Moses. The Brethren "said unto him, Thou seest, brother, how many thousands of Jews there are which believe; and they are all zealous of the law:

"And they are informed of thee, that thou teachest all the Jews which are among the Gentiles to forsake Moses, saying that they ought not to circumcise their children, neither to walk after the customs.

"What is it therefore? the multitude must needs come together: for they will hear that thou art come.

"Do therefore this that we say to thee: We have four men which have a vow on them;

"Them take, and purify thyself with them, and be at charges with them, that they may shave their heads: and all may know that those things, whereof they were informed concerning thee, are nothing; but that thou thyself also walkest orderly, and keepest the law.

"As touching the Gentiles which believe, we have written and concluded that they observe no such thing, save only that they keep themselves from things offered to idols, and from blood, and from strangled, and from fornication.

"Then Paul took the men, and the next day purifying himself with them entered into the temple, to signify the accomplishment of the days of purification, until that an offering should be offered for every one of them" (Acts 21:20–26).

There is no question that Peter and the other Brethren knew that the law of Moses was fulfilled. The doctrinal question was settled. The law was no longer a requirement for salvation now that Jesus had made the Atonement. Missionary work among the gentile nations could go forth directly and without impediment. But there was a conflict between culture and doctrine. The Brethren were clear on the matter, but long-standing culture and tradition persisted among many Jewish members of the Church even after the doctrinal question had been settled. Latter-day revelation leaves no doubt that the law of Moses was fulfilled in Christ (3 Nephi 15:4–5; Moroni 8:8; D&C 74).

In like manner today there may be points about which the doctrinal foundation is clear but about which tradition or custom or the ways of the world are so strong that the Brethren hope, as did the New Testament leaders, that the Holy Ghost will eventually cause the adherents to forsake tradition, academic popularity, and peer pressure for the word of God. Perhaps the theory of organic evolution, some political and economic issues, the doctrine of election as pertaining to the Abrahamic covenant, and several other points are in this category requiring time to elapse and changes to occur before definitive pronouncements can be made beyond what is already in the revelations. At any rate, the book of Acts gives our present generation an informative model of how both members and nonmembers react when revelation confronts tradition and long-standing custom. Only living prophets could correctly handle the situation then. Only living prophets can do so now.

NOTES

1. See William Byron Forbush, *Fox's Book of Martyrs* (Philadelphia: Universal Book and Bible House, 1926), 1–5; M. R. James, *The Apocryphal New Testament* (Oxford: Clarendon Press, 1969), 14–15n., and such geographic areas as Persia and India as are listed in the index).
2. Joseph Smith, *Teachings of the Prophet Joseph Smith,* sel. Joseph Fielding Smith (Salt Lake City: Deseret Book, 1976), 199.

CHAPTER SEVEN

PAUL AMONG THE PROPHETS: OBTAINING A CROWN

MICHAEL W. MIDDLETON

Paul's exemplary life and preeminent writings mark the path toward eternal life. Considered together, Paul's life and his writings paint a stunningly complete picture of what it means to be an "example of the believers" and a special witness of Christ. In many ways Paul is the shining gem of the New Testament writers. He is without peer in his role as a witness of the resurrected Lord and as a minister of the gospel of Jesus Christ (Acts 26:16). Certainly that is not to suggest that Paul preached more powerfully than Peter, or wrote more eloquently than Luke, or loved the Lord more than John, or was any more of a martyr than Stephen; however, when studied in the light of the restored gospel, Paul is, perhaps, our best example of what a servant must do and what an individual must become to receive exaltation. With the exception of the Son of God, the life and writings of the apostle Paul are the best paradigm the New Testament has to offer of a mortal coming unto the Father by following the strait and narrow until his calling and election was made sure.

Three primary considerations make Paul's example preeminent. First is the extent of Paul's writings. Although not everything Paul wrote is in the New Testament, we know more about his life than that of any other New Testament personality. Of the New Testament's 260 chapters, 118 were written either by Paul or about him, more chapters than were written by or about anyone else, save Jesus only. In fact, the 100 chapters of Paul's recorded epistles and the 18 chapters of Acts that detail

☐ ☐ ☐ ☐ ☐

Michael W. Middleton, a writer for "Music and the Spoken Word," is an administrator and instructor at Brigham Young University.

his activities compose a little more than 45 percent of the chapters of the New Testament. Moreover, 123 of the 404 pages of the New Testament, just less than one-third of the entire work, express Paul's written witness of the Savior; another 31 pages recount events of his ministry.

Second is the content of Paul's writings. Unlike some of the other apostolic authors in the New Testament, Paul's writing was not primarily evangelistic; he was writing not to convince his audiences that Jesus was the Christ but rather to instruct, regulate, and reform members of the ancient Church who already knew and believed the basic doctrines of the gospel of Christ. In purpose and audience, Paul's writings are more like John's gospel and Peter's epistles than other New Testament books.[1] In light of Paul's experiences and his personality, it is no surprise that his epistles often offer "strong meat" for believers instead of milk for the unbelieving (Hebrews 5:13–14); without question, Paul's life and his letters were intended to invite the Saints, both ancient and modern, to seek a crown of eternal life.

Third, Paul is a magnificent type of Christ. His life and writings become even more powerful when they are considered against the backdrop of prophetic history and compared with the lives and contributions of others among the Lord's anointed. Paul was intimately acquainted with the prophets who preceded him, with the witnesses of Christ contemporary to the Savior's ministry, and with the apostles and prophets who were called after His death. Unmistakable similarities between Paul's life and the experiences of other chosen servants of God give remarkable insights into the life of the man who wrote more of the New Testament than any other.

As a type of Christ, Paul unveils the pattern of his prophetic brethren. When the canon of scripture is complete, much of what we now know about Paul may well prove to be true of all of the prophets who have ministered to mankind, from Adam down to the the latter days. Each of those apostles and prophets is unquestionably unique, but they have in common characteristics that are as revealing as fingerprints and as binding as pedigrees. These characteristics identify and unite the servants of the living God.

By learning more about Paul, we become more intimately acquainted with the Lord Jesus Christ and with those men whom the Savior has called to be his prophets and apostles. The peace of God and other unimagined spiritual benefits await the Saints of latter days who, like Timothy, come to fully know Paul's doctrine, his manner of life, and his faith (2 Timothy 3:10). Consider the magnitude of the promises the Lord made to us through Paul: "Eye hath not seen, nor ear heard, neither have entered into the heart of man, the things which God hath prepared for them that love him" (1 Corinthians 2:9), and "the peace of God, which passeth all understanding, shall keep your hearts and minds through Christ Jesus" (Philippians 4:7). Elements of Paul's life light the path for all who would follow Christ to obtain a crown of their own. In so many ways Paul urges us, "So run, that ye may obtain" (1 Corinthians 9:24). Examined here are eight aspects of the life and writings of Paul that illuminate that path to conversion, sanctification, and exaltation. The atonement of Jesus Christ opened the way for mankind to inherit eternal life. The life and ministry of Paul demonstrate with rare clarity and completeness what the children of men must do to dwell in the third heaven.

"MARVEL NOT THAT ALL MANKIND MUST BE BORN AGAIN"

Saul the Pharisee, like Alma the Younger, went through a conversion process that while extraordinary and miraculous, actually differed little from the way most converts come into the church of God. After Christ opened Saul's spiritual eyes and Ananias restored his physical sight, Saul's conversion continued, and he received the gospel, including its first principles and ordinances.

There is little doubt that the Christian world of his day had no more ardent enemy than Saul of Tarsus before his first vision. He later acknowledged to the Savior that he had "imprisoned and beat in every synagogue them that believed on [Christ]" (Acts 22:19). Energized by his success in persecuting the Christians in Jerusalem, Saul continued "breathing out threatenings and slaughter against the disciples of the Lord" (Acts 9:1). His zeal is demonstrated by his willingness to travel on foot roughly one hundred and forty miles, beyond the borders of Palestine into Syria, bent on taking the Christians of Damascus "bound into Jerusalem" (Acts 9:2) for punishment.[2]

Although Christ, the "author and finisher" (Hebrews 12:2) of all true conversions, made Saul's conversion possible, it also appears that Saul was ready to hear the word of the Lord. As Elder Neal A. Maxwell explains in *Men and Women of Christ,* Saul was "in a preparation" to learn the truth at the time of his vision. Apparently some element of God's truth or Saul's nature told the young Pharisee that his opposition to Christianity was wrong, though he doggedly kicked against the pricks of conscience. Elder Maxwell wrote: "Then the Lord revealed Himself in His true identity—as Jesus! There could be no mistaking by Paul."[3] His heart turned, his life changed, and "forgetting those things which [were] behind," he began to press forward "toward the mark for the prize of the high calling of God in Christ Jesus" (Philippians 3:13–14).

The conversion stories of Saul and Alma the Younger share some similarities, but the differences between them are also instructive. Alma the Younger, apparently "past feeling" (1 Nephi 17:45) at the time of his vision, was not experiencing any "pricks" (Acts 9:5). He was rebelling against the light and knowledge he had received; he had "rejected [his] Redeemer, and denied that which had been spoken of by [his] fathers" (Mosiah 27:30). Conversely, Saul was engaged in activities he believed were just and right; though misguided, he saw his efforts as pious service to his religion and his God. He later explained to Timothy that despite his violent persecution of the Christians before his vision, he had "obtained mercy, because [he] did it ignorantly in unbelief" (1 Timothy 1:13). The vision of Alma the Younger came as an answer to the faithful pleadings of his righteous father, who had prayed that his wayward son might be "brought to the knowledge of the truth" and convinced of "the power and authority of God" (Mosiah 27:14). Saul's vision, on the other hand, constituted the calling of a "chosen vessel" who was beginning to be shown "how great things he must suffer for [Christ's] name's sake" (Acts 9:15–16). Those differences make it easier to understand why Alma was rebuked by an angry angel who knocked him to the ground twice, whereas Saul fell once and was privileged to converse with the gently reproving Son of God. Consider also the after-math of each man's experience. Saul went without food and sight for three days (Acts 9:9); Alma the Younger was immobi-lized for three days and three nights and was "racked, even with the pains of a damned soul" (Alma 36:16).

The name *Saul* means "asked"[4] or "asked for."[5] We do not know whether Saul, recognizing he lacked wisdom, asked in faith for an experience to show him the truth, but it is obvious that he was invited, or "asked," to the wedding feast of the Lamb. Like the second group of guests in the Savior's parable, Saul was bidden from the highway (Matthew 22:8–10); his response, however, was strictly up to him. There are many dif-ferent, broad roads, all of which lead to Damascus; but to be saved, all mankind must eventually look up, as Saul did, and ask Christ, "Lord, what wilt thou have me to do?" (Acts 9:6).

Saul's vision did not make him anything more than one seek-ing the truth. The order of the priesthood of God was not ignored by the Lord, even in calling one of his chosen vessels. Saul's vision did not promote him to any Church office or enti-tle him to any priesthood power; instead, the Savior sent Saul to those in authority to teach the gospel and to minister in the ordinances thereof. In *The Spirit of Revelation*, Joseph Fielding McConkie explains that Saul "was instructed to go into Damascus and wait. Then the Lord directed Ananias, a local priesthood leader, to go to Paul, restore his sight, teach him the gospel, and baptize him." Blind, bewildered, and in des-perate need of answers and ordinances, Saul was "led . . . by the hand" into Damascus (Acts 9:8; compare D&C 112:10). McConkie concludes that Ananias "had every answer that Paul needed, and it was from him that Paul must get it, if the Lord's house was to remain a house of order."[6]

Saul accepted the first principles and ordinances of the gospel: faith, repentance, baptism, and the gift of the Holy Ghost. Having learned and received, he taught the same prin-ciples and administered the same ordinances to others. For example, he knew from experience about the cleansing power of "godly sorrow" (2 Corinthians 7:10), and without question he received the gift of the Holy Ghost in the same manner in which he later bestowed it upon others—by the laying on of hands (Acts 19:2–6).

It is obvious that Saul did not achieve complete conversion while conversing with Christ in vision one day on the road near Damascus. After three years at the Savior's side, associating and conversing with the Messiah during most of his mortal ministry, the faithful Peter was admonished, "When thou art converted, strengthen thy brethren" (Luke 22:32). Likewise, Saul had to follow the path of supplication, obedience, and revelation by which men and women of Christ "wax stronger and stronger in their humility" and firmer and firmer in their faith (Helaman 3:35), even after receiving divine manifestations or having sublime spiritual experiences.

True conversion is usually a process, not an event. Saul prepared in the desert and grew in wisdom before beginning his ministry (Acts 9:22). Sperry wrote: "We are uncertain how long Saul remained in Arabia; neither are we told just where he sojourned in that land. . . . But we can be sure that through prayer and meditation Saul came to peace with himself and his God in the desert place. Like Moses and the Christ before him, in such solitary places was he prepared for his ministry; doubtless, . . . he became the recipient of divine revelations instructing him in the truths of his new faith."[7]

Perhaps the result of Saul's sojourn in the desert could be described in the words of the testimony of Alma the Younger: "Do ye not suppose that I know of these things myself? Behold, I testify unto you that I do know that these things whereof I have spoken are true. And how do ye suppose that I know of their surety? Behold, I say unto you they are made known unto me by the Holy Spirit of God. Behold, I have fasted and prayed many days that I might know these things of myself. And now I do know of myself that they are true; for the Lord God hath made them manifest unto me by his Holy Spirit; and this is the spirit of revelation which is in me" (Alma 5:45–46). These remarkable words become even more poignant when it is recognized that Alma's days of earnest fasting and humble prayer came after he had seen the angel. Saul's vision of the risen Lord would likewise have been a powerful catalyst, compelling him to seek additional light and knowledge for years after his first vision.

As with Alma and Peter, Saul's vision and conversation with the Savior were the beginning, not the end, of his conversion. He gloried in the many "visions and revelations of the Lord" that he received (2 Corinthians 12:1) and asserted, "The gospel which was preached of me is not after man. For I neither received it of man, neither was I taught it, but by the revelation of Jesus Christ" (Galatians 1:11–12). The gift of the Holy Ghost, which he received after baptism, was given to him to guide him back into the Savior's presence. He was preparing not for another brief conversation with Christ but for the opportunity to enter everlastingly into the rest of the Lord, there to partake of exaltation and life eternal with the Father and the Son.

Through baptism, the "old man" of sin, Saul, was put to death, and Paul was raised up to "walk in newness of life" (Romans 6:6, 3). When Alma the Younger went through a similar spiritual rebirth, the Lord taught him: "Marvel not that all mankind . . . must be born again; yea, born of God, changed from their carnal and fallen state, to a state of righteousness, being redeemed of God, becoming his sons and daughters; and thus they become new creatures" (Mosiah 27:25–26). Like King Saul of the Old Testament, the Spirit of the Lord had come upon Saul of Tarsus and turned him into a new man (1 Samuel 10:6). So real was the change that Saul was given a new name. He who had been "asked," or called, as he journeyed toward Damascus had responded; Saul returned from the desert as Paul, a disciple of Christ who was seeking to be chosen.

"A MAN OF SORROWS"

The Prophet Joseph Smith described Paul's physical appearance in these words: "He is about five feet high; very dark hair; dark complexion; dark skin; large Roman nose; sharp face; small black eyes, penetrating as eternity; round shoulders; a whining voice, except when elevated, and then it almost resembled the roaring of a lion."[8] Neither Paul's "form nor comeliness" (Isaiah 53:2) made people listen to him and love him. Paul's greatness as a person and as an apostle was not diminished by his lack of stature or established by his extensive education.

When individuals accepted the gospel of Christ through the preaching of Paul, it was likely despite his appearance and his personality, not because of them. Yet Paul's physical features were the very reason some rejected his message. President Spencer W. Kimball taught: "The swiftest method of rejection of the holy prophets has been to find a pretext, however false or absurd, to dismiss the man so that his message could also be dismissed. . . . Instead of responding to Paul's message, some saw his bodily presence as weak and regarded his speech as contemptible. Perhaps they judged Paul by the timbre of his voice or by his style of speech, not the truths uttered by him."[9]

As with the ruddy-cheeked David, God looked on Paul's heart and honed what he found there (1 Samuel 16:7). Paul was chastened and shaped until he was a man of the stature of Christ (Ephesians 4:13), despite what the world saw or thought. With all he suffered and all he endured, he must have appeared to be a "man of sorrows," condemned by fate or circumstances to be closely "acquainted with grief" (Isaiah 53:3). Few who have not experienced it understand the abrasive opposition by which God allows his jewels to be polished (Malachi 3:14–18). Joseph Smith described the process in these words: "I am like a huge, rough stone rolling down from a high mountain; and the only polishing I get is when some corner gets rubbed off by coming in contact with something else, striking with accelerated force against religious bigotry, priest-craft, lawyer-craft, doctor-craft, lying editors, suborned judges and jurors, and the authority of perjured executives, backed by mobs, blasphemers, licentious and corrupt men and women—all hell knocking off a corner here and a corner there. Thus I will become a smooth and polished shaft in the quiver of the Almighty."[10] Paul was similarly tested, chastened, and refined with trials, tribulations, and persecutions (Hebrews 12:5–7), yet he gloried in such things (D&C 127:2), knowing that "all that will live godly in Christ Jesus shall suffer persecution" (2 Timothy 3:12). Like Christ, Paul "learned . . . obedience by the things which he suffered" (Hebrews 5:8).

Like other righteous individuals, Paul was opposed by Satan and the spirits that follow him. The degree to which Paul shook the powers of hell and removed the devil's influence from the hearts of the children of men (Alma 48:17) is suggested by the evil spirit's chiding mention of Jesus and Paul in the same breath, associating the two (Acts 19:15). As with the Prophet Joseph Smith, Satan must have been painfully aware that Paul was "destined to prove a disturber and an annoyer of his kingdom" (Joseph Smith–History 1:20). Paul received a "thorn in the flesh" and buffetings from Satan (2 Corinthians 12:7), but he was undeterred and unafraid. Like others among the Lord's anointed, Paul was exposed to the power and opposition of Satan; through experience he gained a more perfect ability to prize the sweet and to love the Lord (Moses 6:55).

The great God of heaven created mortality to be an arena of opposites; mankind's legacy from the Fall is to discern good from evil, for the one cannot exist except where it is defined and opposed by the other (2 Nephi 2:11). Moses recorded that his experiences with both God and Satan allowed him to discern between the two and to rebuke the deceiver with power gained from the comparison; Moses told Satan, "I can judge between thee and God" (Moses 1:15, 18). Similar sentiment from similar experience is found in Paul's assertion to the Corinthians, "Lest Satan should get an advantage of us . . . we are not ignorant of his devices" (2 Corinthians 2:11).

Paul understood that divine justice limits Satan's power to tempt and try mankind so that opposition is provided without agency being constrained. To the Saints of Corinth he wrote, "God is faithful, who will not suffer you to be tempted above that ye are able; but will with the temptation also make a way to escape, that ye may be able to bear it" (1 Corinthians 10:13).

Like other prophets and the Savior himself, Paul submitted to God in all things with a sustaining, childlike faith, and the Lord supported him in his trials and temptations. Like Alma and Joseph Smith, Paul declared he was delivered by the Lord in all that he was called upon to suffer and to experience (2 Timothy 3:11; Alma 36:27; D&C 127:2). He understood the importance of descending below some things to follow Jesus, who descended below all things, and he taught that "God . . . provided some better things for them through their sufferings, for without sufferings they could not be made perfect" (JST Hebrews 11:40).

"SPECIAL MIRACLES"

The Savior himself decreed that certain miraculous signs would follow those who believed on his name (Mark 16:17). In recording the acts of the apostles, Luke wrote, "God wrought special miracles by the hands of Paul" (Acts 19:11). At first the phrase "special miracles" may seem redundant, but we cannot closely examine the mighty miracles Paul performed in the name of Jesus Christ without being impressed by their uniqueness and their frequency. Miracles, like those performed by Paul, are always found in the true church of Christ; they include healing the sick, casting out devils, speaking in tongues, and bringing the dead back to life.

Paul's first experience with the healing power of the priesthood came in Damascus when Ananias "entered into the house; and putting his hands on him said, Brother Saul, the Lord, even Jesus . . . hath sent me, that thou mightest receive thy sight" (Acts 9:17). Having received so great a blessing in his own life, Paul's heart was ever more tender and his soul ever more compassionate to those whose burdens could be lifted through the divine authority that he held. Acts 28 records Paul's healing of the sick and diseased on the island of Melita by prayer and by the laying on of hands, almost exactly as James describes the ordinance (Acts 28:8–9; James 5:14).

Paul exercised the healing power that was in him not only through the laying on of hands but also through other means. The scriptures record that Paul healed a cripple who had faith to be made whole merely by speaking to him (Acts 14:8–10); others were healed without even seeing Paul by receiving handkerchiefs or aprons that were brought to them from him (Acts 19:12). Stories of similar healings are found in the ministry of the Savior (Matthew 8:8, 13; Mark 2:10–12) and in the accounts of Lydia Knight[11] and other Latter-day Saints[12] who were healed by handkerchiefs sent from the hand of the Prophet Joseph Smith.

Paul cast out devils in the name of Jesus Christ. These exorcisms merited such acclaim that certain Jews thought they could duplicate the apostle's results, without authority, simply by mimicking his words and his manner (Acts 19:13–16). Their resounding failure brought even more souls to God (Acts

19:17–20). Apparently evil spirits were also cast out by means of handkerchiefs and aprons brought from Paul (Acts 19:12).

Another spiritual gift Paul exercised was the gift of tongues; in fact, in rebuking the Corinthian Saints' misuse and misunderstanding of the gift, he bluntly stated, "I thank my God, I speak with tongues more than ye all" (1 Corinthians 14:18). He understood the power and the value of the gift of tongues in teaching the gospel of Jesus Christ to individuals who spoke other languages. He taught that "tongues are for a sign . . . to them that believe not," just as the gift of prophecy is a sign and a blessing unto the believers (1 Corinthians 14:22).

Like Elisha (2 Kings 4), Nephi (3 Nephi 7), Peter (Acts 9), and the Savior (Matthew 9; Luke 7; John 11), Paul used the priesthood of God to restore the dead to life. The multitude at Troas may have forgotten what Paul said in his hours of "long preaching," but they probably always remembered Paul's embracing the body of Eutychus and bringing him back to life (Acts 20:7–12). It is likely that the "comfort" the Saints received as a result of this miracle surpassed emotional relief at one young man's return to life. Paul had shown them a beautiful shadow of the Savior's loving embrace that will lift and restore to life each member of the human family, forever breaking the cords of death.

Another sign described by the Savior as being found among true Christians is divine protection from deadly poisons and serpent bites. Paul's ministry shows these miracles also were manifest in his life. Probably wet, cold, and preoccupied after being shipwrecked, Paul "gathered a bundle of sticks, and laid them on the fire," when "there came a viper out of the heat, and fastened on his hand" (Acts 28:3). The kindly barbarians who had kindled the fire for the shipwrecked Paul thought he would die from the venomous bite. But when the divinely protected apostle received no harm, their opinion of him changed from unpunished murderer to deity (Acts 28:4–6).

"AN EXAMPLE OF THE BELIEVERS"

Paul scrupulously followed the admonition that he gave to Timothy to be an example of the believers (1 Timothy 4:12). He believed that "the Lord ordained that they which preach the gospel should live . . . the gospel" (1 Corinthians 9:14). In the

Epistle to the Romans, he stressed the importance of teachers adhering to their own counsel, asking, "Thou therefore which teachest another, teachest thou not thyself? thou that preachest a man should not steal, dost thou steal?" (Romans 2:21). Called of God to teach others, he recognized the importance of being a doer of the word, "lest that by any means, when I have preached to others, I myself should be a castaway" (1 Corinthians 9:27).

The scriptures record many instances of Paul's living what he taught. For example, he not only taught the Saints to be temperate (1 Corinthians 9:25) and hard-working (1 Thessalonians 4:11) but was himself industrious and self-reliant (2 Corinthians 11:9). Like King Benjamin, he supported himself with his own hands, laboring as a tentmaker (Acts 18:3, 20:34) rather than depending upon those who looked to him as a leader (1 Corinthians 9:18; Mosiah 2:14).

Paul taught the worth of souls by serving missions himself (Colossians 1:28–29). From the beginning, he honored his calling as a minister and a witness; during his three missionary journeys, he traveled thousands of miles and shared the gospel with people throughout most of the Mediterranean world. By epistle and by example he taught the threefold mission of the church of Christ: to proclaim the gospel (Romans 10:13–15), to perfect the Saints (Ephesians 4:11–14), and to redeem the dead (1 Corinthians 15:29).

Like Lehi's son Jacob, Paul was conscientious in his ministry that the blood of those who heard him or read his epistles would not come upon him (Acts 18:6; Jacob 1:19). Paul's phrase "I would not have you ignorant" appears six times in his New Testament writings; Sperry contended Paul used this introduction specifically to preface subjects of unusual importance.[13] And indeed, Paul addressed many such subjects; he has not left those who read his writings ignorant of some of the most fundamental and glorious truths of the Restoration: the three degrees of glory (1 Corinthians 15:40–47), the teaching power of the Holy Ghost (1 Corinthians 2:10–16), the purpose and continuity of the family unit (1 Corinthians 11:11), and baptism for the dead (1 Corinthians 15:29). He taught in plainness these and a host of other essential and exalting doctrines. The lack of vibrato with which he presented these concepts suggests that they were common knowledge to the Saints of his day. Many of these precious truths were distorted after Paul's death but have been restored to their former fulness by latter-day revelation.

A PARTAKER OF THE DIVINE NATURE

Peter urged the ancient Saints to "give diligence to make your calling and election sure" by becoming "partakers of the divine nature" (2 Peter 1:10, 4). Paul's life and writings specifically established the pattern for obtaining those "great and precious promises" (2 Peter 1:4). Elements of the divine nature, revealed in summary to Joseph Smith in 1829 (D&C 4:5–7), are ubiquitous in Paul's New Testament epistles. The characteristics of deity he addresses most frequently are faith, hope, and charity.

Perhaps the most beautiful and detailed treatise on faith in the canon of scripture is Hebrews 11. Using the phrases "by faith" and "through faith" eighteen times, Paul summarized what sixteen Old Testament luminaries (fourteen men and two women) accomplished by exercising their faith in Christ. Paul's intention was to perfect the faith of the Saints (1 Thessalonians 3:10), for "without faith it is impossible to please [God]" (Hebrews 11:6). His inspired image of faith as the shield that a person wearing the whole armor of God must take "above all," because of faith's ability to quench the fiery darts of the wicked (Ephesians 6:16), resonates through the centuries.

Paul was also a man of hope, who realized the word's true meaning. He made fifty-two of the New Testament's fifty-nine references to hope, including the only New Testament reference to Christ as the "hope of Israel" (Acts 28:20). Hope, as taught by Paul, is founded on Christ (1 Timothy 1:1). It is apparent that the apostle understood the difference between hoping gospel principles are true and possessing "a hope in Christ" (Jacob 2:19) that allows us to believe that we can obtain "a better world, yea, even a place at the right hand of God" (Ether 12:4). He instructs us to "lay hold upon the hope set before us," contending that it can provide a sure and steady anchor to the faithful who long to enter within the veil (Hebrews 6:18–20).

Paul wrote the earliest and arguably the most complete

treatment of charity found in the scriptures (1 Corinthians 13). The doctrinal aspects shared by 1 Corinthians 13 and Mormon's discourse in Moroni 7 are strong and significant. Like Mormon, Paul lived what he taught. He understood that charity is the essence of the gospel of Jesus Christ—lovingly doing for others that which they cannot do for themselves; looked at in this light, most of his many travels and his extensive writings were acts of charity. As he taught Timothy, the "end of the commandment is charity out of a pure heart, and of a good conscience, and of faith unfeigned" (1 Timothy 1:5).

Perhaps to a greater degree than any other biblical writer, Paul extolled the many aspects of the divine nature. In addition to faith, hope, and charity, his writings teach us about love (Ephesians 5:2), virtue (Philippians 4:8), knowledge (Ephesians 4:13), temperance (Philippians 4:5),[14] patience (Romans 15:4), brotherly kindness (Romans 12:10), godliness (1 Timothy 4:8), humility (Colossians 3:12), and diligence (2 Corinthians 8:7). As Paul himself worked on developing these divine attributes, receiving grace for grace (D&C 93:20), he became a partaker of the divine nature and qualified himself for sacred spiritual experiences which, although available to all, are obtained by few of the children of men.

"ONE BORN OUT OF DUE SEASON"

As a witness of the resurrection of the Savior Jesus Christ, Paul's apostolic ministry links him to individuals of all dispensations who hold this same calling. Not only did Paul have much in common with the prophets and apostles that preceded and followed him but he communed with them. The welding link between prophets of various dispensations is much stronger than is commonly recognized. Paul was taught by the prophets and patriarchs who preceded him and in turn assisted with the restoration in the latter days. Like Joseph Smith (D&C 90:3), David W. Patten (D&C 124:130), and a multitude of others (D&C 128:19–21), after his death Paul continued to hold both the priesthood authority and the keys he had received in mortality.

One explanation for Paul's statement that "the spirits of the prophets are subject to the prophets" (1 Corinthians 14:32) is that the prophets and apostles who have departed from mortality continue to assist their mortal counterparts in building the kingdom of God. Referring to this verse Robert L. Millet wrote, "There is an order, a hierarchy if you will, even among those called as chosen oracles and mouthpieces of the Almighty."[15] Elder Boyd K. Packer's remarks at the funeral services for President Ezra Taft Benson explain further: "The prophets who preceded [President Benson], ancient and modern, have on occasion communed with the servants of the Lord on this earth. So it well may be that we have not seen the last of this great prophet of God.

"I testify that the veil between this mortal realm and the spirit world opens to such revelation as the needs of the church and kingdom of God on earth may require."[16]

By definition, the power and authority of the Melchizedek Priesthood entitle those who magnify it "to have the privilege of receiving the mysteries of the kingdom of heaven, to have the heavens opened unto them, to commune with the general assembly and church of the Firstborn" (D&C 107:18–19). Elder Bruce R. McConkie wrote, "The Church of the Firstborn is made up of the sons of God, . . . those who are destined to be joint-heirs with Christ in receiving all that the Father hath."[17] Though the prophets cannot convey all they understand to contemporaries who are unwilling to give away all their sins to know God (Alma 22:18), the world's wickedness does not prevent the prophets from communing with other members of the Church of the Firstborn.

There is sacred power and divine order in the transfer of keys, authority, and information from one generation of prophets to the next, from the prophet at the head of one dispensation to the prophet at the head of the next. Prophets and prophetic keys link the dispensations together; the priesthood keys and the gospel truths God entrusts to earthly curators are carefully conveyed from one dispensation to the next. The scriptures record many examples of this prophetic brotherhood: Moses and Elijah giving authority and instruction to Peter, James, and John on the Mount of Transfiguration (Matthew 17); the Three Nephites ministering to Mormon and Moroni (Mormon 8:11); and the appearances of Peter, James, John,

Moses, Elijah, Elias, and others to latter-day apostles and prophets (D&C 27; 110; 128).

In like manner, the Prophet Joseph Smith revealed, Paul was tutored by Abel, for Abel had been resurrected, still holding the keys of his dispensation, and "was sent down from heaven unto Paul to minister consoling words, and to commit unto him a knowledge of the mysteries of godliness."[18] How did Paul know what he wrote about Abel in Hebrews 11? It was taught to him by Abel himself.

The Prophet wrote that Abel "magnified the Priesthood which was conferred upon him, and died a righteous man, and therefore has become an angel of God."[19] The choice of the term *angel* is especially significant in light of Mormon's assertion that angels have not "ceased to minister unto the children of men" (Moroni 7:29). Subject unto Christ, these angels "minister according to the word of his command, showing themselves unto them of strong faith and a firm mind in every form of godliness" (Moroni 7:30). Part of an angel's ministry is to "prepare the way among the children of men, by declaring the word of Christ unto the chosen vessels of the Lord, that they may bear testimony of him" (Moroni 7:31).

The Prophet also taught that Enoch is a ministering angel, appointed "to minister to those who shall be heirs of salvation, and appeared unto Jude as Abel did unto Paul." Further, Joseph stated, "Paul was also acquainted with this character [Enoch], and received instructions from him."[20]

In like manner did Paul minister to Joseph Smith. The Prophet was intimately familiar with Paul's appearance and his teachings because he had been taught by him face-to-face.[21] "I've known a few scholars who claim to be the world's leading experts on Paul," wrote Truman G. Madsen. "One man, I suspect, knows more than they. That is Paul. Apparently he is one who taught Joseph Smith."[22] John Taylor could have been speaking of Paul as easily as of Joseph Smith when he said, "He seemed to be as familiar with these [past prophets] as we are with one another."[23]

THE BLOOD OF MARTYRS

Like many of the Lord's elect, Paul was required to seal his testimony with his blood (D&C 135:3). From his own inspired words we learn, "For where a testament is, there must also of necessity be the death of the testator" (Hebrews 9:16). His blood joined that of the martyred multitude whose altar John saw; his voice, now roaring like a lion, joined those that cry with a loud voice, "How long, O Lord, holy and true, dost thou not judge and avenge our blood on them that dwell on the earth?" (Revelation 6:10).

Paul's trial and his execution trace the pattern established by the Savior and followed by many others who have laid down their lives for Christ. Like the Savior (Matthew 12:14), Lehi (1 Nephi 1:20), Zenos (Helaman 8:19), Ezias (Helaman 8:20), Isaiah,[24] and countless others, Paul found his life in peril because of his teachings (Acts 9:23). Luke records that more than forty Jews banded together and plotted to kill Paul; they bound themselves with an oath that they would neither eat nor drink until they had accomplished their evil design (Acts 23:12–15). Because of Paul's rabbinical training (Acts 22:3; 26:5), his testimony that Jesus, whom they had crucified, was indeed the long-awaited Messiah must have been especially piercing and repugnant to the Jewish authorities. Paul could have declared in the words of Jesus, "If I had not come and spoken unto them, they had not had sin: but now they have no cloke for their sin" (John 15:22). Both the Savior and Paul were protected from their enemies at times when their lives were in peril (John 8:59; 10:31–39; Acts 9:23–25). Like Abinadi, they testified of the truth while in the midst of their enemies but were preserved by God until they had delivered the message they were sent forth to give (Mosiah 13:2–3).

Calling Joseph Smith and Paul "parallel prophets," Richard Lloyd Anderson pointed out that both "predicted safety in earlier persecutions, but . . . accurately predicted their own deaths."[25] Paul wrote to Timothy, "I am now ready to be offered, and the time of my departure is at hand" (2 Timothy 4:6). Joseph, who had borrowed *Foxe's Book of Martyrs* from the Edward Stevenson family and used the Urim and Thummim to examine the lives of the early Christian martyrs,[26] stated, "I must seal my testimony to this generation with my blood."[27]

Paul and Joseph Smith each proclaimed their innocence and blamelessness before their martyrdom. Headed toward

Jerusalem, "not knowing the things that [would] befall [him] there," Paul stated, "Wherefore I take you to record this day, that I am pure from the blood of all men" (Acts 20:22, 26). Riding toward Carthage, Joseph declared, "I am going like a lamb to the slaughter; but I am calm as a summer's morning; I have a conscience void of offense towards God, and towards all men" (D&C 135:4).

Paul endured many persecutions as he approached the time of his martyrdom; there are a number of notable parallels between his life and the Savior's. Like the Savior, Paul was smitten by the Jews with the high priest present (John 18:22; Acts 23:2). Like the Christ, Paul was arraigned before both Jewish and Roman tribunals; both the Savior and his apostle were arraigned three times before Roman rulers as the Jews sought the death sentence their own jurisdictions could not provide. The absence of credible witnesses against them during their trials showed both Christ and Paul to have been falsely accused (Mark 14:55–56; Acts 25:7). And, like Pilate, Agrippa was "almost persuaded" (Acts 26:28) and would have freed Paul had it not been for the Jews and his consideration of Caesar (John 19:12; Acts 26:32). Although Paul was not crucified, he was stoned and left for dead outside the city. Like Christ, who was slain outside the city gate and, though placed in a tomb, did not see corruption (Psalm 16:10), Paul also arose and continued his ministry (Acts 14:19–20).

For thirty years following Paul's conversion, the Savior repeatedly showed him the "great things he must suffer for [Christ's] name's sake" (Acts 9:16). Paul's sufferings as a minister of Christ were varied, protracted, and intense (2 Corinthians 11:23–29), yet he endured, even unto martyrdom. His motto was ever, "I reckon that the sufferings of this present time are not worthy to be compared with the glory which shall be revealed in us" (Romans 8:18).

A WITNESS THAT HE PLEASED GOD

Joseph Smith outlined what an individual must do to qualify to receive the Second Comforter: "After a person has faith in Christ, repents of his sins, and is baptized for the remission of his sins and receives the Holy Ghost, (by the laying on of hands) . . . let him continue to humble himself before God, hungering and thirsting after righteousness, and living by every word of God, and the Lord will soon say unto him, Son, thou shalt be exalted. When the Lord hath thoroughly proved him, and finds that the man is determined to serve Him at all hazards, then the man will find his calling and his election made sure."[28]

The Prophet explained the blessings that await those who receive this more sure word of prophecy: "Then it will be his privilege to receive the other Comforter, which the Lord hath promised the Saints. . . . Now what is this other Comforter? It is no more nor less than the Lord Jesus Christ Himself; and this is the sum and substance of the whole matter; that when any man obtains this last Comforter, he will have the personage of Jesus Christ to attend him, or appear unto him from time to time, and even He will manifest the Father unto him, and they will take up their abode with him, and the visions of the heavens will be opened unto him . . . and he may have a perfect knowledge of the mysteries of the Kingdom of God; and this is the state and place the ancient Saints arrived at when they had such glorious visions—Isaiah, Ezekiel, John on the Isle of Patmos, St. Paul in the three heavens, and all the Saints who held communion with the general assembly and Church of the Firstborn."[29]

Once converted, Paul lived and died with his eye single to the glory of God; he looked forward with an eye of faith (Alma 32:40) and saw his worthy soul entering into the presence of God. Paul made his calling and election sure, obtaining an incorruptible crown with which he will reign in the celestial kingdom for all time and eternity. He compiled through the example of his life and the doctrines of his ministry one of the most complete accounts of what an individual must do to receive the "more sure word of prophecy" (2 Peter 1:19).

Paul was perfected by his sufferings, his struggles, and his obedience. As Paul wrote of Christ, "Though he were a Son, yet learned he obedience by the things which he suffered; and being made perfect, he became the author of eternal salvation unto all them that obey him" (Hebrews 5:8–9). Expressing a similar sentiment, the Prophet Joseph Smith wrote, "Men have to suffer that they may come upon Mount Zion and be exalted above the heavens."[30] Through diligence, obedience, faith, and sacrifice, righteous men and women can come unto Christ, being approved and received by him.

Paul wrote that Abel, through his "more excellent" sacrifice, had "obtained witness that he was righteous" (Hebrews 11:4). He also wrote that before Enoch's translation, "he had this testimony, that he pleased God" (Hebrews 11:5). There is little room for doubt that Paul also received similar divine witness that he had pleased God and was sealed up unto eternal life. Paul wrote that he knew a man in Christ who was "caught up to the third heaven" (2 Corinthians 12:2). Joseph Smith asserted, "I know a man that has been caught up to the third heavens, and can say, with Paul, that we have seen and heard things that are not lawful to utter."[31] The Lord told Joseph Smith in a revelation received in 1843, "I seal upon you your exaltation, and prepare a throne for you in the kingdom of my Father, with Abraham your father" (D&C 132:49). Other individuals who received this ultimate divine approbation are Alma the Elder (Mosiah 26:20) and Nephi (Helaman 10:4–7).

The good fight fought, the crown obtained, the victory won, Paul reached the point where the presence of the Lord personally attended and taught him. He received the Second Comforter[32] and, like Joseph Smith[33] and the brother of Jared (Ether 3:20, 25–26), was sealed up unto eternal life.

Paul's is the consummate example of the process required to complete the course of conversion. We see in Saul of Tarsus a person who progressed from breathing out threatenings against the Church, to desiring to do what the Lord would have him do, to entering again into his presence.

As we study the life and writings of Paul, an apostle of the Lord, we come to know a man who was caught up to the third heaven as we strive to understand Paul and endeavor to follow the path he has marked. By precept and by example, Paul prompts us to leave the broad, well-worn road to Damascus in order to journey on Christ's strait and narrow path; like Paul, we may each one day hear and see and know for ourselves. Moreover, Paul's life teaches that embarking on the road to exaltation is only the first step of a lifelong journey—the process of progression. Paul received the necessary ordinances, was born again, suffered for Christ's sake, and grew from grace to grace. As a minister of Christ, he took upon himself the divine nature and, purified from sin (3 Nephi 8:1; D&C 50:27–29), performed miracles in the name of Jesus. Finally, having proven that he was actually willing to serve God at all hazards and to stand as a witness of him at all times and in all things and in all places he was in, even until death (Mosiah 18:9), he made his calling and election sure. Just before his death, he wrote to Timothy in words that ring with eternal triumph, "I have fought a good fight, I have finished my course, I have kept the faith: henceforth there is laid up for me a crown of righteousness, which the Lord, the righteous judge, shall give me at that day" (2 Timothy 4:7–8). A similar coronation awaits all who are willing to follow Paul's example by coming unto Christ, fighting the good fight, and running "with patience the race that is set before us, looking unto Jesus the author and finisher of our faith" (Hebrews 12:1–2).

NOTES

1. Bible Dictionary, LDS edition of the King James Version of the Bible, 743, s.v. "Pauline Epistles"; compare "Gospels," 682–83.
2. Sidney B. Sperry, *Paul's Life and Letters* (Salt Lake City: Bookcraft, 1987), 15–16.
3. Neal A. Maxwell, *Men and Women of Christ* (Salt Lake City: Bookcraft, 1991), 32.
4. Bible Dictionary, 769, s.v. "Saul."
5. Sperry, *Paul's Life and Letters,* 1.
6. Joseph Fielding McConkie, *The Spirit of Revelation* (Salt Lake City: Deseret Book, 1984), 45, 46.
7. Sperry, *Paul's Life and Letters,* 24.
8. Joseph Smith, *Teachings of the Prophet Joseph Smith,* sel. Joseph Fielding Smith (Salt Lake City: Deseret Book, 1938), 180.
9. Spencer W. Kimball, *The Teachings of Spencer W. Kimball,* ed. Edward L. Kimball (Salt Lake City: Bookcraft, 1988), 466.
10. Smith, *Teachings of the Prophet Joseph Smith,* 304.
11. Susa Young Gates, *Lydia Knight's History* (Salt Lake City: Juvenile Instructor, 1883), 52–55.
12. Wilford Woodruff, *Leaves from My Journal,* in *Three Mormon Classics,* comp. Preston Nibley (Salt Lake City: Bookcraft, 1944), 79.
13. Sperry, *Paul's Life and Letters,* 97.
14. See Kimball, *Teachings of Spencer W. Kimball,* 132.
15. Robert L. Millet, "Joseph Smith among the Prophets," in *Joseph Smith:*

The Prophet, the Man, ed. Susan Easton Black and Charles D. Tate Jr. (Provo: Brigham Young University Religious Studies Center, 1993), 21.

16. Boyd K. Packer, "We Honor Now His Journey," *Ensign,* July 1994, 32–34.

17. Bruce R. McConkie, *Mormon Doctrine,* 2d ed. (Salt Lake City: Bookcraft, 1979), 139.

18. Smith, *Teachings of the Prophet Joseph Smith,* 169.

19. Ibid.

20. Ibid., 170.

21. Ibid., 180.

22. Truman G. Madsen, *Joseph Smith the Prophet* (Salt Lake City: Bookcraft, 1989), 44.

23. John Taylor, in *Journal of Discourses,* 26 vols. (London: Latter-day Saints' Book Depot, 1854–86), 21:94.

24. Bible Dictionary, 707, s.v. "Isaiah."

25. Richard Lloyd Anderson, "Parallel Prophets: Paul and Joseph Smith," *Brigham Young University 1982–83 Devotionals and Firesides* (Provo, Utah: Brigham Young University Publications, 1983), 182.

26. Madsen, *Joseph Smith the Prophet,* 63–64.

27. *Brother Joseph,* comp. Kay W. Briggs (Salt Lake City: Bookcraft, 1994), 40.

28. Smith, *Teachings of the Prophet Joseph Smith,* 150.

29. Ibid., 150–51.

30. Ibid., 323.

31. Ibid.

32. *The Words of Joseph Smith,* ed. and comp. Andrew F. Ehat and Lyndon W. Cook (Orem: Grandin Book, 1993), 5.

33. Smith, *Teachings of the Prophet Joseph Smith,* 301.

CHAPTER EIGHT

WALKING IN NEWNESS OF LIFE: DOCTRINAL THEMES OF THE APOSTLE PAUL

ROBERT L. MILLET

It is given to but few to wield a more powerful influence over Christian history than to Saul of Tarsus, the persecutor who became a prophet, the Pharisee who became the Apostle to the Gentiles. The life and teachings of the apostle Paul stand as bright reminders of the power of Christ to transform the souls of men and women, to remake the human heart, and to re-focus one's misdirected zeal into the way of the Master. When the risen Lord appeared in vision to Ananias of Damascus and instructed him to send for the stricken and blinded Saul, Ananias answered: "Lord, I have heard by many of this man, how much evil he hath done to thy saints at Jerusalem: and here he hath authority from the chief priests to bind all that call on thy name." The response that followed bespeaks the Redeemer's insight into the wonders that would be done at Paul's hand: "Go thy way: for he is a chosen vessel unto me, to bear my name before the Gentiles, and kings, and the children of Israel" (Acts 9:11–15).

Other chapters in this volume discuss the early life, education and training, and conversion of Saul. I will consider briefly some of the more significant doctrinal messages from his epistles. Many of those are, in the language of Simon Peter, "things hard to be understood, which they that are unlearned and unstable wrest, as they do also the other scriptures, unto their own destruction" (2 Peter 3:16). I begin with the testimony

▢ ▢ ▢ ▢ ▢

Robert L. Millet is dean of Religious Education and professor of ancient scripture at Brigham Young University.

that the message of Paul was a proclamation of the gospel—Jesus Christ and him crucified—and that he was no more the originator of Christianity (as some foolishly suppose) than Abraham was the originator of the everlasting covenant. Further, as F. F. Bruce observed: "Paul himself is at pains to point out that the gospel which he preached was one and the same gospel as that preached by the other apostles—a striking claim, considering that Paul was neither a companion of Christ in the days of His flesh nor of the original apostles, and that he vigorously asserts his complete independence of these."[1] And yet Paul knew as Peter knew. He knew as Thomas knew. And what he knew—whether from the teachings of Stephen, from the other apostles, from his own study of the Old Testament with new eyes, or by means of personal revelation—he taught. And he taught with a power, a persuasion, and a holy zeal known only to those who, like Alma and the sons of Mosiah, have gone from darkness to light and whose whole soul yearns to lead others to that same light.

"ALL HAVE SINNED"

One cannot fully appreciate the need for medicine until one is aware of a malady. One does not pant after the cooling draught until one has nearly died of thirst. In the same way, as President Ezra Taft Benson observed, people do not yearn for salvation in Christ until they know why they need Christ, which thing they cannot know until they understand and acknowledge the Fall and its effects upon all mankind.[2] The atonement of Jesus Christ is inextricably and eternally tied to the fall of Adam and Eve. To teach the Atonement without discussing the Fall is to teach the Atonement in the abstract, to lessen its impact, to mitigate its transforming power in the lives of men and women. Thus the apostle Paul began at the beginning; he laid stress where it needed to be. Quoting the Psalmist, he affirmed: "There is none righteous, no, not one: there is none that understandeth, there is none that seeketh after God. They are all gone out of the way, they are together become unprofitable; there is none that doeth good, no, not one" (Romans 3:10–12; compare Psalms 14:1–3; 53:1–3).

Though we as Latter-day Saints do not subscribe to the belief held by many in the Christian world about the depravity of

humankind, yet the burden of scripture, including the New
Testament, is that there was a Fall and that it does take a measured toll on all humanity. Paul taught plainly that men and
women must be extricated and redeemed from the Fall.
Because our first parents partook of the forbidden fruit, death
and sin entered the world. We are, as God taught Adam in the
earliest ages, "conceived in sin," such that when children "begin
to grow up, sin conceiveth in their hearts, and they taste the
bitter, that they may know to prize the good" (Moses 6:55). In
the words of Lehi, God revealed to the ancients that all persons
"were lost, because of the transgression of their parents" (2
Nephi 2:21). Truly, "because of the fall our natures have
become evil continually" (Ether 3:2).

We do not believe that there is sin in the sexual act, so long
as it is undertaken within the bonds of marriage. Nor do we
subscribe to the belief in the inability of men and women even
to choose good over evil. To say that we are conceived in sin is
to say, first of all, that we are conceived into a world of sin.
But, more significantly, it is to declare that conception is the
vehicle, the means by which a fallen nature, what we know as
mortality or what Paul calls "the flesh," is transmitted to all the
posterity of Adam and Eve. The revelations declare that little
children are innocent, not because they are that way by nature
but rather because Christ's atonement declares them to be so
(Moroni 8:8, 12, 22; D&C 29:46; 74:7). In short, "as in Adam, or
by nature, they fall, even so the blood of Christ atoneth for their
sins" (Mosiah 3:16). Thus all of us struggle not only for forgiveness for individual sins but also for relief and redemption from
a fallen nature that yields to sin. That is to say, salvation in
Christ consists not only in meeting and satisfying the demands
of God's justice (which forbids uncleanness) but also in enjoy-
ing the renovating and cleansing powers of Christ's blood such
that we begin to die as pertaining to unrighteousness and the
ways of sin.

"All have sinned, and come short of the glory of God," Paul
wrote to the Romans (Romans 3:23). In speaking of life before
coming unto Christ, Paul further taught: "For when we were in
the flesh, the motions of sins, which were not according to the
law, did work in our members to bring forth fruit unto death.

. . . For I know that in me, that is, in my flesh, dwelleth no good thing; for to will is present with me"—that is, to do what is right is in my heart—"but to perform that which is good I find not, only in Christ." (JST Romans 7:5, 19). Herein lies the solution to the problem of the Fall: though all of us are subject to sin and to the pull of the flesh, there is hope for liberation through Jesus. The Son of God has "delivered us from the power of darkness" (Colossians 1:13). He truly "hath abolished death, and hath brought life and immortality to light through the gospel" (2 Timothy 1:10).

JUSTIFICATION BY FAITH

The scriptures are consistent in their declaration that "no unclean thing can enter into [God's] kingdom" (3 Nephi 27:19). In theory there are two ways by which men and women may inherit eternal life. The first is simply to live the law of God perfectly, to make no mistakes. To do so is to be justified—pronounced innocent, declared blameless—by works or by law. To say that another way, if we keep the commandments completely (including receiving the ordinances of salvation), never deviating from the strait and narrow path throughout our mortal lives, then we qualify for the blessings of the obedient. And yet we have just attended to the terrible truth that all are unclean as a result of sin. All of us have broken at least one of the laws of God and therefore disqualify ourselves for justification by law. Moral perfection may be a possibility, but it is certainly not a probability. Jesus alone trod that path. "Therefore," Paul observed, "by the deeds of the law"—meaning the law of Moses, as well as any law of God—"there shall no flesh be justified in his sight" (Romans 3:20; compare 2 Nephi 2:5).

The second way to be justified is by faith, for the sinner to be pronounced clean or innocent through trusting in and relying upon the merits of him who answered the ends of the law (Romans 10:4; compare 2 Nephi 2:6–7). Jesus, who owed no personal debt to justice, is that Holy One who can now "claim of the Father his rights of mercy which he hath upon the children of men" (Moroni 7:27). Because we are guilty of transgression, if there had been no atonement of Christ, no quantity of good deeds on our part, no nobility independent of divine intercession, could make up for the loss. Truly, "since man had fallen he could not merit anything of himself" (Alma 22:14). Thus he who loved us first (1 John 4:10, 19) reaches out to the lost and fallen, to the disinherited, and proposes a marriage. The Infinite One joins with the finite, the Finished with the unfinished, the Whole with the partial, in short, the Perfect with the imperfect. Through covenant with Christ and thus union with the Bridegroom, we place ourselves in a condition to become fully formed, whole, finished—to become perfect in Christ (Moroni 10:32).

The means by which the Savior justifies us is wondrous indeed. It entails what might be called the great exchange. It is certainly true that Jesus seeks through his atoning sacrifice and through the medium of the Holy Spirit to change us, to transform us from fallen and helpless mortals into "new creatures in Christ." But there is more. Jesus offers to exchange with us. In his epistle to the Philippians, Paul speaks of his eagerness to forsake the allurements of the world in order to obtain the riches of Christ. "I count all things but loss," he said, "for the excellency of the knowledge of Christ Jesus my Lord: for whom I have suffered the loss of all things, and do count them but dung, that I may win Christ"—and now note this important addition—"and be found in him, not having mine own righteousness, which is of the law, but that which is through the faith of Christ, the righteousness which is of God by faith" (Philippians 3:8–9). Paul's point is vital: justification comes by faith, by trusting in Christ's righteousness, in his merits, mercy, and grace (Romans 10:1–4; compare 2 Nephi 2:3; Helaman 14:13; D&C 45:3–5).

Though our efforts to be righteous are necessary, they will forevermore be insufficient. Paul teaches a profound truth—that as we come unto Christ by the covenant of faith, our Lord's righteousness becomes our righteousness. He justifies us in the sense that he imputes—meaning, he reckons to our account—his goodness and takes our sin. This is the great exchange. To the Corinthians Paul explained that "God was in Christ, reconciling the world unto himself, not imputing their trespasses unto them. . . . For he [God the Father] hath made him [Christ the Son] to be sin for us, who knew no sin; that we might be made the righteousness of God in him" (2 Corinthians 5:19, 21). As

Paul explained elsewhere, Christ "hath redeemed us from the curse of the law, being made a curse for us" (Galatians 3:13; compare Hebrews 2:9). Sidney Sperry thus spoke of being justified as a matter not only of "acquittal" from guilt and sin but also of "being regarded as 'righteous' in a future Divine judgment."[3] Those who enter the gospel covenant and thereafter seek to do their duty and endure to the end the Lord "hold[s] guiltless" (3 Nephi 27:16; compare D&C 4:2). It is not that they are guiltless in the sense of never having done wrong; rather, the Holy One removes the blame and imputes—accounts or decrees to the repentant sinner, the one who comes unto Christ by covenant—His righteousness. "For as by one man's disobedience"—the fall of Adam—"many were made sinners, so by the obedience of one"—Jesus Christ—"shall many be made righteous" (Romans 5:19).

One Protestant theologian, John MacArthur, has written: "Justification may be defined as an act of God whereby he imputes to a believing sinner the full and perfect righteousness of Christ, forgiving the sinner of all unrighteousness, declaring him or her perfectly righteous in God's sight, thus delivering the believer from all condemnation. . . . It is a forensic reality that takes place in the court of God."[4] MacArthur also explained: "Justification is a divine verdict of 'not guilty—fully righteous.' It is the reversal of God's attitude toward the sinner. Whereas He formerly condemned, He now vindicates. Although the sinner once lived under God's wrath, as a believer he or she is now under God's blessing. Justification is more than simple pardon; pardon alone would still leave the sinner without merit before God. So when God justifies He imputes divine righteousness to the sinner. . . . Justification elevates the believer to a realm of full acceptance and divine privilege in Jesus Christ." The harsh reality is that "the law demands perfection. But the only way to obtain perfect righteousness is by imputation—that is, being justified by faith."[5] "Therefore being justified by faith, we have peace with God through our Lord Jesus Christ: by whom also we have access by faith into this grace wherein we stand, and rejoice in hope of the glory of God" (Romans 5:1–2). Since all have sinned and come short of the glory of God, we are "justified only by his grace through the redemption that is in Christ Jesus," or in other words, "justified by faith alone without the deeds of the law" (JST Romans 3:24, 28). The comforting message of the gospel is that Jesus the Messiah has, "according to his mercy," offered to save us, "by the washing of regeneration, and renewing of the Holy Ghost; which he shed on us abundantly . . . ; that being justified by his grace, we should be made heirs according to the hope of eternal life" (Titus 3:5–7).

SALVATION BY GRACE

As we are all aware, the theological debate between whether we are saved by grace or by works has continued for centuries. In reality, it is a meaningless argument that radiates more heat than light. Perhaps because Latter-day Saints have been so hesitant to acknowledge any virtue in the argument that we are saved by grace alone, some of us have not taken the apostle Paul seriously enough; sadly, we have too often robbed ourselves of sacred insights, understanding, and comfort to be found not only in the New Testament but also in the Book of Mormon.

Paul certainly understood that the works of righteousness are necessary to our salvation. He taught that God "will render to every man according to his deeds" (Romans 2:6). Of course we must receive the ordinances of salvation. Of course we must strive to live a life befitting that of our Christian covenant. Of course we must do all in our power to overcome sin, put off the natural man, and deny ourselves of all ungodliness. These things evidence our part of the gospel covenant. They allow us, in fact, to remain in the covenant with Christ, even as we occasionally stumble and fall short of the ideal. The question is not whether good works are necessary—they are. As we have already observed, they are not sufficient. The harder questions are, In whom do I trust? On whom do I rely? Is my reliance on Christ's works, or do I strive to save myself?

Paul asked: "What shall we say then that Abraham our father, as pertaining to the flesh, hath found? For if Abraham were justified by the law of works, he hath to glory in himself; but not of God. For what saith the Scripture? Abraham believed God, and it was counted unto him for righteousness. Now to him who is justified by the law of works, is the reward reckoned, not of grace, but of debt. But to him that seeketh not to be justified by the law of works, but believeth on him who justifieth not the ungodly, his faith is counted for righteousness" (JST Romans 4:1–5). Abraham's faith—his willingness to believe the promises of God, trust in Jehovah's power to accomplish what to him seemed impossible, and thus to sacrifice Isaac—was what gained him the approval of the Almighty. It is with us as it was with Abraham; if in fact we are saved by our deeds and our merits alone, then we might have something about which to boast, namely that our own genius, our own resources, our own righteousness were what allowed us to bound into glory.

It isn't that Paul believed that only those who do not work receive eternal life but rather that those who labor, knowing their own fallibility and limitations, never trust in their own works. Paul taught what James taught—that true faith is always manifest in righteous works (James 2) and that one who relies wholly on the merits of Christ, who has faith in him, will evidence that faith through noble actions and Christian conduct. To argue that we are saved by our works is to argue that Christ's atoning mission was unnecessary. "I do not frustrate the grace of God," Paul wrote, "for if righteousness come by the law, then Christ is dead in vain" (Galatians 2:21). John MacArthur has suggested that the word *grace* makes an acronym for a glorious concept—"God's Riches At Christ's Expense."[6]

"How else could salvation possibly come?" Elder Bruce R. McConkie asked. "Can man save himself? Can he resurrect himself? Can he create a celestial kingdom and decree his own admission thereto? Salvation must and does originate with God, and if man is to receive it, God must bestow it upon him, which bestowal is a manifestation of grace. . . . Salvation does not come by the works and performances of the law of Moses, nor by 'circumcision,' nor by 'the law of commandments contained in ordinances'. . . , nor does it come by any good works standing alone. No matter how righteous a man might be, no matter how great and extensive his good works, he could not save himself. Salvation is in Christ and comes through his atonement."[7]

NEW CREATURES IN CHRIST

Paul taught that to come unto Christ is to enter into a new realm of existence, a spiritual realm. It is to forsake death and come unto life, to put away evil and darkness and learn to walk in righteousness and light. "Know ye not," Paul asked the Romans, "that so many of us as were baptized into Jesus Christ were baptized into his death? Therefore we are buried with him by baptism into death: that like as Christ was raised up from the dead by the glory of the Father, even so we also should walk in newness of life. For if we have been planted together in the likeness of his death, we shall be also in the likeness of his resurrection: knowing this, that our old man is crucified with him, that the body of sin might be destroyed, that henceforth we should not serve sin" (Romans 6:3–6).

The new life in Christ entails a new energy, a new dynamism, a new source of strength and power. That power is Christ. So often people simply go through the motions, do good and perform their duties but find little satisfaction in doing so. One Christian writer offered this thought: "There are few things quite so boring as being religious, but there is nothing quite so exciting as being a Christian!

"Most folks have never discovered the difference between the one and the other, so that there are those who sincerely try to live a life they do not have, substituting religion for God, Christianity for Christ, and their own noble endeavors for the energy, joy, and power of the Holy Spirit. In the absence of reality, they can only grasp at ritual, stubbornly defending the latter in the absence of the former, lest they be found with neither!

"They are lamps without oil, cars without gas, and pens without ink, baffled at their own impotence in the absence of all that alone can make man functional; for man was so engineered by God that the presence of the Creator within the creature is indispensable to His humanity. Christ gave Himself for us to give Himself to us! His presence puts God back into the man! He came that we might have life—God's life!

"There are those who have a life they never live. They have come to Christ and thanked Him only for what He did, but do not live in the power of who He is. Between the Jesus who 'was' and the Jesus who 'will be' they live in a spiritual vacuum, trying with no little zeal to live for Christ a life that only He can live in and through them."[8]

The disciples of Jesus must strive to do what is right. They should do their duty in the Church and in the home, even when they are not eager to do so. They cannot just leave the work of the kingdom to others because they have not been changed and reborn. But that doesn't mean they must always remain that way. Each of us may change; we can change; we should change; and it is the Lord who will change us. Coming unto Christ entails more than being cleansed, as important as that is. It entails being filled. We speak often of the importance of being cleansed, or sanctified. It is to have the Holy Spirit, who is not only a revelator but a sanctifier, remove filth and dross from our souls. We refer to this process as a baptism by fire. To be cleansed is essential, but to stop there is to stop short of great blessings. Paul presents the idea of (in a sense) nailing ourselves to the cross of Christ—nailing our old selves, the old man of sin. He wrote: "I am crucified with Christ: nevertheless I live; yet not I, but Christ liveth in me: and the life which I now live in the flesh I live by the faith of the Son of God, who loved me, and gave himself for me" (Galatians 2:20).

This is a new life in Christ. To the Ephesian Saints Paul wrote: "For by grace are ye saved through faith; and that not of yourselves: it is the gift of God: not of works, lest any man should boast. For we are his workmanship, created in Christ Jesus unto good works, which God hath before ordained that we should walk in them" (Ephesians 2:8–10). To the Hebrews he said: "Now the God of peace, that brought again from the dead our Lord Jesus, that great shepherd of the sheep, through the blood of the everlasting covenant, make you perfect in every good work to do his will, working in you that which is wellpleasing in his sight, through Jesus Christ" (Hebrews 13:20–21). When we have been filled, the Spirit is with us and Christ comes to dwell in us through that Spirit. Then our works begin to be motivated by that Holy Spirit and they are no longer our works; they are his works.

The risen Lord said to the Nephites that certain things were required before his church would be truly his Church: it must have his name, and it must be built upon his gospel. If these two conditions are met, then the Father would show forth his own works in it (3 Nephi 27:5–10). How? Through the body of Christ, through the members of the Church. The Father's Spirit motivates them to greater righteousness. It is not expected that we "go through the motions" all our lives. There can come a time when the Spirit changes our motives, desires, and yearnings, and we begin to do works the way God would do them, because he has now begun to live in us through that Spirit.

On one occasion Paul wrote: "Wherefore, my beloved, as ye have always obeyed, not as in my presence only, but now much more in my absence, work out your own salvation with fear and trembling." If we stop our reading there, and that's usually where we stop, we wonder about the phrase "work out your own salvation." How? There's not a person living on this earth that can work out his own salvation, at least not without divine assistance. There aren't enough home teaching visits; there aren't enough cakes and pies to be delivered to the neighbors; there aren't enough prayers to be uttered for a person to work out his own salvation. But Paul didn't stop there: "For it is God which worketh in you both to will and to do of his good pleasure" (Philippians 2:12–13). The works are the Lord's works through us, and thus we are doing not our works but his works.

Through the atonement of Christ we do more than enjoy a change of behavior; our nature is changed. "Therefore, if any man be in Christ, he is a new creature: old things are passed away; behold, all things are become new" (2 Corinthians 5:17). Isn't that what the angel taught King Benjamin—that the natural man is an enemy to God and will stay that way unless and until he yields himself to the enticings of the Holy Spirit? (Mosiah 3:19). John Stott explained: "We may be quite sure that Christ-centredness and Christ-likeness will never be attained by our own unaided efforts. How can self drive out self? As well expect Satan to drive out Satan! For we are not interested in skin-deep holiness, in a merely external resemblance to Jesus Christ. We are not satisfied by a superficial modification of behaviour patterns. . . . No, what we long for is a deep inward change of character, resulting from a change of nature and leading to a radical change of conduct. In a word we want to be *like Christ*, and that thoroughly, profoundly, entirely. Nothing less than this will do."[9]

Elder Glenn Pace put it this way: "We should all be striving for a disposition to do no evil, but to do good continually. This isn't a resolve or a discipline; it is a disposition. We do things because we want to, not just because we know we should. . . . Sometimes we overlook the fact that a spiritual transformation or metamorphosis must take place within us. It comes about through grace and by the Spirit of God, although it does not come about until we have truly repented and proven ourselves worthy. . . . My conclusion is that we will not be saved by works if those works are not born of a disposition to do good, as opposed to an obligation to do good."[10] That, of course, is what President Ezra Taft Benson meant when he taught that although the world deals in externals, the Lord works from the inside out.[11]

Bob George, a Protestant writer, described the spiritual transformation this way: "Being made into a new creation is like a caterpillar becoming a butterfly. Originally an earthbound crawling creature, a caterpillar weaves a cocoon and is totally immersed in it. Then a marvelous process takes place, called metamorphosis. Finally a totally new creature—a butterfly—emerges. Once ground-bound, the butterfly can now soar above the earth. It now can view life from the sky downward. In the same way, as a new creature in Christ you must begin to see yourself as God sees you.

"If you were to see a butterfly, it would never occur to you to say, 'Hey, everybody! Come look at this good-looking converted worm!' Why not? After all, it *was* a worm. And it was 'converted.' No, now it is a new creature, and you don't think of it in terms of what it was. You see it as it is now—a butterfly."[12]

THE FRUIT OF THE SPIRIT

The apostle Paul declared that one mark of true discipleship, one significant evidence of our growth into the new life in Christ, is the degree to which we enjoy the fruit of the Spirit. In three different books of scripture the Lord discusses the gifts of the Spirit—such things as discernment, tongues, interpretation of tongues, administration, prophecy, healing, and so forth. In 1 Corinthians 12 Paul suggested that the gifts of the Spirit are intended to enhance, build up, and make perfect the body of Christ, meaning the Church. They are for the good of the Church and kingdom. In addition, Paul spoke of the fruit of the Spirit. In Galatians 5, he contrasted the works of the flesh with the fruit of the Spirit: "Now the works of the flesh are manifest, which are these; adultery, fornication, uncleanness, lasciviousness, idolatry, witchcraft, hatred, variance, emulations, wrath, strife, seditions, heresies, envyings, murders, drunkenness, revellings, and such like: of the which I tell you before, as I have also told you in time past, that they which do such things shall not inherit the kingdom of God" (Galatians 5:19–21).

There is a natural birth and there is a spiritual birth. The natural birth comes with mortality, and the natural birth creates the natural man. The spiritual birth comes later. The natural birth has its own set of fruits, or works. Paul mentioned several of them. The spiritual man or woman brings forth his or her own fruits. "But the fruit of the Spirit is love, joy, peace, longsuffering, gentleness, goodness, faith, meekness, temperance: against such there is no law. And they that are Christ's have crucified the flesh with the affections and lusts. If we live in the Spirit, let us also walk in the Spirit" (Galatians 5:22–25).

Some of the gifts we know as the gifts of the Spirit may have begun to develop within us before we came here.[13] Many aptitudes, capacities, and talents may thus come quite naturally for us. For some, the gift of speaking or the gift of teaching come naturally, and these are spiritual gifts. For others, discernment or wisdom is an integral part of their lives. But there are people who are wonderful speakers and poor Christians. There are people who do remarkable things in the classroom and hurtful things outside the classroom. Talk to their family, secretary, staff, or co-workers. The gifts of the Spirit are one thing; the fruit of the Spirit, another. Patience, mercy, meekness, gentleness, longsuffering, and of course, charity, or the pure love of Christ—these characterize men and women who have begun to live in Christ. Such persons are simply more Christlike. Elder Marion D. Hanks frequently asked a haunting question, one that strikes at the core of this matter of being Christlike. He would inquire: "If you were arrested and were to be tried for being a Christian, would there be enough evidence to convict you?"

The interesting thing about the fruit of the Spirit is that attitudes and actions do not seem to be situational. In other words, a person is not just very fruitful in the Spirit only while the sun shines, pleasant and kindly only when circumstances are positive. Rather, those who enjoy the fruit of the Spirit feel "love for those who do not love in return, joy in the midst of painful circumstances, peace when something you were counting on doesn't come through, patience when things aren't going fast enough for you, kindness toward those who treat you unkindly, goodness toward those who have been intentionally insensitive to you, faithfulness when friends have proved unfaithful, gentleness toward those who have handled you roughly, self-control in the midst of intense temptation."[14]

NOT ALL ISRAEL ARE ISRAEL

Once Christ came into his life, nothing was quite the same for Saul of Tarsus. The scriptures, our Old Testament, were a new book to him. He saw the life and ministry of Jesus Christ in and through all things, and he became a witness that all things bear testimony of the Redeemer (Moses 6:63). Paul knew, for example, that the gathering of Israel was first and foremost a gathering to Christ and only secondarily a gathering to lands of inheritance. He taught that to be a true son or daughter of the covenant was to be fully Christian, to have accepted completely Jesus Christ, the mediator of God's new covenant with Israel. "They are not all Israel, which are of Israel," he pointed out. "Neither, because they are all children of Abraham, are they the seed" (JST Romans 9:6–7). Descent from Abraham, Isaac, and Jacob was significant to the degree that one received the God of Abraham, Isaac, and Jacob. In Nephi's words, "as many of the Gentiles as will repent are the covenant people of the Lord; and as many of the Jews as will not repent shall be cast off; for the Lord covenanteth with none save it be with them that repent and believe in his Son, who is the Holy One of Israel" (2 Nephi 30:2).

In bearing witness of Christ, Paul drew upon the prophetic promise that through Abraham's seed all humanity would be blessed (Genesis 12:1–3; 17:1–7; JST Genesis 17:11–12). "Now to Abraham and his seed were the promises made. He saith not, And to seeds, as of many; but as of one, And to thy seed, which is Christ" (Galatians 3:16). Paul's point might be restated as follows: although it is certainly true that through Abraham's seed all nations would be blessed—meaning that through his endless posterity the blessings of the gospel, the priesthood, and eternal life would be dispensed to the world (Abraham 2:8–11)—the ultimate fulfillment of the Abrahamic promise came through the One who was truly the Chosen Seed, Jesus of Nazareth, son of David and thus son of Abraham (Matthew 1:1–16).

Paul also taught that many of the performances and ordinances of the ancients (animal sacrifice being the most obvious) had their fulfillment and thus ultimate meaning in Christ and his redemption. For example, circumcision was given originally as a token of God's covenant with Abraham, a commandment that male children were to be circumcised at eight days as a reminder that because of the Atonement little children are not accountable until they are eight years old (JST Genesis 17:11–12). "For he is not a Jew, which is one outwardly," he wrote, "neither is that circumcision, which is outward in the flesh: but he is a Jew, which is one inwardly; and circumcision is that of the heart, in the spirit" (Romans 2:28–29). Stated another way, "in Jesus Christ neither circumcision availeth any thing, nor uncircumcision; but faith which worketh by love" (Galatians 5:6). Truly, in Christ we "are circumcised with the circumcision made without hands, in putting off the body of the sins of the flesh by the circumcision of Christ: buried with him in baptism, wherein also [we] are risen with him through the faith of the operation of God, who hath raised him from the dead" (Colossians 2:11–12).

In short, Paul's message to those who took pride and license in their lineage was clear. He declared boldly that it is a blessed privilege to be a chosen people, to be heirs to the adoption, the glory, the covenants, and the promises (Romans 9:4). But true heirship is to be secured through adoption into the family of the Lord Jesus Christ. "For there is no difference between the Jew and the Greek: for the same Lord over all is rich unto all that call upon him. For whosoever shall call upon the name of the Lord shall be saved" (Romans 10:12–13). "For ye are all the children of God by faith in Christ Jesus. For as many of you as have been baptized into Christ have put on Christ. There is neither Jew nor Greek, there is neither bond nor free, there is neither male nor female: for ye are all one in Christ Jesus. And if ye be Christ's, then are ye Abraham's seed, and heirs according to the promise" (Galatians 3:26–29; compare Colossians 3:11).

A NAME ABOVE ALL OTHERS

Paul affirmed that Jesus Christ transcends all things, is superior to the gods of the pagans, has preeminence over the mystical deities of the Gnostics, and is, under the Eternal Father, the One before whom all creatures bow in humble reverence. Paul wrote to the Ephesians that he did not cease to "give thanks for you, making mention of you in my prayers; that the God of our Lord Jesus Christ, the Father of glory, may give unto you the spirit of wisdom and revelation in the knowledge of him." The apostle then added that the Father's power had been "wrought in Christ, when he raised him from the dead, and set him at his own right hand in the heavenly places, far above all principality, and power, and might, and dominion, and every name that is named, not only in this world, but also in that which is to come: and hath put all things under his feet, and gave him to be the head over all things to the church, which is his body, the fulness of him that filleth all in all" (Ephesians 1:16–17, 20–23).

Many of the ancients believed that names held power and that to know the name of a deity was to possess power with or over it. Paul let it be known that Christ was the name above all other names and that salvation, the greatest of all the gifts of God, was to be had only in and through that holy name. "Let this mind be in you," he pleaded with the Philippian Saints, "which was also in Christ Jesus: who, being in the form of God, thought it not robbery to be equal with God: but made himself of no reputation, and took upon him the form of a servant, and was made in the likeness of men: and being found in fashion as a man, he humbled himself, and became obedient unto death, even the death of the cross. Wherefore God also hath highly exalted him, and given him a name which is above every name: that at the name of Jesus every knee should bow, of things in heaven, and things in earth, and things under the earth; and that every tongue should confess that Jesus Christ is Lord, to the glory of God the Father" (Philippians 2:5–11; compare Ephesians 3:15).

The united testimony of the apostles and prophets is that God the Eternal Father has delivered us from the power of darkness and "translated us into the kingdom of his dear Son: in whom we have redemption through his blood, even the forgiveness of sins: who is the image of the invisible God, the firstborn of every creature"—meaning, all creation—"for by him were all things created, that are in heaven, and that are in earth, visible and invisible, whether they be thrones, or dominions, or principalities, or powers: all things were created by him, and for him: and he is before all things, and by him all things consist. . . . For it pleased the Father that in him should all fulness dwell" (Colossians 1:13–17, 19; compare Hebrews 1:1–3). Thus in adoration and worship, Elder Bruce R. McConkie wrote: "The name of Jesus—wondrous name—the name in which the truths of salvation are taught; the name in which the ordinances of salvation are performed; the name in which miracles are wrought, in which the dead are raised and mountains moved;

"The name of Jesus—wondrous name—the name by which worlds come rolling into existence; the name by which redemption comes; the name which brings victory over the grave and raises the faithful to eternal life;

"The name of Jesus—wondrous name—the name by which revelation comes and angels minister; the name of him by whom all things are and into whose hands the Father hath committed all things; the name of him to whom every knee shall bow and every tongue confess in that great day when the God of Heaven makes this planet his celestial home."[15]

CONCLUSION

I love the apostle Paul. I love his personality—his wit, his charm, his firmness, his unquestioned allegiance to the Christ who called him. I love his breadth, his vision, his flexibility, and his capacity to be "all things to all men" (1 Corinthians 9:22). And, most important, I love his doctrine—particularly as revealed in his epistles, the timely but timeless messages in that regulatory correspondence by which he set in order the branches of the Church. Jesus of Nazareth, Savior and King, was the Lord of his life and the burden of his message to the world.

As he closed his last epistle, Paul said: "I am now ready to be offered, and the time of my departure is at hand. I have fought a good fight, I have finished my course, I have kept the faith: henceforth there is laid up for me a crown of righteousness, which the Lord, the righteous judge, shall give me at that day: and not to me only, but unto all them also that love his appearing" (2 Timothy 4:6–8). The "chosen vessel" (Acts 9:15) ran the race of life and did all he had been commanded to do, namely, open the eyes of the people far and wide to the gospel of Jesus Christ and "turn them from darkness to light, and from the power of Satan unto God, that they [might] receive forgiveness of sins, and inheritance among them which are sanctified" (Acts 26:18). And surely his was a glorious reunion with the Master whose name he had declared and whose gospel he had defended. In Christ Paul found a newness of life, and through Christ Paul inherited the greatest of all the gifts of God—that life which is eternal and everlasting.

NOTES

1. F. F. Bruce, *The New Testament Documents: Are They Reliable?* (Grand Rapids, Mich.: William B. Eerdmans Publishing, 1960), 79.
2. Ezra Taft Benson, *A Witness and a Warning* (Salt Lake City: Deseret Book, 1988), 33.
3. Sidney B. Sperry, *Paul's Life and Letters* (Salt Lake City: Bookcraft, 1955), 176.
4. John F. MacArthur, *The Gospel According to Jesus,* rev. ed. (Grand Rapids, Mich.: Zondervan Publishing, 1994), 197.
5. John F. MacArthur, *Faith Works: The Gospel According to the Apostles* (Dallas: Word Publishing, 1993), 89–90.
6. Ibid., 57.
7. Bruce R. McConkie, *Doctrinal New Testament Commentary,* 3 vols. (Salt Lake City: Deseret Book, 1965–73), 2:499–500.
8. W. Ian Thomas, Foreword to *Classic Christianity,* by Bob George (Eugene, Oreg.: Harvest House Publishers, 1989), n.p.
9. John Stott, *Life in Christ* (Wheaton, Ill.: Tyndale House, 1991), 109; emphasis in original.

10. Glenn L. Pace, *Spiritual Plateaus* (Salt Lake City: Deseret Book, 1991), 62–63.

11. Ezra Taft Benson, "Born of God," *Ensign,* Nov. 1985, 6.

12. George, *Classic Christianity,* 78.

13. Bruce R. McConkie, *A New Witness for the Articles of Faith* (Salt Lake City: Deseret Book, 1985), 4, 34, 359.

14. Charles Stanley, *The Wonderful, Spirit-Filled Life* (Nashville: Thomas Nelson Publishers, 1992), 108.

15. Bruce R. McConkie, *The Promised Messiah* (Salt Lake City: Deseret Book, 1978), 300.

CHAPTER NINE

WHAT IS A MORTAL MESSIAH?

CRAIG J. OSTLER

Christians desire to understand the Jesus Christ whom they worship. The divinity and the mortality of Christ are intriguing, especially as they relate to the image we have of Christ in regard to ourselves. Often when we read, write, or speak of Christ, he is placed so far above our human condition that we may lose sight of his mortal life. A topic of great debate in the early Christian church through the fifth century after Christ was the divinity versus the mortality of Jesus Christ.[1] That debate has continued into the modern era.[2] Even within the membership of The Church of Jesus Christ of Latter-day Saints there is confusion in our understanding of the nature of the mortal Messiah. To better comprehend the Lord, we should examine the writings of the apostle Paul about the mortal Messiah. He addressed such questions as, What is a mortal Messiah? How can the Lord Jesus Christ relate to the frailties of mortal beings? What influence did Christ's premortal life have on his earth life?

Paul was a special witness of Christ, a divinely appointed apostle[3] to teach and testify of Jesus Christ as the Son of God. His teachings on the interplay between Christ's premortality and mortality illuminate our individual lives and give us a glimpse of what our coming into mortality entails. Understanding the similarities between our premortal and our mortal situations and those of Jesus Christ helps us better understand both him and the plan of salvation in which we participate. On the other hand, Jesus Christ is unique among God's children, and Paul's writings help us understand why He is worthy of our faith in Him.

□ □ □ □ □

Craig J. Ostler is an instructor in Church history at Brigham Young University.

THE DIVINITY AND MORTALITY OF JESUS CHRIST

Paul taught the Philippians concerning the divinity and mortality of Christ: "Let this mind be in you, which was also in Christ Jesus: who, being in the form of God, thought it not robbery to be equal with God: but made himself of no reputation, and took upon him the form of a servant, and was made in the likeness of men: and being found in fashion as a man, he humbled himself, and became obedient unto death, even the death of the cross" (Philippians 2:5–8).

The Greek verb used by Paul in this passage, rendered "he made himself of no reputation," is a derivative of the word *kenosis,*[4] meaning "to make empty."[5] Bible scholars translate Paul's writings to say literally that the Christ "emptied himself" (Philippians 2:7; NIV study notes).[6] Other translations interpret Paul's writings to say he "made himself nothing" (NEB Philippians 2:7)[7] or "of his own free will he gave up all he had" (GNNT Philippians 2:7).[8] Referring to Philippians 2:5–8, the scholars who contributed to Dummelow's *Commentary on the Holy Bible* stated: "We take the sense of the passage to be, that Christ, while divine in His proper nature, did not, when the call came to serve others, hold fast in self-assertion His God-like state, but divested Himself of this by assuming a servant's form . . . and leading an earthly life such as our own."[9]

But what did Christ empty himself of or give up? The Savior answered this question in a revelation given through Joseph Smith the Prophet: "John saw and bore record of the *fulness of my glory* . . . saying: I saw his *glory,* that he was in the beginning, before the world was. . . . And I, John, bear record that I beheld his *glory,* as the *glory* of the Only Begotten of the Father, *full* of grace and truth, even the Spirit of truth, which came and dwelt in the flesh, and dwelt among us. And I, John, saw that he received not of the *fulness* at the first, but received grace for grace; and he received not of the *fulness* at first, but continued from grace to grace, until he received a *fulness;* and thus he was called the Son of God, because he received not of the *fulness* at the first" (D&C 93:6–7, 11–14; emphasis added).

John also recorded the petition of Christ in which he appealed to his Father in prayer, "And now, O Father, *glorify* thou me with thine own self with the *glory* which I had with thee *before* the world was" (John 17:5; emphasis added). Therefore, it was the fulness of glory that Christ had enjoyed in his premortal state of which he emptied himself in being born into mortality.

THE PREMORTAL GLORY OF JESUS CHRIST

What glory did Christ enjoy before he was born on earth? What glory did he give up to experience mortality? To understand Paul's teachings concerning the condescension[10] of Christ to mortality, we must consider his testimony of who Jesus is in the eternal sense. Paul distinguished Christ as the "firstbegotten" (Hebrews 1:6) or "the firstborn" (Romans 8:29). Paul's testimony to the Roman Saints was that God foreordained Christ before his mortal birth to be glorified (Romans 8:29–30). The scriptural account of the plan of salvation presented in the premortal councils pivots on the appointment of a redeemer or savior to atone for the sins of mankind.[11] Paul wrote of this plan as "the gospel of God, Concerning his Son Jesus Christ our Lord" (Romans 1:1, 3). His testimony was that Jesus Christ was the appointed Redeemer and Savior.[12]

Paul recorded that Jesus was given "a name which is above every name: that at the name of Jesus every knee should bow . . . and that every tongue should confess that Jesus Christ is Lord" (Philippians 2:9–11). The word translated "Lord" is the Greek *kurios,* which has several possible meanings.[13] In what way for Paul was Jesus *kurios,* or Lord? In this passage Paul was quoting the words of Jehovah[14] to Isaiah that "unto me every knee shall bow, every tongue shall swear" (Isaiah 45:23). Paul testified that Jesus is the Lord, Adonai, the Hebrew substitute for the divine name of God, Jehovah. Further, he explained to the Saints in Ephesus that God the Father "created all things by Jesus Christ" (Ephesians 3:9); he wrote to the Hebrews[15] that it was by Christ that the Father "made the worlds" (Hebrews 1:1–2).[16] In teaching of Christ as the Lord and the Creator, Paul established that the premortal Jesus had been involved in divine activity before he was born in Bethlehem. He stood apart as one who was in "the brightness of [God's] glory" (Hebrews 1:3). Paul boldly asserted to critics of his claim for Jesus as the Lord that Jesus "thought it not robbery to be equal with God" (Philippians 2:6). Paul reasoned that the appointment of Christ as the Creator and his position in the family of God as the firstborn gave him preeminence.[17]

To summarize, Paul wrote as a witness of Christ that Jesus was the firstborn, that he was the creator of worlds before he was born into mortality, and that he was in a position of pre-eminence in the family of God from before the foundations of the world. Jehovah appeared to mortals in glory.[18] He was praised and glorified as the God of Israel before he was born on earth. Paul's teachings help us understand the glory of which Christ emptied himself. We can better appreciate what was comprised for him to give up all that he had in being born into mortality.

JESUS CHRIST AS A MORTAL MESSIAH

The questions now become, How do we understand a God who has emptied himself of his glory in coming to earth? How much of the mortal experience did Jesus undergo? In what ways was Christ like or different from other mortals? Was his mortal body like that of yours or mine?

Paul's teachings illuminate the mortality of the Messiah. He wrote to the Hebrews that Jesus Christ was made "so much better than the angels. . . . For unto which of the angels said he at any time, Thou art my Son, this day have I begotten thee? . . . And again, when he bringeth in the firstbegotten into the world, he saith, And let all the angels of God worship him" (Hebrews 1:4–6).[19] Yet, even though Christ was "so much better than the angels" and was the Only Begotten Son of God, Paul informed his readers that in coming into mortality the Messiah "was made a little lower than the angels" (Hebrews 2:9).[20] Paul's writings testify again and again that Christ was made of flesh and blood[21] as the seed of Abraham.[22] Furthermore, Paul taught that the Messiah was sent as the Son of God, "made of a woman" (Galatians 4:4). Given the tendency of some in Paul's day to remove mortality from Jesus, the apostle's teachings on this point were of great importance.[23] In contrast, Paul gave special recognition to Abraham and the lineage of Israel "of whom as concerning the flesh Christ came" (Romans 9:5). Paul taught that Christ did not seize or cling to his glorified condition, but "being found in fashion as a man, he humbled himself" (Philippians 2:8) and "emptied himself" of his glory to be born on earth as a mortal being in order to save all persons. The similarity between Christ and humankind is made explicit in the Epistle to the Hebrews: "Forasmuch then as the children are partakers of flesh and blood, he also himself likewise took part of the same. . . . For verily he took not on him the nature of angels; but he took on him the seed of Abraham. Wherefore in all things it behooved him to be made like unto his brethren" (Hebrews 2:14, 16–17). Therefore, Christ began his mortal sojourn like all of the rest of Adam's seed, as a babe, born helpless and dependent upon others. He continued his mortal life, growing and maturing to manhood.[24] Elder Bruce R. McConkie, a latter-day apostle and fellow with Paul in his appointment as a special witness of Jesus Christ, wrote that the Savior underwent the ordeals of mortality: "Jesus walked the same road from infancy to manhood that has been trod by every adult mortal. . . . As a babe he began to grow, normally and naturally, and there was nothing supernatural about it. He learned to crawl, to walk, to run. He spoke his first word, cut his first tooth, took his first step—the same as other children do."[25]

In reference to Christ's being mortal and experiencing the weaknesses of the mortal body, John recorded that Jesus was "wearied with his journey" (John 4:6) as he sat upon Jacob's well in Samaria. He also recorded that the scripture was fulfilled when Jesus uttered, "I thirst" (John 19:28) while he hung upon the cross. Clearly, Paul and other witnesses testified that the Messiah had taken upon him all of the physical aspects of mortality. His body of flesh and blood was like that of all mortal beings.

THE MORTAL MESSIAH SUFFERED TEMPTATIONS

The temptations common to mortality were also part of the Messiah's mortal experience. The gospels record some of the temptations of the Messiah,[26] and Paul assured his readers that Jesus Christ "was in all points tempted like as we are" (Hebrews 4:15). Paul added that Christ did not give in to temptation nor indulge in sin, for he was "tempted like as we are, *yet without sin*" (Hebrews 4:15; emphasis added).

We might ask why the plan for the mortal Messiah would include temptation. Paul explained that being "in all points tempted like as we are," Christ is able to "be touched with the feeling of our infirmities" (Hebrews 4:15). He is a being who is filled with compassion.[27] Moreover, Paul pointed out, "for in that he himself hath suffered being tempted, he is able to succor them that are tempted" (Hebrews 2:18.)[28] In reference to Paul's teachings on the mortality and temptations of Christ, Stephen E. Robinson wrote: "A remarkable doctrine is taught here. The same Jesus Christ who is God the Son is also one of us. He was human in every respect ('in all things')—right down to being tempted like other human beings. And because he personally has been tempted, Christ can understand what temptation is. From his own personal experience of the human condition, he understands what we are dealing with here, and he can empathize with us and help us overcome temptation just as he overcame it."[29]

The extent of the similarity between Christ and his mortal brothers and sisters and the purpose of Christ's temptations were explained by Elder McConkie: "Jesus was tempted—if we may so say—to fulfill all righteousness. It was part of the eternal plan. It gave him the experiences he needed to work out his own salvation."[30] Part of the plan of salvation is that God's spirit children have a mortal experience, including temptation. But comfort and hope come to us in our weakness from a clearer understanding of the mortal life of the Messiah, which was like our own with respect to being tempted.

THE PHYSICAL SUFFERINGS OF THE MORTAL MESSIAH

That the mortality of Christ included physical suffering was made clear by Paul.[31] His message to the Jews, as he reasoned with them in the synagogue in Thessalonica, was that the scriptures testified "that Christ must needs have suffered, and risen again from the dead; and that this Jesus, whom I preach unto you, is Christ" (Acts 17:3). The Book of Mormon confirms and amplifies Paul's message concerning the sufferings of Jesus. King Benjamin prophesied that the Messiah "shall suffer temptations, and pain of body, hunger, thirst, and fatigue, even more than man can suffer" (Mosiah 3:7).[32] Alma taught the people in Gideon that the Son of God "shall go forth, suffering pains and afflictions and temptations of every kind" (Alma 7:11).

But for what purpose? Why would the plan of God include a Messiah who must undergo the sufferings of mortality? What benefit could come from a suffering Son of God? The answer is similar to that of the need for the Messiah to undergo temptation. As the "author of eternal salvation" (Hebrews 5:9), Christ did more than write the book on salvation and the integral part that suffering plays in progression; he experienced the plan himself. Even "though he were a Son, yet learned he obedience by the things which he suffered; and being made perfect, he became the author of eternal salvation unto all them that obey him" (Hebrews 5:8–9).[33] Richard Anderson explained: "For many years Paul probably faced that question [of what benefit could come from a suffering savior] of ridicule or confusion. His answer is that a suffering Savior knows us better and is better known by us. Having learned obedience through mortal trials, Christ can be trusted totally to lead 'all them that obey him' to 'eternal salvation' (Hebrews 5:9). . . . The Savior does not call from a distant height but from a little ahead on the rocky path that his disciples climb: 'For we do not have a High Priest who cannot sympathize with our weaknesses, but was in all points tempted as we are, yet without sin' (Hebrews 4:15, NKJB). Jesus was once on this earth, fully felt its pressures, and met its challenges. He not only died for the sins of all but lived as the example for all. Could anyone believe that perfection is attainable unless someone had attained it? And could anyone have confidence in divine mercy unless the Lord knew personally the terrible realities of life?"[34]

Moreover, in the course of his writings Paul made two further points about the need for a Messiah who was subject to the full extent of mortality. The first point was that it was necessary for the Messiah to become mortal "for the suffering of death" (Hebrews 2:9). Salvation for mankind could be accomplished only if the bands of death could be broken.[35] Christ's sufferings and death were made possible by his mortality. The Father gave him the power to break the bands of death[36] and to claim victory for all mortal beings.[37] The plan of God was perfect, and Paul affirms to the Corinthians that "death is swallowed up in victory . . . thanks be to God, which giveth us the victory through our Lord Jesus Christ" (1 Corinthinans 15:54, 57).

The second point Paul made about the purpose for a suffering mortal Messiah deals with the spiritual salvation of mankind. He taught that "without shedding of blood is no remission" of sins (Hebrews 9:22). One element that separates mortal from immortal beings is blood.[38] Christ needed to be mortal in order to have the blood that he shed for the salvation of humanity. The Roman Saints were taught that it was through the blood of Christ that they could be justified before God (Romans 5:9). In the epistle to the Hebrews Paul declared that "Jesus also, that he might sanctify the people with his own blood, suffered without the gate" (Hebrews 13:12). Paul's message was that Christ had suffered for the sins of all mankind through the shedding of his blood and the giving of his life.

Confirming the writings of Paul, Alma gave three reasons for the mortal sufferings of the Messiah: "[1] he will take upon him death, that he may loose the bands of death which bind his people; [2] and he will take upon him their infirmities, that his bowels may be filled with mercy, according to the flesh, [3] that he may know according to the flesh how to succor his people according to their infirmities" (Alma 7:12). In Alma's confirmation of Paul's writings, we find the answer to an important question. Given that Christ was the creator of worlds, the God of the Old Testament—even Jehovah[39]—and that his mortal experiences were to aid in his understanding of the human condition, how could he have dealt with and understood human weaknesses and sufferings in the time before his own mortal experience? Alma reasoned, "Now the Spirit knoweth all things" (Alma 7:13). Therefore, the premortal Messiah was able to understand the human experience to the extent that it was made known to him by the Spirit. His dealings with his mortal brothers and sisters before his own mortal life were aided by the understanding and empathy given to him of the Spirit. "Nevertheless," Alma emphasizes, "the Son of God suffereth according to the flesh that he might take upon him the sins of his people, that he might blot out their transgressions according to the power of his deliverance" (Alma 7:13). Christ's mortality was necessary to fulfill his premortal appointment as Redeemer and Savior. The Atonement required that the Redeemer have a body of flesh and blood and be subject to the physical sufferings of mortality.

THE SPIRITUAL SUFFERINGS OF THE MORTAL MESSIAH

Another point, one philosophical in nature, is important in

understanding the experiences of the mortal Messiah. Not all of the experiences of mortality can be understood vicariously or objectively. As a divine being Christ could not fully experience humanity unless he also experienced spiritual death. All humanity are spiritually dead, or "cut off from the presence of the Lord" (Helaman 14:16). I propose that the Spirit could not objectively give Christ the experience of knowing spiritual death, by its very definition, which is to be without the Spirit of God. That could only be understood through the subjective experience—to actually have the Spirit forsake him, to suffer in both body and soul the effects of separation. The separation from the Spirit allowed the condescension of the Son of God to be complete. While on the cross "Jesus cried with a loud voice, saying, Eli, Eli, lama sabachthani? that is to say, My God, my God, why hast thou forsaken me?" (Matthew 27:46; see also Mark 15:34). The Savior explained to Joseph Smith and Martin Harris that they had "in the least degree . . . tasted" the suffering of separation that Christ experienced during his atonement and crucifixion "at the time I withdrew my Spirit" (D&C 19:20). Brigham Young taught: "The Father withdrew His spirit from His Son, at the time he was to be crucified. . . . at the hour when the crisis came for him to offer up his life, the Father withdrew Himself, withdrew His Spirit, and cast a vail over him. That is what made him sweat blood. If he had had the power of God upon him, he would not have sweat blood; but all was withdrawn from him, and a veil cast over him."[40] As the Savior explained, the suffering that caused him to "tremble because of pain, and to bleed at every pore" included a suffering of "both body and spirit" (D&C 19:18). The Lord has provided Latter-day Saints a unique comprehension of Paul's teachings of the mortality of the Messiah. The depth of the Savior's becoming "like his brethren in all things" adds to our acknowledgment of Jesus Christ as Lord, even as we bow the knee to the Son of God who "descended below" all things.[41]

THE VEIL OF MORTALITY AND THE MESSIAH

But what of Jesus' mental capabilities? Given that he was God before he was born on this earth, did he have the advantage over his mortal brethren? Did Christ come with memory of his premortal life? Christ's experience of mortality was not limited to his physical makeup but extended to his mental and spiritual faculties as well.[42] Paul clarified the mortality of Christ as being "in all things made like unto his brethren" (Hebrews 2:17). Paul's writings assert that the condescension was complete. Because all humanity come to earth without a memory of their former life, being like his brethren in "all things" includes the loss of memory of the premortal life. Christ did not come to earth with a memory of his premortal divinity and activities. As we have previously seen, he gave up all that he had, he "emptied himself"! Elder James E. Talmage confirmed this point that "over His mind had fallen the veil of forgetfulness common to all who are born to earth, by which the remembrance of primeval existence is shut off."[43]

THE DIVINITY OF THE MESSIAH DURING MORTALITY

Paul's teachings concerning the place of Christ's divinity during his mortal life take us again to Philippians. Paul explained to them that Christ "took upon him the form of a servant" (Philippians 2:7). We are reminded of Joseph who was sold into Egypt as a servant. He had the outward appearance of a servant. The coat given to him by his father, Jacob, had been removed, and he was no longer in the presence of his father as a favored son. He was made a servant and later cast into prison. Yet, he was still Joseph! Those who could discern spiritual characteristics recognized the greatness of Joseph (Genesis 39:3, 21–23; 41:38). In a similar way, Christ emptied himself of the glory of God, came to earth, and "took upon him the form of a servant."[44] Yet, he was still Jehovah! Circumstances of the world did not dictate the character of the Son of God. Regardless of his lowly birth, family, and situation in life, Jesus of Nazareth was divine, and those who received his testimony recognized him as the Messiah.[45]

By way of further illustration, Paul referred to Jesus as one "though he was rich, yet for your sakes he became poor" (2 Corinthians 8:9). If the glory of the premortal Messiah is likened unto riches, then he was truly the richest of all.[46] Again one is reminded of an Old Testament personality. Job was the richest of all of the men of the east. In sudden disasters he lost everything he possessed and suffered physical afflictions. Yet, he was still Job! His indomitable spirit triumphed over all of the testing and tribulations that mortality had to offer.[47] Likewise, Christ may have made himself poor for us, yet, once again, he was still Jehovah. Elder McConkie explained: "When we pass from preexistence to mortality, we bring with us traits and talents there developed. True, we forget what went before because we are here being tested, but the capacities and abilities that then were ours are yet resident within us. . . . And all men with their infinitely varied talents and personalities pick up the course of progression where they left it off when they left the heavenly realms."[48] Christ "brought with him from that eternal world the talents and capacities, the inclinations to conform and obey, and the ability to recognize truth that he had there acquired."[49]

That Jesus of Nazareth excelled above all mankind during his mortal sojourn is due to his character, spiritual sensitivity, and obedience to his Father in Heaven. In time the divinity of Christ was made manifest. He could be emptied of all he possessed, and still he was the being whom the Father recognized as capable of exemplifying perfect righteousness and atoning for the salvation of humanity.[50]

CONCLUSION

Paul testified of Christ's divinity and of his mortality. As a special witness of Christ, Paul taught the truth concerning the Messiah and his mortal life on earth and gave us the information we need to understand our Lord and Savior. Paul's readers thereby gain a firm foundation upon which to build their faith in Christ. He is the Lord and creator of all things. He has undergone the experiences of mortality and shown us the path to walk. He understands our mortal situation and is able to strengthen us in temptation and save us from sin. In every way he is worthy of our praise and love. He is one with us in partaking of mortality, as we hope to become one with him in partaking of immortality and eternal life.[51]

NOTES

1. James L. Barker, *Apostasy from the Divine Church* (Salt Lake City: Kate Montgomery Barker, 1960), 328–412.

2. Michael Goulder, ed., *Incarnation and Myth: The Debate Continued* (Grand Rapids, Mich.: William B. Eerdmans Publishing, 1979).

3. Doctrine and Covenants 107:23 reveals that the calling of the Twelve Apostles is to be special witnesses of the name of Christ in all the

world. Paul identified himself as an apostle in several instances (Romans 1:1; 1 Corinthians 1:1; 15:9; 2 Corinthians 1:1; Galatians 1:1, 17; Ephesians 1:1; Colos-sians 1:1; 1 Timothy 1:1; 2 Timothy 1:1, 11; Titus 1:1.)

4. *The Word Study New Testament,* ed. Ralph D. Winter and Roberta H. Winter (Pasadena: William Carey Library, 1978), 635. George V. Wigram and Ralph D. Winter, *The Word Study Concordance* (Pasadena: William Carey Library, 1978), entry 2758.

5. *Theological Dictionary of the New Testament,* ed. Gerhard Kittel (Grand Rapids, Mich.: William B. Eerdmans Publishing, 1965), 661.

6. *The NIV Study Bible* (Grand Rapids, Mich.: Zondervan Publishing, 1985), 1805.

7. *The New English Bible* (Oxford and Cambridge: Oxford University Press and Cambridge University Press, 1970), 252. J. R. Dummelow's commentary expounds further on the concept of the Messiah emptying himself, "the verb 'emptied' in v. 7 supplies the theological term *kenosis* for the deprivation of divine attributes or powers involved in the incarnation of our Lord. However far this diminution went—and we cannot pretend to define its limits—since it was a *self*-emptying, an act of our Lord's sovereignty, it involved no forfeiture of intrinsic Deity." J. R. Dummelow, *A Commentary on the Holy Bible* (New York: Macmillan, 1973), 973.

8. *Good News New Testament* (New York: American Bible Society, 1976), 500.

9. Dummelow, *Commentary,* 973.

10. In 1 Nephi 11 the coming of the Son of the Eternal Father into mortality is called the "condescension of God."

11. See 2 Nephi 2:8, 26–27; 9:4–13; Alma 12:23–24; 18:39; 21:9; 22:13–14; 34:14–16; 42:15; Abraham 3:27; Moses 4:1–2; 6:51–62.

12. Acts 13:23; Romans 3:24; Galatians 1:3–4; Titus 2:13–14.

13. *Theological Dictionary of the New Testament,* 1041–58.

14. I will use the name *Jehovah* for the Hebrew designation *Yahweh.* This is the common term used by Latter-day Saints, as it is found in the King James Version of the Bible.

15. Some question the authorship of Hebrews. Protestant scholarship generally rejects the Pauline authorship of the epistle, but Catholic scholarship accepts it. For an LDS discussion of these two points of view, see Sidney B. Sperry, *Paul's Life and Letters* (Salt Lake City: Bookcraft, 1955), 268–72, and Richard Lloyd Anderson, *Understanding Paul* (Salt Lake City: Deseret Book, 1983), 197–201.

16. See Colossians 1:16–17; D&C 38:1; 76:23–24.

17. See 1 Corinthians 8:6; Colossians 1:15–18.

18. Exodus 16:10; 19:18–20; 24:15–17; Deuteronomy 5:24; 1 Nephi 1:9; Moses 1:1–5, 13–15, 25.

19. That the angels had literally worshipped the Savior is shown in the account of the Nativity recorded by Luke. See Luke 2:6–14.

20. Paul is quoting Psalm 8:4–5, in which the Hebrew for the word translated *angels* should be translated *gods.*

21. Romans 8:3; 2 Corinthians 5:16; Ephesians 1:7; 2:13; Colossians 1:14, 22; 1 Timothy 3:16.

22. Romans 9:5; Hebrews 2:16–17.

23. These explanations were made not by apostles but by theologians who used the philosophies of Greece and mingled them with apostolic teachings. Among those theologians was Cerinthus, a man trained in Egypt who propounded that the man Jesus and the divine Christ were two separate entities. He taught that the Christ, or the divine spirit, descended upon Jesus in "bodily shape" (Luke 3:22) after he was baptized. The spirit of the divine Christ thus gave the mortal Jesus the power of God to perform miracles and to declare the will of the Father. In regard to the sufferings of the Atonement, Cerinthus taught that the Christ left the mortal Jesus before the Passion. Therefore, it was the mortal Jesus who suffered and died. Meanwhile, the Christ remained untouched by the mortal suffering recorded in the gospels. *The Interpreter's Dictionary of the Bible,* ed. George A. Buttrick (New York: Abingdon Press, 1962), 1:549. For a discussion of heretical teachings concerning the nature of Christ, see also F. F. Bruce, *New Testament History* (Garden City: Anchor Books, Doubleday, 1972), 416. Another school of thought was that of the Docetists. They believed that physical matter was inherently evil and that Christ was a divine being; therefore Jesus only "appeared" to have a mortal body, for it was an illusion. *Interpreter's Dictionary of the Bible,* 1:860.

24. Luke 2:40, 52.

25. Bruce R. McConkie, *The Mortal Messiah,* 4 vols. (Salt Lake City: Deseret Book, 1979), 1:367–68. In writing about the childhood of Christ, Dr. Geikie maintained: "Mysterious as it is to us, we must never forget that, as a child, He passed through the same stages as other children. As Irenaeus says, 'He sanctified childhood by passing through it.' Neither His words nor acts, His childish pleasures nor His tears, were different from those of His age. Evil alone had no growth in Him: His soul gave back to the heavens all their sacred brightness. The ideal of humanity from His birth, He never lost the innocence of childhood, but He was none the less completely like other children in all things else." Cunningham Geikie, *The Life and Words of Christ* (New York: D. Appleton, 1897), 165.

26. Matthew 4:1–10; Mark 1:13; Luke 4:1–13.

27. 3 Nephi 17:6; D&C 101:9.

28. The Savior himself testified to the early members of the Church that

he "knoweth the weakness of man and how to succor them who are tempted" (D&C 62:1).

29. Stephen E. Robinson, *Believing Christ* (Salt Lake City: Deseret Book, 1992), 112.

30. McConkie, *Mortal Messiah,* 1:417.

31. Hebrews 5:8; 13:12. In addition, Christ taught from the scriptures that the Messiah ought to have suffered (Luke 24:25–27).

32. Following a recital of the perils and travails that the Prophet Joseph Smith had suffered consequent to the persecutions in Missouri, the Savior informed him, "The Son of Man hath descended below them all" (D&C 122:8).

33. The Joseph Smith Translation manuscripts of the Bible state that Hebrews 5:7–8 is "a parenthesis alluding to Melchizedek and not to Christ." Bruce R. McConkie contends that "these verses make clear reference to Christ and his mortal ministry. . . . The fact is verses 7 and 8 apply to both Melchizedek and to Christ, because Melchizedek was a prototype of Christ." *Doctrinal New Testament Commentary,* 3 vols. (Salt Lake City: Bookcraft, 1973), 3:157. See also Robert J. Matthews, *"A Plainer Translation": Joseph Smith's Translation of the Bible, A History and Commentary* (Provo, Utah: Brigham Young University Press, 1975), 383–84; Anderson, *Understanding Paul,* 227, n. 56.

34. Anderson, *Understanding Paul,* 204.

35. 2 Nephi 9:7–13.

36. Acts 2:24; Hebrews 13:20.

37. 1 Corinthians 15:21–22; 2 Nephi 2:8; 9:12; Mosiah 13:35; Mormon 9:13.

38. The Prophet Joseph Smith taught that the bodies of resurrected beings are quickened by spirit and there will be no blood in these bodies. *Teachings of the Prophet Joseph Smith,* sel. Joseph Fielding Smith (Salt Lake City: Deseret Book, 1974), 367.

39. Exodus 3:14; D&C 29:1; 38:1; 39:1; 110:2–4.

40. Brigham Young, in *Journal of Discourses,* 26 vols. (London: Latter-day Saints' Book Depot, 1854–86), 3:206.

41. D&C 122:8; "The Son descended in suffering below that which man can suffer; or, in other words, suffered greater sufferings, and was exposed to more powerful contradictions than any man can be. But, notwithstanding all this, he kept the law of God, and remained without sin, showing thereby that it is in the power of man to keep the law and remain also without sin." Joseph Smith, *Lectures on Faith,* comp. N. B. Lundwall (Salt Lake City: N. B. Lundwall, n.d.), 5:2.

42. Bruce R. McConkie wrote that "it seems perfectly clear that our Lord grew mentally and spiritually on the same basis that he developed physically." *Mortal Messiah,* 1:369. Elder McConkie further explained that Christ "was subject to the restrictions and testings of mortality." *Doctrinal New Testament Commentary,* 1:111.

43. James E. Talmage, *Jesus the Christ* (Salt Lake City: Deseret Book, 1976), 111.

44. For more examples of Joseph of Egypt as a type for Christ, see *Old Testament: Genesis–2 Samuel (Religion 301) Student Manual* (Salt Lake City: The Church of Jesus Christ of Latter-day Saints, 1980), 97.

45. Matthew 16:13–17; John 4:25–29, 41–42; 9:25–38; 11:27.

46. Abraham 3:16–19.

47. Job 1:1–2:10; 42:10–13.

48. McConkie, *Mortal Messiah*, 1:25.

49. Ibid., 1:369.

50. Moses 1:6; 4:2; Abraham 3:27.

51. John 17:11; D&C 35:2; Moses 1:39; 6:68.

CHAPTER TEN

THE HOLY GHOST BRINGS TESTIMONY, UNITY, AND SPIRITUAL GIFTS

REX C. REEVE JR.

The Greek world in Paul's day had very little concern for moral law. There was an emphasis on the joys of physical existence, and typical of many societies, outward appearance, rhetoric, discussion, and physical possessions were more important than personal righteousness. Corinth, with its sailors, freighters, and diverse population, had its share of wickedness and moral corruption. And yet in Corinth Paul found many good people prepared and willing to receive and learn to live the gospel of Jesus Christ.

Corinth was a very active business and commercial center and the meeting point of many nationalities. The chief town of the Roman province of Achaia, it was destroyed in 146 B.C. during the Roman conquest, but because of its important location, it was rebuilt by Julius Caesar about 50 B.C. It was situated on the isthmus connecting the Peloponnese peninsula with the mainland of Greece and had harbors on both the eastern and western sides. Much of the ancient trade between Asia and Western Europe passed through its harbors. To avoid the long and dangerous voyage around the Peloponnese, merchants unloaded their goods at one harbor, transported them overland across the isthmus, and reloaded them on ships to continue their journey to all parts of the world.

"This trade center was also a center of wickedness. . . . The big cities of the Roman empire were like today's big cities in

□ □ □ □ □

Rex C. Reeve Jr. is associate professor of ancient scripture at Brigham Young University.

offering the best and the worst. . . . Yet the existence of bad society does not make all society bad. The Lord stood before Paul in vision and commanded him to stay and gather his people out of this worldly center."[1]

Paul first visited Corinth about A.D. 50 during his second missionary journey. He began teaching in the Jewish synagogue as was his custom. When persecution arose, the Lord instructed Paul to remain in Corinth and continue teaching among the Gentiles, because the Lord had many people in that city. Paul labored about eighteen months in Corinth, during which time many believed and were baptized (Acts 18:1–11).

Paul wrote 1 Corinthians about A.D. 57 while he was in Ephesus on his third missionary journey. He had received several reports of problems that had developed among the Church members in Corinth. From the household of a woman named Chloe he learned of contentions and factions in the branch (1 Corinthians 1:11). He learned of serious moral sins among the members (1 Corinthians 5:1–3) and that there was misunderstanding about the use and purpose of spiritual gifts (1 Corinthians 12:1–2). In addition to those problems, the Corinthians had written to Paul asking important questions that needed answers (1 Corinthians 7:1). The challenge for Paul was to help these early Church members understand "that your faith should not stand in the wisdom of men, but in the power of God" (1 Corinthians 2:5). The solutions to their problems and the answers to their questions could only be found as they better understood the doctrines and conformed their lives to the teachings of the gospel of Jesus Christ. Paul therefore taught the Saints to seek the companionship of the Holy Ghost, which brings testimony, unity, and all the benefits of spiritual gifts.

SEEK THE COMPANIONSHIP OF THE HOLY GHOST

Having the companionship of the Holy Ghost is the key gift that all should seek and develop. With that companionship individuals can know and testify that Jesus is the Lord and can have access to a diversity of other spiritual gifts. "Wherefore I give you to understand, that no man speaking by the Spirit of God calleth Jesus accursed: and that no man can say that Jesus is the Lord, but by the Holy Ghost. Now there are diversities of gifts, but the same Spirit" (1 Corinthians 12:3–4). Individuals may say things without the aid of the Holy Ghost, but they may not be assured of eternal truths without the influence of that member of the Godhead. The Prophet Joseph Smith said that 1 Corinthians 12:3 should be translated "no man can *know* that Jesus is the Lord, but by the Holy Ghost."[2] As members have more companionship with the Holy Ghost, in addition to a stronger personal testimony of Christ, they will experience the spiritual gift of unity, which is essential in the church of Christ.

UNITY IN CHRIST

By building on the foundation of a personal testimony of Jesus Christ, members of the Church in Corinth were reminded to understand the doctrine of unity in Christ, which overrides all divisions. Paul's discussion at this point is part of the answer to a larger question faced by the early Church: How does the gospel of Jesus Christ really work when applied to every nation, kindred, tongue, and people? How can one mix the great cultural extremes of Jew and Gentile or the economic and social extremes of bond and free and have the unity required by Christ?

Paul's answer is simple yet profound. He said: "For as the body is one, and hath many members, and all the members of that one body, being many, are one body: so also is Christ. For by one spirit are we all baptized into one body, whether we be Jews or Gentiles, whether we be bond or free; and have been all made to drink into one Spirit. For the body is not one member, but many" (1 Corinthians 12:12–14). The body of Christ represents the Church, which is made up of many different people who have different backgrounds and different gifts but who are united with Christ through baptism and the reception of the Holy Ghost. Each member of the Church is part of the body of Christ (or part of the church of Christ) and individually represents Christ in the world.

Paul continues teaching by comparing members of the Church, the body of Christ, to a human physical body, with such different parts as eyes, ears, and so forth. Just as all parts of the body are necessary, so are all the members necessary and important in the church of Christ. "But now hath God set the members every one of them in the body, as it hath pleased him. . . . But now are they many members, yet but one body.

And the eye cannot say unto the hand, I have no need of thee: nor again the head to the feet, I have no need of you" (1 Corinthians 12:18–21).

To achieve the unity in the Church that Christ requires, each member must view himself first and foremost as a true follower of Jesus Christ. Members must also recognize that every other member, regardless of background and circumstance in life, is a true follower of Christ. Whether they be Jew, Gentile, bond, free, male, female, black, or white, all are united in Christ. If members see themselves or others primarily as Jew or Gentile, or bond or free, or male or female, the Spirit is offended and unity is destroyed.

Paul builds on his theme of unity by teaching: "God hath tempered the body together . . . that there should be no schism in the body [church]; but that the members should have the same care one for another. And whether one member suffer, all members suffer with it; or one member be honoured, all the members rejoice with it" (1 Corinthians 12:24–26). Unity requires that members care for others, serve one another, and share the sorrows and joys of this life. The key is to achieve unity while at the same time remembering that each member is unique and has the potential to make a special contribution. Paul said it this way, "Now ye are the body of Christ, and members in particular" (1 Corinthians 12:27).

SPIRITUAL GIFTS: THE LORD'S SYSTEM OF SERVICE

Adding to the uniqueness of each individual is the doctrine that through the administration of the Holy Ghost each member of the Church has access to differing spiritual gifts. Paul said: "Now there are diversities of gifts, but the same Spirit. And there are differences of administrations, but the same Lord. And there are diversities of operations, but it is the same God which worketh all in all. But the manifestation of the Spirit is given to every man to profit withal" (1 Corinthians 12:4–7).

Paul listed some of the spiritual gifts Church members may experience. "For to one is given by the Spirit the word of wisdom; to another the word of knowledge by the same Spirit; to another faith by the same Spirit; to another the gifts of healing by the same Spirit; to another the working of miracles; to another prophecy; to another discerning of spirits; to another

divers kinds of tongues; to another the interpretation of
tongues; but all these worketh that one and the selfsame Spirit,
dividing to every man severally as he will" (1 Corinthians
12:8–11).[3]

At first glance one might think that every person's experiencing a different spiritual gift would emphasize differences
and further divide the Saints. Nevertheless, the opposite is true:
spiritual gifts are given by the Lord to perfect and unite the
Saints in true service one to another. Paul's words combined
with the other scriptures clearly teach the uniting power of spiritual gifts.

According to the wisdom and pleasure of the Lord, every
Church member has at least one spiritual gift, as Paul said,
"dividing to every man severally as he will" (1 Corinthians
12:11). Moroni taught, "And all these gifts come by the Spirit of
Christ; and they come unto every man severally, according as
he will" (Moroni 10:17). No member would have all the spiritual gifts; some may have one gift, and some another; a few
members may have several gifts; but among the group, all of
the spiritual gifts would be present in the Church. The Lord
revealed to Joseph Smith, "For all have not every gift given
unto them; for there are many gifts, and to every man is given
a gift by the Spirit of God" (D&C 46:11).

Individual Church members are given spiritual gifts for their
own benefit and for the benefit of all other Church members.
Paul taught, "But the manifestation of the Spirit is given to
every man to profit withal . . . forasmuch as ye are zealous of
spiritual gifts, seek that ye may excel to the edifying of the
church" (1 Corinthians 12:7; 14:12). Moroni said that the gifts of
God "are given by the manifestations of the Spirit of God unto
men, to profit them" (Moroni 10:8). The Lord said, "To some is
given one, and to some is given another, that all may be profited thereby" (D&C 46:12). These gifts are available to those
"who love me and keep all my commandments, and him that
seeketh so to do" (D&C 46:9).

How is it possible to benefit from the spiritual gift of another
person? It could work this way. Let's say I was not given the
gift of faith. My faith may be weak, and I may be struggling
with things in the Church or in my life. I have the opportunity

to associate with Jim, who has the special gift of strong faith. As the Lord's system works, if my faith is weak, I can associate with Jim and benefit from his gift of faith. As we continue to associate, my faith can actually increase; he can render real service to me in sharing his spiritual gift. Now think of other members with different spiritual gifts. As we associate with them, we can grow in testimony, wisdom, knowledge, and so on. In turn we share our individual spiritual gifts with others, and we are edified together. There are no unimportant gifts in the Lord's system. Just as every part of a physical body is important, so every individual Church member, with his or her special gift, is important to other members and to the welfare of the Church as a whole.

Each member of the Church is responsible to identify his or her spiritual gifts, develop them, and share them with others. Through this process the individual and the whole Church are united in Christ and are blessed.

To safeguard the purity and purpose of spiritual gifts and to ensure that gifts come from God and are used for his purposes, some Church leaders are given the gift of discernment. "And unto the bishop of the church, and unto such as God shall appoint . . . are to have it given unto them to discern all those gifts lest there shall be any among you professing and yet be not of God" (D&C 46:27). Paul is an example of how this gift works. As a Church leader responsible for the Corinthian Saints, he was able to discern and correct the false gifts and the misuse of true gifts that existed among them.

The prophet of God is given all of the spiritual gifts, so he can stand as an example and as a light to the Saints who will follow him. "That unto some it may be given to have all those gifts, that there may be a head, in order that every member may be profited thereby" (D&C 46:29). By looking to the prophet, individual members can see the functioning of every spiritual gift. Just as members benefit from sharing spiritual gifts with other members, they benefit from sharing the spiritual gifts of the prophet.

THE GIFTS OF TONGUES, PROPHECY, AND CHARITY

The spiritual gifts most visible to other people are the gift of speaking in tongues and the gift of prophecy. Paul discussed those two gifts, compared their importance, and outlined their proper use. Their external visibility made the proper use of these gifts very important to the functioning of the true Church. Joseph Smith said: "There are several gifts mentioned here, yet which of them all could be known by an observer . . . ? There are only two gifts that could be made visible—the gift of tongues and the gift of prophecy. . . . The greatest, the best, and the most useful gifts would be known nothing about by an observer."[4]

In the use of these two gifts, especially speaking in tongues, the Corinthian Saints had been deceived. They seemed to think the confusion of many people speaking in some unknown tongue at the same time was the highest gift and indicated a superior level of spirituality for those involved. They were judging the worth of individuals according to their use of these more visible spiritual gifts.

To help the Corinthian Saints gain a proper perspective, Paul stated very strongly that the less-visible gifts of faith, hope, and charity, especially charity—which is the pure love of Christ— exceed all others. He said, "Though I speak with the tongues of men and of angels, and have not charity, I am become as sounding brass, or a tinkling cymbal. And though I have the gift of prophecy, . . . and have not charity, I am nothing" (1 Corinthians 13:1–2). Elder Bruce R. McConkie taught: "Above all the attributes of godliness and perfection, charity is the one most devoutly to be desired. Charity is more than love, far more; it is everlasting love, perfect love, the pure love of Christ which endureth forever. It is love so centered in righteousness that the possessor has no aim or desire except for the eternal welfare of his own soul and for the souls of those around him."[5]

To further emphasize the importance of charity over that of other spiritual gifts, Paul taught that the need for the gifts of tongues and prophecy, as we know them, will end when Christ returns to the earth, but charity, the pure love of Christ, will never end. It will abide forever. He said: "Charity never faileth: but whether there be prophecies, they shall fail; whether there be tongues, they shall cease; . . . But when that which is perfect is come, then that which is in part shall be done away.

. . . And now abideth faith, hope, charity, these three; but the greatest of these is charity" (1 Corinthians 13:8–13).

Elder McConkie taught, "Shall the gifts of the Spirit cease? Is there to be a day when the saints shall no longer possess the gifts of prophecy and tongues? . . . Yes, in the sense that these shall be swallowed up in something greater, and shall no longer be needed in the perfect day."[6] Keeping in mind their relative importance and their temporary nature, we can see that the spiritual gifts of speaking and interpreting tongues are important when used in the right way and for the right reasons. Both gifts should be used to edify and uplift the Church.

The gift of tongues works in two ways. The first, to "speak with the tongues of men," is to speak to people in their own language even when the speaker does not know that language. One proper use of this gift of tongues was on the day of Pentecost. The apostles spoke and were clearly understood by many people who spoke different languages (Acts 2:1–18). The result was that those hearing the gospel understood and were edified. The second, to "speak with the tongue of angels," is for an individual to speak in a language unknown to both the speaker and the hearer. Elder McConkie suggested, "Sometimes it is the pure Adamic language which is involved."[7] For this gift to be beneficial it must be communicated in an orderly way and there must be someone with the gift to interpret the unknown language. Paul said, "If any man speak in an unknown tongue, let it be by two, or at the most by three, and that by course; and let one interpret. But if there be no interpreter, let him keep silence in the church; and let him speak to himself, and to God" (1 Corinthians 14:27–28). The purpose of this gift is for the individuals possessing it to receive revelation, knowledge, prophesying, or doctrine, that all may be edified.

Joseph Smith warned the Saints about the gift of tongues: "Speak not in the gift of tongues without understanding it, or without interpretation. The devil can speak in tongues; the adversary will come with his work; he can tempt all classes; can speak in English or Dutch. Let no one speak in tongues unless he interpret, except by the consent of the one who is placed to preside; then he may discern or interpret, or another may."[8] The Prophet also said: "Be not so curious about tongues, do not speak in tongues except there be an interpreter present; the ultimate design of tongues is to speak to foreigners. . . . The gifts of God are all useful in their place, but when they are applied to that which God does not intend, they prove an injury, a snare and a curse instead of a blessing."⁹

Paul taught the Corinthians that their false understanding and application of the gift of tongues would not help the Church or those investigating the Church: "For he that speaketh in an unknown tongue speaketh not unto men, but unto God: for no man understandeth him; . . . If therefore the whole church be come together into one place, and all speak with tongues, and there come in those that are unlearned, or unbelievers, will they not say that ye are mad?" (1 Corinthians 14:2, 23). In the Lord's church, all speaking and teaching should be under-standable and done in proper order to edify the individual and the Church. To emphasize this point Paul said, "I thank my God, I speak with tongues more than ye all: yet in the church I had rather speak five words with my understanding, that by my voice I might teach others also, than ten thousand words in an unknown tongue" (1 Corinthians 14:18–19).

In a hierarchy of spiritual gifts, the gift of prophecy is greater than the gift of tongues. Elder Bruce R. McConkie said: "Prophecy is revelation; it is testimony; it is Spirit speaking to spirit; it is knowing by revelation that Jesus is the Lord, that sal-vation is in Christ, that he has redeemed us by his blood. Prophecy is walking in paths of truth and righteousness; it is living and doing the will of Him whose we are. . . . Prophecy is for all: men, women, and children, every member of the true Church; and those who have the testimony of Jesus have the spirit of prophecy."¹⁰ Paul said, "Desire spiritual gifts, but rather that ye may prophesy. . . . He that prophesieth speaketh unto men to edification, and exhortation, and comfort. . . . He that prophesieth edifieth the church. . . . Wherefore, brethren, covet [be eager, zealous] to prophesy, and forbid not to speak with tongues" (1 Corinthians 14:1, 4, 39).

Even with the special gift of prophecy it is important to avoid confusion and disorder in the Church. Paul instructs the Corinthian Saints that when the prophets (those who have the testimony of Jesus) speak, others should listen and give their full attention, so that by partaking of the same Spirit as the speaker all may be edified together: "Let the prophets speak two or three, and let the other judge . . . For ye may all prophesy one by one, that all may learn, and all may be comforted. . . . For God is not the author of confusion, but of peace, as in all churches of the saints. . . . Let all things be done decently and in order" (1 Corinthians 14:29, 31, 33, 40). When things are done according to the will of the Lord and when the spirit is right, "he that preacheth and he that receiveth, understand one another, and both are edified and rejoice together" (D&C 50:22).

SUMMARY

The companionship of the Holy Ghost brings a true testimony of Jesus Christ, unity in Christ, and access to spiritual gifts. Spiritual gifts come from God, through the Holy Ghost, and are one sign of the true Church in every age. Christ taught the Nephites, "And if it so be that the church is built upon my gospel then will the Father show forth his own works in it" (3 Nephi 27:10). Spiritual gifts are one of the manifestations of the works of the Father. Elder Bruce R. McConkie taught: "Whence come spiritual gifts? Paul says they come from the Spirit, meaning the Holy Ghost. The latter-day revelation on spiritual gifts says they come from God, meaning the Father. Moroni calls them the gifts of God, but says they come from Christ and also that they come by the Spirit of Christ, meaning the light of Christ which proceedeth forth from the presence of God to fill the immensity of space.

"And all of these inspired declarations are true; each is in perfect harmony with all of the others. Certainly they are the gifts of the Father, and of the Son, and of the Holy Ghost . . . which exemplifies the perfect unity and oneness of the members of the Godhead."[11]

Members of the Church must seek spiritual gifts. The Lord will not force them upon an individual, but they are available to all who make the effort to obtain them. One way a person demonstrates love for the Lord is by seeking and sharing spiritual gifts. President David O. McKay said: "The only thing which places man above the beasts of the field is his possession of spiritual gifts. Man's earthly existence is but a test as to whether he will concentrate his efforts, his mind, his soul upon things which contribute to the comfort and gratification of his physical instincts and passions, or whether he will make as his life's end and purpose the acquisition of spiritual qualities."[12] Elder McConkie taught, "By the grace of God—following devotion, faith, and obedience on man's part—certain special spiritual blessings called *gifts of the Spirit* are bestowed upon men. Their receipt is always predicated upon obedience to law, but because they are freely available to all the obedient, they are called gifts. They are signs and miracles reserved for the faithful and for none else. . . . Their purpose is to enlighten, encourage, and edify the faithful so that they will inherit peace in this life and be guided toward eternal life in the world to come."[13] Whenever the gospel and the priesthood are on the earth these gifts will be available, through the Holy Ghost, to members of the Church who seek them. One sign of apostasy for individuals and for the Church is the absence of spiritual gifts.

There are many different gifts, including healing, tongues, faith, prophecy, and so forth. The purpose of each gift is to encourage, edify, unite, and help perfect the individual and, in turn, to bless other members of the Church. Every member has at least one gift; some may have several; but only the prophet has them all. Individuals have the responsibility to identify, develop, and share their gifts with others. In sharing their gifts, members render real service to others, and each member with his or her special gift is an important part of the Church.

Spiritual gifts can be misused, their purpose can be misunderstood, and there are even false gifts that do not come from the Lord. To protect Church members from these deceptions, the Lord gives Church leaders the gift of discernment. Another sure protection for Church members is a personal relationship with Heavenly Father, a firm testimony of Christ, and the companionship of the Holy Ghost.

There should be order and peace in the use of spiritual gifts, especially such gifts as prophecy and speaking in tongues, which are outwardly visible. To Paul the gift of charity, the pure love of Christ, is the ultimate, lasting gift. After the coming of Christ, most gifts will become part of the outpouring of the

Lord's Spirit, but the gift of charity, which never faileth, will endure forever.

When the gifts of the Spirit are used properly and in unity with the will of the Lord, all will understand, rejoice, and be edified together.

N O T E S

1. Richard Lloyd Anderson, *Understanding Paul* (Salt Lake City: Deseret Book, 1983), 93–94.
2. Joseph Smith, *Teachings of the Prophet Joseph Smith,* sel. Joseph Fielding Smith (Salt Lake City: Deseret Book, 1938), 223.
3. In other places and at other times Moroni and Joseph Smith listed the same spiritual gifts, with some variations.
4. Smith, *Teachings of the Prophet Joseph Smith,* 246.
5. Bruce R. McConkie, *Doctrinal New Testament Commentary,* 3 vols. (Salt Lake City: Bookcraft, 1965–73), 2:378.
6. Ibid., 2:380.
7. Ibid., 2:383.
8. Smith, *Teachings of the Prophet Joseph Smith,* 162.
9. Ibid., 247–48.
10. McConkie, *Doctrinal New Testament Commentary,* 2:386–87.
11. Ibid., 2:371.
12. David O. McKay, in Conference Report, Oct. 1951, 9.
13. Bruce R. McConkie, *Mormon Doctrine,* 2d ed. (Salt Lake City: Bookcraft, 1966), 314.

CHAPTER ELEVEN

A TRIUMPH OF FAITH: PAUL'S TEACHINGS IN SECOND TIMOTHY

JOHN G. SCOTT

Second Timothy is Paul's last letter recorded in the New Testament.[1] It was written from a prison in Rome to his beloved friend Timothy sometime between late A.D. 65 and 67.[2] Paul took one more opportunity to speak to Timothy, and to us, about faith and why faith always triumphs. Shortly Paul would be executed because he was a Christian,[3] yet the vision we have of him in 2 Timothy is as the victor, not the vanquished, a man calm and confident in the face of imminent death.

Paul's confidence came from knowing his eternal destiny. As a true believer in Christ and a valiant worker in the kingdom, he could say with complete assurance: "I have fought a good fight, I have finished my course, I have kept the faith: henceforth there is laid up for me a crown of righteousness" (2 Timothy 4:7–8). More important than the vision of Paul as victor is the vision he gives to all Christians of the possibilities of their victory: "There is laid up for me a crown of righteousness, which the Lord, the righteous judge, shall give me at that day: and not to me only, but unto all them also that love his appearing" (2 Timothy 4:8). Second Timothy is an avowal of personal triumph, but it is also, and more importantly, instruction for us on how to fight the good fight, finish the course, and keep the faith.

ENDURE TRIALS AS A GOOD SOLDIER OF JESUS CHRIST

Being a Christian in the empire of Nero was not easy. Elder James E. Talmage pointed out: "During the latter part of his

□ □ □ □ □

John G. Scott is a teacher in the Church Educational System and resides in Afton, Wyoming.

infamous reign, a large section of the city of Rome was destroyed by fire. He [Nero] was suspected by some of being responsible for the disaster; and, fearing the resentment of the infuriated people, he sought to implicate the unpopular and much-maligned Christians as the incendiaries, and by torture tried to force a confession from them."[4] Under these trying circumstances Paul was imprisoned a second time in Rome, an imprisonment that was a great deal harsher than his first.[5] Paul joined hundreds of other Christians scapegoated for the incineration of Rome. Facing death with a stout heart and unflinching faith, he chose the metaphor of a soldier to illuminate to Timothy his idea of dedication to God: "Therefore endure hardness, as a good soldier of Jesus Christ" (2 Timothy 2:3).

Being a good soldier of Jesus Christ implies commitment to the Savior and his kingdom. Paul told Timothy he was capable of such commitment when he reminded Timothy of his inheritance of faith: "I call to remembrance the unfeigned faith that is in thee, which dwelt first in thy grandmother Lois, and thy mother Eunice; and I am persuaded that in thee also" (2 Timothy 1:5).

Their troubled times made it a challenge to maintain faith in Jesus Christ. That Paul was imprisoned and would soon meet a cruel death indicates the severity of the trial; however, Paul told Timothy: "For God hath not given us the spirit of fear; but of power, and of love, and of a sound mind. Be not thou therefore ashamed of the testimony of our Lord, nor of me his prisoner: but be thou partaker of the afflictions of the gospel according to the power of God. Who hath saved us, and called us with an holy calling, not according to our works, but according to his own purpose and grace, which was given us in Christ Jesus before the world began" (2 Timothy 1:7–9).

Paul thus admonished Timothy to replace fear with faith. The apostle reminded his friend that even though he was a prisoner, God was in control of the situation. Paul wanted Timothy to understand that God had called them to the work for God's "own purpose." Because God was in control of all things, they must rely on him. Thus, though Paul's physical body may have been at the mercy of the Roman government, he could declare triumphantly: "I am not ashamed: for I know whom I have believed, and am persuaded that he is able to keep that which I have committed unto him against that day" (2 Timothy 1:12). Captive or not, he was firm in that faith which is built upon Jesus Christ. He would not let the terror of his imprisonment control him.

Being a good soldier of Jesus Christ also meant being committed to protecting, defending, and advancing the causes of the kingdom of God. Paul said, "No man that warreth entangleth himself with the affairs of this life; that he may please him who hath chosen him to be a soldier" (2 Timothy 2:4). Paul thus described for Timothy the level of commitment that one must attain to "fight the good fight." Only total commitment to the kingdom will "please him who hath chosen him to be a soldier." Paul told Timothy to "endure as a good soldier," and he tells us the same thing. We endure when our faith, through our complete reliance on God, triumphs over the pitfalls and persecutions around us. We endure as good soldiers when we totally commit ourselves to the causes of the kingdom.

SHUN STRIFE AND CONTENTION

Strife and contention are tools of the devil. Paul's Master prayed unto the Father that his followers "may be one" (John 17:21). Unity is vital to the reception of the Holy Ghost. Without unity, the Holy Ghost cannot have full effect upon the followers of Christ. Satan knows that, and during Paul's time stirred up contention within the Church about such fundamental matters as the sequence of the resurrection and other basic doctrines.

Paul took a firm stand on the issue of contending over doctrines. He advised Timothy to "study to shew thyself approved unto God, a workman that needeth not to be ashamed, rightly dividing the word of truth. But shun profane and vain babblings: for they will increase unto more ungodliness" (2 Timothy 2:15–16). Here, Paul encouraged study of the doctrines and precepts of the gospel and denounced "profane and vain babblings" as the antithesis of godliness. Additionally he warned that "their word will eat as doth a canker: of whom is Hymenaeus and Philetus" (2 Timothy 2:17). A canker is "that which corrodes, corrupts, or destroys."[6] Paul's use of the word *canker* impressed on Timothy that the contention arising from vain babblings was something that could destroy him and the Church. This warning should also impress on us the need to avoid "vain babblings" before they canker us today. In the modern Church this is a matter of increasing concern. Many brothers and sisters who could have gone on to exaltation have instead become ungodly because of their unbridled and faithless intellectualism, which induces them to wrongly "[divide] the word of truth" (2 Timothy 2:15). Unfortunately, errors can be made about even such solidly established doctrines as the Book of Mormon being what it claims to be, women and the priesthood, or the divinity of Jesus Christ. Paul's example of men who erred concerning true doctrine was Hymenaeus and Philetus, who had debated about the doctrine of the sequence of the resurrection until they "erred." That mistake was severe enough to "overthrow the faith of some" (2 Timothy 2:18), which concerned Paul, who had the gift of seership and knew that the Apostasy would come from those who had allowed themselves to succumb to that ungodliness.

In 2 Timothy 2:22 we find Paul's admonition to his friend to avoid vain babblings by "[fleeing] also youthful lusts: but follow righteousness, faith, charity, peace, with them that call on the Lord out of a pure heart." Paul was not necessarily talking about immorality when he wrote of "youthful lusts." J. R. Dummelow explained Paul's meaning as to "avoid a young man's desires after novelty in teaching. (There is apparently no reference to the desires of the flesh.) Avoid foolish questions or speculations which gender strife, and pursue a steadfast course of piety with sincere believers, not entering into controversial disputations, but correcting opponents with gentleness and meekness, not for the sake of victory, but for their good."[7] Certainly the doctrines of the gospel must be defended and correctly taught, but, Paul stressed, it must be done for the right reason.

Second Timothy 2:21 heightens our understanding of our responsibility when we are tempted to dispute the Brethren concerning doctrine or any other issue that is vital to our exaltation. Paul used a term familiar to Christians when he said, "If a man therefore purge himself from these, he shall be a vessel unto honor, sanctified, and meet for the master's use, and prepared unto every good work." Ordinarily, Paul might have used this sequence of words to speak of some moral temptation. Instead, the context of the entire chapter indicates that Paul was speaking about the temptation to ask "foolish and unlearned questions" (2 Timothy 2:23). Paul taught that the tendency to question, to contradict, to debate the fundamental doctrines of the Church must be treated as any other sin would be treated: we must purge it from our souls. Only in this way can we securely study the gospel and safely arrive at our appointed destination, the celestial kingdom.

Paul had considerable experience in this area. Only a few decades before he had been carried away with the doctrines of the learned men around him. Years of reflection must have humbled him as he thought how he, too, had once been a man deceived by his own vain and babbling words (see Acts 8:1–3; 9:1–43). Is it any wonder that Paul counseled: "The servant of the Lord must not strive; but be gentle unto all men, apt to teach, patient, in meekness instructing those that oppose themselves; if God peradventure will give them repentance to the acknowledging of the truth; and that they may recover themselves out of the snare of the devil, who are taken captive by him at his will" (2 Timothy 2:24–26). For Paul, who at one time persecuted those who disagreed with him in doctrine, this was a triumph of faith. It is a triumph of faith we also must achieve: to study the gospel so we will know the truth and accept without question the doctrines that allow us, as Christians, to become one with our Savior.

GUARD AGAINST PERILOUS TIMES

After Paul warned Timothy about the things in his life that he must avoid in order to remain faithful, he warned him about the conditions that would soon engulf the Church. His description is a vivid portrayal of certain attitudes prevalent in his day and also in our day, just before the Second Coming. These attitudes can lead to apostasy, and Paul's warning against them should not be taken lightly. He termed the last days as "perilous" because these attitudes threaten not only the stability of the individual but also that of the Church itself.

He stated: "For men shall be lovers of their own selves, covetous, boasters, proud, blasphemers, disobedient to parents, unthankful, unholy, without natural affection, trucebreakers, false accusers, incontinent, fierce, despisers of those that are good, traitors, heady, highminded, lovers of pleasures more than lovers of God; having a form of godliness, but denying the power thereof: from such turn away. For of this sort are they which creep into houses, and lead captive silly women laden with sins, led away with divers lusts, ever learning, and never able to come to the knowledge of the truth. Now as Jannes and Jambres withstood Moses, so do these also resist the truth: men of corrupt minds, reprobate concerning the faith" (2 Timothy 3:2–8).

Like a surgeon's knife, Paul's words cut to the very core of the canker which, if left unchecked, would destroy the Church and lead it into apostasy. Paul outlined those injurious attitudes as selfishness and pride (2 Timothy 3:2), immorality (2 Timothy 3:3), betrayal of gospel covenants (2 Timothy 3:4), and deceit (2 Timothy 3:5). He also explained to Timothy that a person of such character would lead others astray and resist the simple truths of the gospel. As Elder Bruce R. McConkie pointed out: "Sin-laden souls are easily led from the truth."[8] Paul warned Timothy and us that those who have fallen away from truth often prey on those who are weak in the faith and become victims of the seducing doctrines of devils (1 Timothy 4:1).

Paul underscored for us the absolute pride these people would have in mentioning Jannes and Jambres as the archetypes of those who oppose the prophets of God. These two men were, according to Jewish tradition, the Egyptian magicians who opposed Moses.[9] Paul said that those who would play a big role in the eventual apostasy of the Church would have a similar attitude with regard to truth. These people would choose not only to disregard gospel truths but would also "resist the truth." To resist something takes serious action and energy. Resistance is not passive; it is very active. People resistant to the truth will denounce gospel truths. In the end, however, "They shall proceed no further: for their folly shall be manifest unto all men, as theirs [the folly of Jannes and Jambres] also was" (2 Timothy 3:9). Paul's statement is abundantly clear. Those who resist and fight against truth will, in the end, gain no victory for their folly but only disappointment, sorrow, and ultimately the same reward as Jannes and Jambres—dismay at the power of God.

To Paul, the attitude of pride is in direct opposition to the teachings of the gospel of Jesus Christ. The apostle highlighted what a true believer in Jesus should be like by using examples from his own life to emphasize gospel characteristics and attitudes. In 2 Timothy 3:10 Paul said, "But thou hast fully known my doctrine, manner of life, purpose, faith, longsuffering, charity, patience." Paul could, after a full life of persecutions, hardships, personal trials, and imprisonment, testify of the goodness of his own life's example. It is an impressive thing that he asked Timothy and us to do, to examine his life, his teachings, his example.

Paul could confidently use his life as an example because Jesus Christ was his strength, his example, his mentor. His testimony comes strongly to us: "Persecutions, afflictions, which came unto me at Antioch, at Iconium, at Lystra; what persecutions I endured: but out of them all the Lord delivered me" (2 Timothy 3:11). Paul endured the perilous times of early Christianity and triumphed because the Lord was his companion. We too face perilous times as we prepare for the Second Coming; we too can triumph over these perils if we put our faith in the Lord Jesus Christ.

RELY ON THE HOLY SCRIPTURES

In his last recorded letter in the New Testament, Paul instructed Timothy about the vital role the scriptures play in maintaining a virtuous and faithful life. (Paul was referring to the parchments of the Old Testament, for the New Testament was not available until much later.[10]) He commended and encouraged Timothy's study of the scriptures: "But continue thou in the things which thou hast learned and hast been assured of, knowing of whom thou hast learned them; and that from a child thou hast known the holy scriptures, which are able to make thee wise unto salvation through faith which is in Christ Jesus" (2 Timothy 3:14–15).

This statement illustrated for Timothy and for us the central role that the scriptures play in the life of a true Christian. Perhaps, by using his gift of seership, Paul understood the significance that the scriptures would have in the Restoration. He said, with reference to the study of scriptures: "that the man of God may be perfect, throughly furnished unto all good works" (2 Timothy 3:17). He knew how much we would need the scriptures and how much our faith would need our belief in the holy word of God.

TEACH THE TRUTHS OF THE GOSPEL

At the end of his letter, Paul, thinking of the destiny of the Church that he had fought so hard to develop, called on his beloved friend and fellow laborer to continue the fight: "I charge thee therefore before God, and the Lord Jesus Christ, who shall judge the quick and the dead at his appearing and his kingdom; preach the word; be instant in season; those who are out of season reprove, rebuke, exhort with all long-suffering and doctrine" (JST 2 Timothy 4:1–2).

For Paul, part of fighting the good fight was to meet the enemy head on through teaching the truths of the gospel. Why should Timothy be similarly engaged in teaching the doctrines of the gospel? Paul's answer is quite clear: "For the time will come when they will not endure sound doctrine; but after their own lusts shall they heap to themselves teachers, having itching ears; and they shall turn away their ears from the truth, and shall be turned unto fables" (2 Timothy 4:3–4).

Richard Lloyd Anderson gives even clearer meaning to this passage: "The prophecy on losing sound doctrine also tells how the members will transform the faith: 'After their own lusts shall they heap to themselves teachers, having itching ears' (2 Tim. 4:3). But these last three words should appear with 'they' and not after 'teachers.' For translations now follow the clear meaning of the Greek, which makes 'having itching ears' apply to Church members: 'Because they have itching ears, they will heap up for themselves teachers' (2 Tim. 4:3, NKJB)."[11]

Obviously Paul understood the problems the Church would face. No longer able to warn the members about the perilous times ahead, the most he could do was enlist Timothy in the cause and encourage his friend to keep the course. Brother Anderson commented on Paul's situation: "The real threat to the Church was not opposition but inner corrosion. Here Paul's last prophecy on the Church fits his last recorded speech on the subject, Acts 20. Both carry the same pessimism about the

Church's future and the same mechanism for its failure. What made Paul's . . . farewell heartrending to him was not his leaving but his realizing that the great flock he had gathered would be divided and spoiled. There would be successors to the apostles, but not true successors, for after Paul left would come 'savage wolves . . . not sparing the flock' (Acts 20:29, NKJB)."[12]

Paul's words of counsel to Timothy are instructive for all Saints. We too are charged to preach the gospel to others. The fight Paul spoke of is the struggle for souls between God and Satan; Paul had done everything God had commanded him to do in this struggle. Likewise, anyone who has committed to God must also fight, struggle, and labor for the children of God.

CONCLUSION

Paul wrote his last letter to Timothy with his own mortal end in full view, but we do not see Paul as a broken old man, viewing the storm clouds of apostasy on the horizon. Instead, he was confident that he did all he could to build up the church of Christ. One scholar observed: "Rather than fret and fume over the apostasy or impending death, [Paul] asked his friend Timothy to come visit him and bring a few necessities, a coat and some books but especially the parchments or scriptures. In the mind's eye one can see an aged, worn apostle whose body has been torn and bruised but whose faith is positive and upbeat because he has discovered the riches of faith."[13]

In relating his feelings Paul taught us what it takes to triumph in faith. Like Paul, we also must endure trials as good soldiers of Jesus Christ. Likewise we must chart a safe path to avoid the perils of our day: pride, strife, contention, and the allures of a world that has gone far astray from the principles and values that Paul taught. We must become thoroughly familiar with the scriptures and use that knowledge to teach others the gospel. That is the pattern for Christianity; and in the end we will be judged by the strength of our own faith in the Lord Jesus Christ, not by what others did or failed to do. May we, like Paul, live the pattern of Christianity so that we may triumph in our faith and be assured of our own "crown of righteousness" in the celestial kingdom.

N O T E S

1. Scholars debate whether Paul actually wrote 2 Timothy. I believe that

he did and that the words we find in 2 Timothy are actually his. For a discussion of why Paul should be considered the author of 2 Timothy, see J. R. Dummelow, ed., *A Commentary on the Holy Bible by Various Writers* (New York: Macmillan, 1927), 994–95, 1001.

2. Bruce A. Van Orden, "The Pastoral Epistles," in *Studies in Scripture, Volume 6: Acts to Revelation,* ed. Robert L. Millet (Salt Lake City: Deseret Book, 1987), 178.

3. Werner Keller, *The Bible as History* (New York: Bantam Books, 1982), 405.

4. James E. Talmage, *The Great Apostasy* (Salt Lake City: Deseret Book, 1968), 68.

5. Sidney B. Sperry, *Paul's Life and Letters* (Salt Lake City: Bookcraft, 1955), 297–98.

6. *Webster's New Collegiate Dictionary,* 2d ed. (Springfield, Mass.: G&C Merriam Co., 1956), 121.

7. Dummelow, *Commentary,* 1003.

8. Bruce R. McConkie, *Doctrinal New Testament Commentary,* 3 vols. (Salt Lake City: Bookcraft, 1973), 3:111.

9. William Smith, *A Dictionary of the Bible* (New York: Thomas Nelson Publishers, 1986), 278.

10. For an excellent, brief treatment of the coming forth of the New Testament, see Robert C. Patch, "New Testament," in *Encyclopedia of Mormonism,* ed. Daniel H. Ludlow, 4 vols. (New York: Macmillan, 1992), 3:1011–14.

11. Richard Lloyd Anderson, *Understanding Paul* (Salt Lake City: Deseret Book, 1983), 376.

12. Ibid., 376–77.

13. Doug Reeder, "Paul and the Riches of Faith," unpublished paper in possession of the writer.

CHAPTER TWELVE

THE JEWISH AND GENTILE MISSIONS: PAUL'S ROLE IN THE TRANSITION

GAYE STRATHEARN

In the 1842 Wentworth Letter the Prophet Joseph prophesied the future missionary endeavors of the Church. He declared: "Our missionaries are going forth to different nations, and in Germany, Palestine, New Holland, Australia, the East Indies, and other places, the Standard of Truth has been erected; no unhallowed hand can stop the work from progressing; persecutions may rage, mobs may combine, armies may assemble, calumny may defame, but the truth of God will go forth boldly, nobly, and independent, till it has penetrated every continent, visited every clime, swept every country, and sounded in every ear, till the purposes of God shall be accomplished, and the Great Jehovah shall say the work is done."[1] Years later, in 1861, Brigham Young told Church members that when he "came into this Church, [he] started right out as a missionary, and took a text, and began to travel on a circuit. Truth [was his] text, the Gospel of salvation [his] subject, and the world [his] circuit."[2] As Latter-day Saints today we take it for granted that the goal of missionary work is to reach out to all the nations of the world. We remember President Spencer W. Kimball's admonition to the members of the Church to "lengthen [their] stride" both by making personal preparation for missionary activity and by petitioning the Lord to open the doors of the nations.[3] In the 1990s we are partaking of the fruit of such activities. Doors are opening and missions are being established in areas that we

□ □ □ □ □

Gaye Strathearn is a Ph.D. student in New Testament studies at Claremont Graduate School.

only dreamed about ten years ago. It is an exciting time in the progression of the Church.

Yet, especially in this context, we often forget that an international organization, consisting of peoples from a melange of social and cultural backgrounds, was not always the central focus of the Church. In fact, during the earliest period of Christianity, while Christ was on earth, the missionary emphasis was almost entirely directed to the house of Israel. Twice the Savior specifically indicated that both his ministry and that of his disciples were restricted to the house of Israel (Matthew 10:5–6; 15:24). Not until the resurrected Savior was about to ascend into heaven did he issue what has come to be known as the great commission. His departing words to his gathered disciples instructed them to expand their missions to include those outside of the house of Israel: "Go ye therefore, and teach all nations, baptizing them in the name of the Father, and of the Son, and of the Holy Ghost: teaching them to observe all things whatsoever I have commanded you" (Matthew 28:19–20).

The key to understanding this great commission is the phrase "teach all nations" (*panta ta ethnē*). The Greek word for "nations" is *ethnos*. In its most basic form *ethnos* means "a multitude associated or living together" and thus came to mean "a mass or host or multitude bound by the same manners, customs or other distinctive features."[4] The Septuagint (the Greek version of the Old Testament), however, used *ethnos* in a more specific sense—that of nations who were not worshipping the true God. In other words, *ethnos* designated pagan, or gentile, nations.

The great commission delivered on top of the Mount of Olives was a watershed event for the early Christian church, but apparently it raised questions in the minds of the disciples. Without doubt, Christ's disciples recognized that it represented a change in the missionary focus of the Church, but who were the "nations" mentioned by the Savior? Did he simply refer to the Samaritans, or did he also mean to include the gentile nations? If the latter, then what was to be the nature of proselyting? As we look back and read the commission, we may think Christ's intent was perfectly clear, but it wasn't necessarily so for the earliest Christians. The available records, both within and without the New Testament canon, indicate that different Christian groups interpreted the commission in varying ways, and the answers took years to crystallize in the minds of the disciples.

Meanwhile, the debate caused considerable tension among various Christian groups. Central to the debate were the apostle Paul and his "opponents." Although Paul never specifically identified his opponents, scholars generally collect them under the rubric of Jewish Christians. Initially this type of Christianity survived within the framework of the organization. Later, however, as the issues became more formalized, some groups broke away from the Church and followed their own interpretation of the gospel. Two such groups were the Ebionites and Elchasaites. Both considered themselves to be Christians but continued to hold to the Jewish practices of circumcision and Sabbath observance.[5]

Against such divisive forces Paul focused his epistles and missionary activity on the universality of the Church. Indeed, through Paul's activities the Lord moved the early Church from an exclusionary view of missionary work to the house of Israel to an expanded view that included peoples from around the world. Paul vigorously argued that the Mosaic law was fulfilled through the atonement of Jesus Christ. In doing so, he followed the precedent set by the Savior himself to the Nephites (3 Nephi 15:1–10). Paul became particularly vocal as he confronted the Jewish Christian groups that insisted on the continuation of the practice of circumcision and table fellowship[6] among gentile converts. One of Paul's primary objections to the Mosaic law centered on the nationalistic connotations associated with it. With Christ's ascension the gospel moved beyond being a national covenant, and it was intolerable to Paul to impose Jewish cultural traditions on converts from other cultures.

THE JEWISH MISSION DURING THE LIFE OF JESUS

To appreciate the struggle Paul encountered over the gentile mission, it is important to understand the mind-set of his opponents. For some, the concept of a gentile mission challenged the very basis of their understanding of Israel's chosen status.

The Lord had promised Abraham, "I will establish my covenant between me and thee and thy seed after thee in their generations for an everlasting covenant, to be a God unto thee, and to thy seed after thee" (Genesis 17:7). Although Gentiles could participate in that covenant, to do so meant that they had to forgo their cultural identity and, for all intents and purposes, become Israelites. This position was reinforced during Christ's mortal ministry as he directed his missionary activities almost exclusively to the house of Israel. Matthew recorded two incidents when Jesus specifically stated that his mission was to the house of Israel alone. The first declaration occurred when he commissioned his twelve disciples. Jesus expressly directed them: "Go not into the way of the Gentiles, and into any city of the Samaritans enter ye not: but go rather to the lost sheep of the house of Israel" (Matthew 10:5–6). The activities of the disciples before the Resurrection certainly reflect their obedience to this commission. The second incident involved the Syro-Phoenician woman who importuned Jesus to cure her possessed daughter. Jesus' initial response to her pleas was to ignore her. When pressed by his disciples to send her away, Jesus replied, "I am not sent but unto the lost sheep of the house of Israel" (Matthew 15:24). Those two instances clearly indicate that Jesus' ministry was to Israel rather than to the Gentiles.

As one looks more closely, however, particularly at the Gospel of Matthew, one finds definite indications that Matthew saw those two events in a larger context. Matthew was very much interested in detailing the shift of emphasis from Israel to the Gentiles. He did that in several ways. First, he bracketed his gospel by beginning and ending with selections involving Gentiles. His is the only Gospel to record the visit of the eastern magi at Jesus' birth. Not only were they foreigners but they recognized the Son of God at a time when Herod, the chief priests, and the scribes did not. Matthew closed his gospel with the great commission whereby Christ instructed his disciples to go forth and include the Gentiles in their teaching sphere. Matthew then reiterated the importance of Jesus' ministry to the Jews but also included in his gospel a record of events that would prepare his readers for the great commission.

The first event involved the healing of the centurion's servant. Matthew and Luke both record the event, although under different circumstances. In Matthew, we read of Jesus healing the lepers and then traveling to Capernaum. In Luke, the centurion sent servants to bring Jesus to him (Luke 7:3–5), but the Matthean account has the centurion approaching Jesus in person, saying, "Lord, my servant lieth at home sick of the palsy, grievously tormented" (Matthew 8:6). Although Jesus offered to go to the house, the centurion declined, saying, "Lord, I am not worthy that thou shouldest come under my roof: but speak the word only, and my servant shall be healed" (Matthew 8:8; Luke 7:6–7). As a result Jesus declared to his followers, "Verily I say unto you, I have not found so great faith, no, not in Israel" (Matthew 8:10). Then, unlike Luke, Matthew records Jesus saying, "Many shall come from the east and west, and shall sit down with Abraham, and Isaac, and Jacob, in the kingdom of heaven. But the children of the kingdom shall be cast out into outer darkness: there shall be weeping and gnashing of teeth" (Matthew 8:11–12). This is the first specific statement by Jesus that covenantal lineage is not sufficient for exaltation and that others will participate in the blessings of Abraham, Isaac, and Jacob. Later, Paul likewise argued from a similar point of view, writing to the Romans, "but glory, honour, and peace, to every man that worketh good, to the Jew first, and also to the Gentile" (Romans 2:10).

The second example of the faith of the Gentiles is the story of the Syro-Phoenician woman. Not to be put off by Jesus' remark, Matthew records, the woman came and "worshipped him, saying, Lord, help me" (Matthew 15:25). Again Jesus rejected the woman's pleas by informing her that "it is not meet to take the children's bread, and to cast it to dogs" (Matthew 15:26). The woman's response is a superb example of humility: "Truth, Lord: yet the dogs eat of the crumbs which fall from their masters' table" (Matthew 15:27). The Savior responded: "O woman, great is thy faith: be it unto thee even as thou wilt" (Matthew 15:28). Thus, although Matthew records Jesus' making very definite statements about the preaching of the gospel to those outside the house of Israel, he also includes examples of Gentiles' faith, which, to some extent, overshadowed that of the covenant people. These examples help to prepare the reader for the declaration given on the top of the Mount of Olives.

THE GREAT COMMISSION AND ITS INTERPRETATION

As Jesus' parting words to his disciples, the great commission represented the new direction and emphasis for the infant Church. It quickly became evident, however, that different groups interpreted its meaning in different ways. Schweizer represents many biblical scholars in saying, "It is undoubtedly true that a long and bitter struggle was fought in the primitive community before the idea of the gentile mission was accepted."[7] To a certain extent we see this struggle played out in the pages of Acts.

Luke records for us three events that took place before Paul's missionary activity began. Each event is an important stepping-stone for the development of the Gentile mission. The first two involved the missionary activities of Philip. It is almost ironic that Acts 8 introduces his missionary activity immediately following the selection about Saul/Paul's persecution of the Christians "throughout the regions of Judaea and Samaria" (Acts 8:1). Philip may have been caught up in that persecution, for verses 3 and 4 tell us that as a result of these persecutions the Christians who were "scattered abroad went every where preaching the word." It is under such circumstances that we find Philip preaching Christ to the inhabitants of the city of Samaria (Acts 8:5). He was apparently quite successful, and Peter and John were then sent to confer the gift of the Holy Ghost upon the converts (Acts 8:14–17). This episode is important because, as we have noted above, when Jesus first commissioned his disciples he specifically forbade them from entering "into any city of the Samaritans" (Matthew 10:5). Clearly Philip, Peter, and John understood that this injunction had been revoked, presumably by the great commission. Therefore, on their way back to Jerusalem, we are told, they "preached the gospel in many villages of the Samaritans" (Acts 8:25).

But it was one thing to preach to the Samaritans, who had some association with the house of Israel, and quite another to preach to the Gentiles. In the remaining two events, Acts records differing responses to gentile conversions, even though in both instances a divine manifestation was the catalyst for the conversion. That such a manifestation was deemed necessary strengthens the hypothesis that the transition to a gentile mission was a significant change in direction for the fledgling Church.

In the first instance, Philip was specifically instructed by an angel of the Lord to journey from Jerusalem down into Gaza. On the way he met an Ethiopian eunuch who appears to have been sympathetic to the Jewish religion because he went to Jerusalem specifically to worship (Acts 8:27). The Ethiopian is never expressly identified as such, but it is possible that he was one of a group of Gentiles known as "God-fearers." This group was an important source of gentile converts for the early Christian missionaries.[8] Many "had been deeply impressed by the tenets of Judaism and were desirous of embracing it as their own religion but were not yet willing to take some final step that would bring them into the fold as proselytes."[9] Even though they were not regarded as full Jews, "they were welcomed . . . in many synagogues."[10] The book of Acts generally uses either the Greek word *eusebēs,* which means "pious" or "religious,"[11] or *sebomenēs,* which means "one who worships," to describe such people. Although the Ethiopian is never described in such specific terms, that he is a Gentile who is going to worship in Jerusalem implies as much. Philip apparently had no reservations about teaching and baptizing a man such as this, and there is no record of any adverse comment from the Christian community, but that may be because the Ethiopian returned to Ethiopia and was not directly associated with the Jerusalem branch of the Church.

The book of Acts outlines a very different reaction to the baptism of Cornelius, a Roman centurion living in the seaside city of Caesarea. Acts 10:2 describes him as a "devout man, and one that feared God with all his house, which gave much alms to the people, and prayed to God alway." The Greek word used here for "devout man" is *eusebēs,* or, as we have noted above, a "God-fearer." Cornelius was instructed in a heavenly vision to travel to Joppa, where he would receive instructions from "Simon, whose surname is Peter" (Acts 10:5–6). Peter was also the recipient of a divine manifestation. The vision of the clean and unclean beasts that Peter was commanded to eat clearly indicates that he did not yet fully understood the implications of the great commission. Nevertheless, after the vision and the meeting with Cornelius, Peter seems finally to have understood that the Gentiles were now to become an integral part of the Church. He then exclaims, "Of a truth I perceive that God is no respecter of persons: but in every nation *[ethnos]* he that feareth him, and worketh righteousness, is accepted of him" (Acts 10:34–35). Luke reports that "while Peter yet spake . . . the Holy Ghost fell on all them which heard the word. And they of the circumcision which believed were astonished . . . because that on the Gentiles also was poured out the gift of the Holy Ghost" (Acts 10:44–45).

Elder Bruce R. McConkie explained the pivotal nature of the Peter's experience with Cornelius. He wrote that "the decree to go to the Gentiles was already in force before Peter received his vision, but the full and true meaning had not yet burst upon the Lord's apostolic ministers. With this heaven-directed experience, Peter finally swung open the gospel door to the gentile nations, although in practice, as Paul was soon to learn, there would yet be difficult doctrinal, administrative, and procedural problems to be solved."[12]

These problems confronted Peter as soon as he returned to Jerusalem. He was immediately required to justify his actions in Joppa. The accusation against him reflects the two practices of the Mosaic law that Paul would confront in his missionary journeys. The Jewish Christians complained that Peter had gone to "men uncircumcised" and he "did eat with them" (Acts 11:3). In other words Peter had ignored the Mosaic requirements of circumcision and table fellowship. These two Mosaic laws became the crux of the debate over the gentile mission.

As a result of the increased missionary activity to the Gentiles, two different approaches emerged. One group advocated that proselytes to Christianity be required to observe all the rules and regulations associated with the law of Moses. That was in keeping with the current manner of proselyting among the Jews.[13] In effect, the gentile proselytes became Jewish Christians rather than gentile Christians. The other

group, championed by Paul, advocated that Christian proselytes
not be encumbered with the outward manifestations of the law.

PAUL'S UNDERSTANDING OF THE MISSION
TO THE GENTILES

Paul's theophany as he traveled on the road to Damascus
transformed a persecuting Pharisee into a proselyting Christian.
From the very beginning, it was apparent that he would play a
profound role in the struggling Church. Ananias, the disciple to
whom the Lord directed Paul, hesitated to receive him, given
Paul's reputation for persecution. But the Lord assuaged his
fears by declaring that Paul was "a chosen vessel" who had
been called to "bear [Christ's] name before the Gentiles, and
kings, and the children of Israel" (Acts 9:15). Although it was
some years before Paul formally embarked on that mission,[14]
the scriptures record that he fulfilled it with a zeal and deter-
mination that has left its mark on the ensuing centuries.

Paul was not the first to take the message of Christ to the
Gentiles. Philip, Peter, Barnabas, and undoubtedly others had
already laid the foundation on which Paul built. The book of
Acts records that as Paul and Barnabas entered new cities, they
generally used the synagogue to introduce their message (Acts
13:5, 14). At Antioch their message met with mixed reactions.
Luke records that Jews, Jewish proselytes, and Gentiles
believed Paul's teachings and followed him, but when the
Jewish leaders witnessed his success, "they were filled with
envy, and spake against those things which were spoken by
Paul, contradicting and blaspheming" (Acts 13:45). This incident
appears to have been the turning point in Paul's mission. He
and Barnabas announced to those assembled that from that
time on they would concentrate on taking the gospel to the
Gentiles: "It was necessary that the word of God should first
have been spoken to you: but seeing ye put it from you, and
judge yourselves unworthy of everlasting life, lo, we turn to the
Gentiles. For so hath the Lord commanded us, saying, I have
set thee to be a light of the Gentiles, that thou shouldest be for
salvation unto the ends of the earth" (Acts 13:46–47).

The change in emphasis brought Paul face-to-face with questions that were fundamental for the Church and its efforts to
declare the word to "all nations." Should the gentile mission

function on the same basis as proselytes to Judaism, or should different criteria be established? How valid was the law of Moses for those outside of blood Israel? In other words, should the gentile mission observe the law of Moses, or not? These and many other questions may have passed through Paul's mind as he contemplated the direction of his mission. Certainly, these are issues that most scholars address when discussing Paul and the gentile mission; but were they really the issue for Paul, or was something more fundamental going on?

Without doubt, the Mosaic law had been Paul's focus for a large part of his life. Of his own account he was thoroughly steeped in Israelite tradition and education. To the Philippians he wrote that he was "circumcised the eighth day, of the stock of Israel, of the tribe of Benjamin, an Hebrew of the Hebrews; as touching the law, a Pharisee" (Philippians 3:5). At another time he wrote to the Galatians about the fervor with which he had once lived the Mosaic law and its traditions. Not only was he a Pharisee, one of the strictest law-observant Jewish sects, but compared with his "equals in mine own nation," he was "more exceedingly zealous of the traditions of my fathers" (Galatians 1:14). This zealousness was undoubtedly fostered under the tutelage of the renowned Jewish teacher Gamaliel (Acts 22:3). Therefore, to address the issue at hand, it is easy to imagine that political and religious analysts of his day would have predicted Paul would side with those who advocated a gentile mission that included the law of Moses. But maybe it wasn't the law of Moses per se that Paul argued against; maybe it was a particular way that the law, or parts of it, were presented by the Jewish Christians with respect to its national and cultural associations.

The events on the road to Damascus brought a new perspective to Paul's understanding of the Mosaic law. Whereas the law, for Paul, had once been the focal point of salvation, suddenly he realized that it was merely a prelude to the atoning sacrifice of Jesus Christ. He would write that "the law was our schoolmaster to bring us unto Christ" (Galatians 3:24). Here the Greek word for "schoolmaster" is *pedagōgos,* which meant a person who taught someone until the pupil reached adulthood. Georg Bertram, commenting on Paul's use of this term, wrote that "education through the Law ends with man's coming of age. Up to that time the minor needs pedagogues, teachers and supervisors. Though a son of the house, he is no different from the slaves. Indeed, he is under them, for the pedagogues, teachers and supervisors . . . were normally domestic slaves."[15] Through the ministry, atonement, and resurrection of Jesus Christ, Israel had now come of age. It no longer needed that tutor.

Paul did not argue that the Mosaic practices had become a part of Jewish tradition and culture, but he took exception when some Jewish Christians sought to impose those traditions on converts of differing cultural backgrounds. The Council of Jerusalem, held some twenty years after Christ's ascension into heaven, was convened specifically because such practices existed within the Church. In Acts 15 we read, "And certain men which came down from Judaea taught the brethren and said, Except ye be circumcised after the manner of Moses, ye cannot be saved" (Acts 15:1).

At other times, the conflict was precipitated by the Mosaic rules of table fellowship. The most prominent example occurred at Antioch, where Paul confronted Peter. Unfortunately, only Paul's side of the argument has survived, in his epistle to the Galatians. There we read that "before . . . certain came from James, [Peter] did eat with the Gentiles: but when they were come, he withdrew and separated himself, fearing them which were of the circumcision" (Galatians 2:12). As Richard Longenecker noted, the imperfect tense of the verb *sunēsthien,* translated as "did eat," suggests that Peter "ate with Gentile believers repeatedly or habitually, and not just once—which is a picture consistent with what we know of him in Acts after he learns not to call anything that God has cleansed unclean (Acts 10:9–23) and during his visit with Cornelius at Caesarea (Acts 10:24–11:18)."[16] Similarly, the phrase *aphōridzen heauton,* "withdrew himself," is also in the imperfect tense signaling "that [Peter's] separation from the Gentile believers was gradual and step by step, and not immediate on the arrival of the delegation from James."[17] Therefore, it is important that we not be hasty in our condemnation of Peter.[18] He too had a history of missionary work among the Gentiles. In fact, Luke's account of the Council of Jerusalem records that Peter was the first to stand up in support of Paul's missionary activities (Acts 15:7–11). We do not know why Peter chose to withdraw from the Gentiles, but given the tension within the Church over these issues, it may be that Paul overreacted in his condemnation of Peter. Paul himself would write to the Corinthians that "unto the Jews I became as a Jew, that I might gain the Jews; to them that are under the law, as under the law, that I might gain them that are under the law. . . . And this I do for the gospel's sake, that I might be partaker thereof with you" (1 Corinthians 9:20, 23). Surely Peter should be allowed the same latitude. Perhaps if we had access to Peter's side of the story, we could understand his reasons for his actions; but regardless, this incident highlights the sensitivities involved in the issue of missionary work to the Gentiles.

In reviewing the role of circumcision and table fellowship in defining the gentile mission, one becomes curious about why those requirements were singled out. Certainly the law of Moses was not restricted to those two commandments. In fact, the rabbis tell us that the law consisted of six hundred thirteen commandments! There must be some explanation of why those two become the center of the debate. One solution may be extrapolated from their place in the Judaism of the time. James Dunn has argued that circumcision and table fellowship were "widely regarded as characteristic and distinctive Jewish practices."[19] Both Jewish and Greco-Roman texts testify of this fact. Circumcision was the sign of the covenant between God and Israel (Genesis 17:11), and as that covenant became the center of the social and political system in Israel, it also signified cultural identity. First Maccabees informs us that under the rule of Antiochus Epiphanes, some Jews wanted to dissociate themselves from their cultural heritage and become a part of Hellenistic culture. To do so, they "removed their marks of circumcision and repudiated the holy covenant" (1 Maccabees 1:14). Paralleling circumcision as a cultural identity marker were the dietary laws. The book of Daniel manifestly describes the way that diet distinguished Jews in Babylonian captivity from their captors (Daniel 1:8–16).

Before the Maccabean revolt, those who made a stand against the Greek invasion "found strength to resist" by "taking a determined stand against eating any unclean food." Instead, they "welcomed death rather than defile themselves and profane the holy covenant" (1 Maccabees 1:62–63).

The Greek and Roman sources from the first and second centuries after Christ paint a similar picture. Petronius, Plutarch, and Tacitus all described circumcision and table fellowship as being the chief characteristics of Jews. Petronius mentioned both circumcision and table fellowship but argued that circumcision was the critical factor in whether a Jew maintained his national identity or pursued the Greek lifestyle. Thus, "the Jew may worship his pig-god and clamour in the ears of high heaven, but unless he also cuts back his foreskin with the knife, he shall go forth from the people and emigrate to Greek cities, and shall not tremble at the fasts of Sabbath imposed by the law."[20] Plutarch recorded a conversation between his brother Lamprias and Callistratus and Polycrates on whether the Jewish refusal to eat pork was "because of reverence or aversion for the pig."[21] Regardless of their conclusions, that they were having such a discussion points to the importance of the issue in the minds of the Greeks. Tacitus likewise wrote to Simplicum, listing both dietary requirements and circumcision among the things that distinguish them from other nations. He said that Jews "abstain from pork" and "adopted circumcision to distinguish themselves from other peoples."[22]

Therefore, it is possible that Paul's confrontations with those who wanted gentile converts to be circumcised and abide by the Mosaic dietary laws stemmed not purely from their relationship to the law of Moses but also from their relationship to national identification. As long as keeping those parts of the law was a requirement for entrance into the Christian community, the Gentiles would have to reject their own cultural background. Was that what the Lord meant when he twice promised Abraham that through him "all the nations of the earth shall be blessed"? (Genesis 12:3; 18:18). Paul certainly did not think so. So that there was absolutely no doubt in his audience's mind about the way he interpreted this blessing, Paul quoted to the Galatians the version in Genesis 12:3. Putting the blessing in context, he wrote that "the scripture, foreseeing that God would justify the heathen through faith, preached before the gospel unto Abraham, saying, In thee shall all nations be blessed" (Galatians 3:8). The reason he quoted the Greek rendition of Genesis 12:3 rather than Genesis 18:8 is that the former uses the word *ethnos* whereas Genesis 18:18 uses *phulai,* which can also be translated as "tribes" and thus be construed as referring to the tribes of Israel rather than the nations of the earth. Therefore, in arguing the position of the Gentiles, Paul turned to the Abrahamic, rather than the Mosaic, covenant. For Paul, the former covenant allowed for a multiplicity of ethnic backgrounds brought together under the covenant. Therefore he could argue to the Saints at Ephesus that both Jew and Gentile had access to the Father because they were now "no more strangers and foreigners, but fellowcitizens with the saints, and of the household of God" (Ephesians 2:19). Along a similar line, he also wrote to the Galatians that in the gospel of Jesus Christ "there is neither Jew nor Greek, there is neither bond nor free, there is neither male nor female: for ye are all one in Christ Jesus" (Galatians 3:28).[23] One scholar noted, however, that "this sentence does not imply that all national, social and physiological distinctions have disappeared. The Greek who becomes a Christian remains a Greek, unlike the Greek proselyte to Judaism, who abandons his own community to become part of another."[24]

Paul argued for unity through diversity rather than unity through uniqueness. In condemning the ritual practices of the Mosaic law, Paul was only "speaking against the too narrow understanding of God's covenant promise and of the law in nationalistic and racial terms."[25] By changing the focus of Christianity's mission to the Gentiles, the Lord through Paul was reaching out to people throughout the Roman world and inviting them all to be a part of the gospel of Jesus Christ. In a similar way President Spencer W. Kimball encouraged people from around the world to "bring all that you have that is good and wholesome with you, and let us add to all that you have, that which we have—the fullness of the gospel and the even greater blessings that can follow unto you through membership in The Church of Jesus Christ of Latter-day Saints."[26]

Paul was keenly sensitive to the implications of expanding the gospel message to include the Gentiles. His experiences as he traveled throughout the world proved that the pull of the Mosaic law was still very strong in some Christian sectors. Paul did not concern himself with the Jews who continued to observe circumcision and the dietary requirements, but he took exception when they tried to impose those rules upon those who were not Jews. For Paul, the law of Moses was no longer a part of the gospel of Jesus Christ. Instead, it was merely a sign of cultural identity for the Jewish Christians—and the implicit message of Paul's teachings is that the separation between gospel and culture should be maintained when one takes the gospel to the world.

CONCLUSION

As we contemplate Paul's struggle with those Jewish Christians who favored a Christian unity built upon the law of Moses, we find some sobering lessons for modern missionaries. The explosion of missionary activity has opened doors into many nations with varied political, social, religious, and cultural systems. President Howard W. Hunter has declared, "The validity, the power, of our faith is not bound by history, nationality, or culture. It is not the peculiar property of any one people or any one age."[27] This was the message of Paul as he confronted those Christians who viewed salvation in terms of the law of Moses. Instead of trying to force people from different cultural backgrounds into one mold, Paul allowed those differences to have their own expression. As one New Testament scholar wrote, "The life in Christ unites those who are different, and alters the relations between them, without destroying the differences."[28] As we approach the twenty-first century, we find ourselves closer than at any other point in history to fulfilling the Lord's command to preach the gospel to all nations. Christ's commission on the Mount of Olives has never been rescinded, and Elder David B. Haight has reconfirmed our commitment to it by declaring that it is also "our mandate."[29] As we work to fulfill our part, it is imperative that we have an approach similar to Paul's—we also must respect the multitude of cultural differences that bring diversity and beauty to the worldwide Church. In so doing we can follow in Paul's footsteps and be the Lord's instruments to take the gospel message to the world, helping to bring to pass the injunction given almost two thousand years ago to "go ye therefore, and teach all nations."

NOTES

1. Joseph Smith, *History of The Church of Jesus Christ of Latter-day Saints,* ed. B. H. Roberts, 2d ed. rev., 7 vols. (Salt Lake City: The Church of Jesus Christ of Latter-day Saints, 1932–51), 4:540.

2. Brigham Young, in *Journal of Discourses,* 26 vols. (London: Latter-day Saints' Book Depot, 1854–86), 9:137.

3. Spencer W. Kimball, *The Teachings of Spencer W. Kimball,* ed. Edward Kimball (Salt Lake City: Bookcraft, 1982), 586.

4. *Theological Dictionary of the New Testament,* ed. Gerhard Kittel, trans. Geoffrey W. Bromiley, 10 vols. (Grand Rapids, Mich.: William B. Eerdmans Publishing, 1964), 2:369, s.v. *"ethnos."*

5. The Ebionites, in particular, are an excellent example of Paul's "opponents." Hippolytus records the Ebionite claim that Jesus became the Christ through observance of the law of Moses. Hippolytus, *Refutation of All Heresies* 7.22, in *The Ante-Nicene Fathers,* ed. Rev. Alexander Roberts and James Donaldson (Grand Rapids, Mich.: William B. Eerdmans Publishing, 1981), 5:114. Irenaeus also refers to the Ebionites by saying that they "use only the Gospel according to Matthew and reject the Apostle Paul, saying that he is an apostate from the law. . . . They circumcise themselves and continue in the practices which are prescribed by the law and by the Judaic standard of living." *St. Irenaeus of Lyons Against the Heresies,* trans. Dominic J. Unger, in *Ancient Christian Writers: The Works of the Fathers in Translation,* ed. Walter J. Burghardt, Thomas C. Lawler, and John J. Dillon (New York: Paulist Press, 1992), 1:90.

6. "Table fellowship" is a technical term that embraces the ancient social laws governing meals. Dennis E. Smith writes that "to the ancients, sharing a meal was embued with ritual meaning and often signified the most solemn and intimate of social relationship." *The Anchor Bible Dictionary,* ed. David Noel Freedman, 6 vols. (New York: Doubleday, 1992), 6:302, s.v. "Table Fellowship." These customs included rules about who should dine together and the food to be shared. For Israel, these rules were particularly important in light of the Mosaic injunctions on "clean" and "unclean" foods (see Leviticus 11; Deuteronomy 14:3–20). By the time of the New Testament, the Levitical dietary rules had been expanded to include injunctions against eating with Gentiles (John 18:28; Acts 10:28).

7. Eduard Schweizer, *The Good News According to Matthew,* trans. David E. Green (Atlanta: John Knox Press, 1975), 529.

8. *The International Standard Bible Encyclopedia,* ed. Geoffrey W.

Bromiley, 4 vols. (Grand Rapids, Mich.: William B. Eerdmans Publishing, 1988), 1:967, s.v. "dispersion."

9. Ibid.

10. John G. Gager, "Jews, Gentiles, and Synagogues in the Book of Acts," in *Christians among Jews and Gentiles: Essays in Honor of Krister Stendahl on His Sixty-Fifth Birthday,* ed. George W. E. Nickelsburg and George W. MacRae (Philadelphia: Fortress Press, 1986), 93.

11. Henry George Liddell and Robert Scott, *A Greek-English Lexicon,* rev. by Henry Stuart Jones (Oxford: Clarendon Press, 1977), s.v. *"eusebeō."*

12. Bruce R. McConkie, *Doctrinal New Testament Commentary,* 3 vols. (Salt Lake City: Bookcraft, 1970), 2:101.

13. That the scribes and Pharisees actively participated in missionary work is attested by the Savior's condemnation of them in Matthew 23:15: "Woe unto you, scribes and Pharisees, hypocrites! for ye compass sea and land to make one proselyte, and when he is made, ye make him twofold more the child of hell than yourselves."

14. We have very little documentation about Paul's activities between his conversion and his first missionary journey. What we do know comes primarily from his epistle to the Galatians. There he writes that he spent some time in Arabia before returning to Damascus. It was about three years from his conversion until he made his first trip to Jerusalem to meet Paul and James (Galatians 1:17–19).

15. *Theological Dictionary of the New Testament,* 5:620.

16. Richard N. Longenecker, *Galatians,* in *Word Biblical Commentary,* ed. David A. Hubbard and Glenn W. Barker, 52 vols. (Dallas, Texas: Word Books, 1990), 41:73.

17. Ibid., 75.

18. President David O. McKay suggested likewise: "It is true that once after this council, so Paul says (see Gal. 2:7), Peter withdrew from the company of some Gentiles because some of the Jews came down from Jerusalem. Paul says he rebuked Peter for his actions on this occasion, but we have no record of what Peter said or did. Knowing Peter as we do, we are safe in concluding that he did not intentionally waver from the right. It seems more probable that Paul misunderstood Peter's motives. At any rate, we may rest assured that what Peter said and did was intended to help those who were influenced by his actions." *Gospel Ideals* (Salt Lake City: Deseret News Press, 1953), 235–36.

19. James D. G. Dunn, "The New Perspective on Paul," in *Bulletin of the John Rylands Library* 65 (Spring 1983), 107. Dunn included the celebration of special days and feasts—the most important of which was the Sabbath. Paul also mentioned feast days in his letter to the Galatians (4:10), but these do not appear to have had the same influence on the Gentile mission debate.

20. Petronius, *Fragmenta* no. 37, in *Greek and Latin Authors on Jews and Judaism,* ed. Menahem Stern, 3 vols. (Jerusalem: Israel Academy of Sciences and Humanities, 1981), 1:444.

21. Plutarch, *Questiones Convivales* 4:4–5:3, in Stern, *Greek and Latin Authors on Jews and Judaism,* 1:554–57.

22. Tacitus, *Histories and Annals* 4:2; 5:2, in Stern, *Greek and Latin Authors on Jews and Judaism,* 2:25–26. See also Juvenal, *Saturnae* 14, in Stern, *Greek and Latin Authors on Jews and Judaism,* 2:102–3.

23. Paul wrote in a similar vein to the Colossians: "Where there is neither Greek nor Jew, circumcision nor uncircumcision, Barbarian, Scythian, bond nor free: but Christ is all, and in all" (Colossians 3:11).

24. Nils Alstrup Dahl, *Studies in Paul: Theology for the Early Christian Mission* (Minneapolis: Augsburg Publishing House, 1977), 16.

25. Dunn, "New Perspective on Paul," 121.

26. Kimball, *Teachings of Spencer W. Kimball,* 552.

27. Howard W. Hunter, "The Gospel—a Global Faith," in *Ensign,* Nov. 1991, 19.

28. Dahl, *Studies in Paul,* 16.

29. David B. Haight, "Jesus of Nazareth," in *Ensign,* May 1994, 78.

INDEX

Aaron, 74

Abraham: covenant of, 92; Paul on, 138–39, 201; Lord's promise to, 191

Abraham's seed, 92

Acts of the Apostles, 3, 51, 96

Adam and Eve, 133

Adoption: spirit of, 80; formulas of, 82; meaning of, 85–86; metaphor of, 86; in Ephesians, 87–88; spirit of, 90; into family of Christ, 146–47

Adoptive-redemption model, 81; in Paul's writings, 84, 92–93

Adultery, 14

Advent, 17

Adversary, 41

Allied invasion of Normandy, 1

Alma, 158

Alma the Younger, 113, 115

Amendments to United States Constitution, 12

American advent of Christ, 25

Ammon, 74

Ananias, 38, 69, 114

Andersen, T. David, 83–84

Anderson, Richard P., 65, 67

Anderson, Richard Lloyd, 126, 157, 185–86

Angels, 125

Anger, 20, 29

Animals forbidden to be eaten, 101

Antioch, 102

Anti-Semitic position of churches, 51

Apostasy, 41, 44, 186

Apostles: death of, 31 n. 23; attributes of true, 36, 111–12

Apostleship: authority of, 14; corporate, 30; Paul called to, 59

Apostolic: revelation, 12, communication, 22–23

Aramaic, 25

Aratus, 68

Areopagus, 68

Atonement, 38; doctrinal issue regarding, 103–4; and fall of Adam and Eve, 133; necessity for, 135–36; and change of nature, 142; requires Christ to have body of flesh and blood, 158; fulfills Mosaic law, 190

Authority, 14, 44, 124

Babblings, vain, 181

Baptism: Old Testament images and, 84–85; rite of, 85, 86; covenant of, 87, 93; redemption through, 92–93; of Saul, 116; for the dead, 121; by fire, 141

Barnabas, 25, 39, 102

Barsabas, 105

Beasts, Peter's vision of, 194–95

Benson, Ezra Taft, 124; on need for Christ, 133; on externals, 143

Bertram, Georg, 197–98

Betrayal of gospel covenants, 183

Betz, Hans Dieter, 60

Biblical adoptive-redemption model, 93

Bickerman, E., 50

Birth, natural and spiritual, 144

Blood: Paul seals testimony with own, 125–26; of Christ shed for salvation of humanity, 158

Body of Christ, 168–69
Bondage, spirit of, 90
Books, Christian, 29
Bruce, F. F., 133
Bullinger, E. W., 77

Calling and election, 122
Canker, 180–81
Cassiodorus, Flavius Magnus Aurelius,
    45
Celestial kingdom, 182, 186
Character, change of, 142–43
Charismatic gifts, 43
Charity: Paul appeals for, 17, 21, 34,
    122–23; as fruit of Spirit, 144; gift
    of, 171–72, 176
Chosen vessel, Paul as, 149
Christianity: Paul's conversion to, 52;
    pattern for, 186; proselytes of, 196
Christians: calling of, 29; Jewish, 190
Church of Jesus Christ: Satan seeks to
    possess, 16–17; as God's temple,
    17; after ascension of Christ, 96;
    prophets and apostles build up,
    97–98; edifying of, 170
Church of Jesus Christ of Latter-day
    Saints, 98, 201, 202
Circumcision: of proselytes, 85;
    emphasis on, 103; spiritual, 146;
    Mosaic requirement of, 195
Commission, great, of Christ, 189, 193
Communication, apostolic, 22–23
Condescension of Christ, 153
Contention, 180
Conversion: true, 115; catalyst for, 194
Converts, 3–4, 18, 190
Corinth, 166; correspondence with
    Saints in, 11, 13, 34, 59; obeisance
    to false gods by people of, 35
Cornelius, 101, 194
Corporate apostleship, 30
Council, Jerusalem, 96, 98–99, 198
Covenant: between Lord and Israel,
    81–82; meal and, 82; renaming as
    expression of, relationship, 83;
    meaning of, 85–86; adoption of

Israel through, 87; of Abraham, 92,
    191; lineage and, 192
Cross, nailing ourselves to, 141
Crown of righteousness, 186
Crucifixion, Paul's writings on, 23
Culture, conflict between doctrine
    and, 108–9
Custom and tradition, 109

Damascus, 114
Daube, D., 50
Davidic credentials of Christ, 11
Davids, Peter, 27
Davies, W. D., 27, 49, 52–54
Dead, restoring the, to life, 120
Dead Sea Scrolls, 48
Deceit, 183
Deliverance from sin, 90–91
Destiny, Paul knew own eternal, 178
Devil, tools of, 180
Devils, Paul cast out, 119
Diaspora Judaism, 49, 53–54
Diet: Jewish restrictions of, 17–18, 20;
    law of Moses and, 101, 199
Diligence, 123
Discernment, gift of, 42, 143–44, 169,
    171
Disciple-preachers, 8
Disciples: Christian standards for, 18;
    true, 34
Discipleship, mark of true, 143
Diversity of gifts, 35
Divine: protection, 12; nature, 122,
    123; approbation, 129
Divorce, 14, 23
Doctrine, conflict between culture
    and, 108–9
Drunkenness, 16
Dummelow, J. R., 181
Dunn, James, 199

Ebionites, 190, 203 n. 5
Elchasaites, 190
Election, doctrine of, 109
Elitism, spiritual, 35
Eloquence, 65–66

Elymas, 40
Endowments, spiritual, 36–37
Enoch, 125
Ephesians, adoption, redemption, and inheritance in, 87–88
Ephesus, 167
Epimenides, 68
Eternal life, 110; and atonement of Christ, 112; Paul inherits, 149
Ethics, rhetoric and, 77
Ethiopian, 194
Ethnos, 189
Ethos, 75
Eupolemus, 57
European Protestants join Church, 98
Eusebius, 24, 27
Eutychus, 39
Evil, 16, 19–20; spirit rebuked, 42; spirits cast out, 120
Evolution, 109
Exchange, great, 136–37
Exorcists, 42
Eyewitnesses of Christ, 9

Faith, 38; treatise on, 122; justification by, 135–36; counted for righteousness, 139; gift of, 170–71; maintaining, in Christ, 179
Faithfulness, 30
Fall, legacy of the, 118, 133
False: prophets, 17; gods, 35; spirits, 41
Family relationships: covenant making and, 82; purpose of, 121
Father-son covenant terminology, 82
Fear, replacing, with faith, 179
Feast: of Passover, 99; of Pentecost, 99
Felix, 69–70
Firstbegotten, Christ as, 153
Firstborn, Christ as, 153
Fitzmyer, Joseph A., 7–8
Foolish, 182
Foreordination of Christ, 153
Forgiveness, 29–30; of sins through Christ, 148

Fruit of the Spirit, 144–45
Furnish, Victor, 53–54

Galatians: adoption in, 91; Paul's epistle to, 105–6
Galilean Twelve, 30
Gamaliel, 37, 47, 55, 197
Gaston, Lloyd, 51
Gathering of Israel, 145
Gentiles: join Church, 102, 104; mission to, 190–91, 196–97; shift of emphasis from Israel to, 191; preaching to, 193–94
Gift: of discernment, 42, 143, 169, 171; of healing, 39, 119, 144, 169; of prophecy, 34, 40, 144, 169, 171–72. *See also* Gifts of Spirit
Gift of Holy Ghost, 101; Saul receives, 114–15
Gifts of Spirit, 34, 42–43; diversity of, 35; cessation of, 44; Lord discusses, 143–44; misunderstanding regarding, 167; and service, 169–70; all, given to prophet of God, 171; members of Church to seek, 175
George, Bob, 143
God-fearers, 194
Godhead, 35
Godliness, 123
Godly persuasion, 74
Gods, false, 35
Gorgias, 67
Gospel: fourth, 2; restoration of fulness of, 41; teachers of, 75–76; taught to non-Jews, 96; entering the, covenant, 137; preaching of, to all nations, 202
Gospels, synoptic: 2; wording in, 4–5; comparing, 5–6
Grace of Jesus Christ, 104, 138
Grant formula, 82
Great commission of Christ, 189, 193
Greek: Matthew's Gospel written in, 24–25; Paul's letters written in, 47;

in India, 55–56; education of Paul,
  59, 68–69

Haight, David B., 202
Half-converts, 86
Hanks, Marion D., 144–45
Hawthorne, G. F., 83
Healing, 39, 119, 144, 169; of
  centurion's servant, 192
Heavenly Father, language of, 74
Hebrew: period of early Church, 25;
  practice of redeemer as kinsman,
  93
Hellenistic Judaism, 48–49, 53–54
Hellenizein, 56, 58
Hengel, Martin, 54–55, 56
Holy Ghost: as conduit for gifts,
  35–36; as witness of Christ, 36–37;
  descends on Twelve, 99; and gift
  of the Holy Ghost, 101; teaching
  power of, 121; Paul teaches Saints
  to seek companionship of, 167–68;
  access to spiritual gifts through,
  169; companionship of, brings
  testimony of Christ, 175; unity
  essential to reception of, 180
Holy Spirit: of promise, 88–89; as a
  sanctifier, 141
Honesty, 27
Hope, 122
Humility, 123
Hunter, Howard W., 202
Hymenaeus, 181

Idols, false, 35
Immorality, 183
Immortality, 15
Inheritance: of land, 82; in Ephesians,
  87–88; in Galatians, 92
Intellectualism, faithless, 181
Isaiah, 74
Israel: covenantal adoption of, 87;
  gathering of, 145; Jesus' ministry
  to, 191
Israelite: concept of redeemer, 81;
  exodus, 85

Jacob, 74
James, 10; epistle of, 26–27;
  martyrdom of, 102
Jannes and Jambres, 183
Jerusalem, 57, 61
Jerusalem Council, 96; date of, 106;
  shortcomings of, 106–7; avoids
  schism, 107; effects of decision of,
  107–8
Jesus Christ: dating religious
  biographies of, 2–3; historical
  accounts of, 4, 9; authority of, 6;
  death and resurrection of, 7, 13;
  appearances of, 8, 11, 12, 16, 24;
  as source, 12; definitions of love
  of, 21; teaching of, 21–22; Paul
  speaks with authority of, 22;
  evidence of early records of, 25;
  on mercy, 27; apostles of, 36; and
  needs of his audience, 74; as
  redeemer and father of Israel,
  81–82; ransom by blood of, 89;
  children of, 93; told Twelve where
  to preach, 99; to change Mosaic
  customs, 100; atonement of, 103–4,
  135–36; grace of, 104; fulfills law
  of Moses, 108; atonement of, and
  eternal life, 112; as hope of Israel,
  122; Paul witnesses resurrection of,
  123; becoming perfect in, 136;
  new life in, 140; Paul bears
  witness of, 145–46; salvation
  through name of, 147–48; divinity
  versus mortality of, 151;
  condescension of, 153;
  foreordination of, 153; empties
  himself of glory, 154; temptations
  of, 155–56; physical suffering of,
  156–57; spiritual sufferings of,
  158–59; spiritual death of, 159;
  knowledge of premortal life of,
  159–60; divinity of, in mortal life,
  160; childhood of, 163 n. 25;
  personal testimony of, 168; Holy
  Ghost brings testimony of, 175;
  issues great commission, 189

Jewish Christians, 190, 197

Jews: dietary convictions of, 17–18, 20, 29; practice ritual cleanliness, 23; proselyte baptism to become one of, 85; observe law of Moses, 108; cultural traditions of, imposed on converts, 190

Job, 160

John, Gospel of, dating, 2

John Mark, 102

Josephus, 55

Judaism, 48–49; Palestinian, 49; Hellenistic, 49; attempt to fit Paul into category of, 51–52; gentile converts to, 99

Jude, 10

Judicial speech, 69–70

Justice, satisfying demands of God's, 134

Justification by faith, 135–36; a matter of acquittal, 137

Kennedy, George A., 69, 71, 77

Keys, transfer of, 124

Kimball, Spencer W., 117; on lengthening stride, 188; on joining Church, 201

Kindness, 123

King Benjamin, 93

Kinship, 81

Kinsman-redeemer, 81, 84, 86, 93

Knight, Lydia, 119

Knowledge, 123

Lamb, wedding feast of, 114

Language: of Paul, 47; power of, 72–73; of Heavenly Father, 74

Last Supper, 11, 13; John's discourse on, 18, 30; apostles share Christ's instruction at, 21; Paul taught about, 24

Law, as a bondage, 92

Law of Christ, 19

Law of Moses: Samaritans and, 100; circumsised represents, 103; Jewish members observe, 108; no flesh

justified by, 135; fulfilled through atonement of Christ, 190; sign of cultural identity, 202

Legal oration, 69–70

Letters of Paul, 3–4, 17, 22

Liddell, Henry George, 56

Lieberman, S., 50

Longenecker, Richard, 198

Love, 20–21; Paul's evaluation of, 21; laws of, 23

Luke, Gospel of: dating, 2; viewpoint of, 9; preface to, 9–10

Lust, 29

MacArthur, John, 137, 139

Mack, Burton L., 77

Madsen, Truman G., 125

Mark, Gospel of, dating, 2, 11

Marriage, sexual act within bonds of, 134

Matthew, Gospel of, 17; dating, 2; and equivalents to Paul's words, 24; written in Greek, 24–25; record of oracles in, 28

Matthias, 99

Maxwell, Neal A.: on endowment, 37; on Saul, 113

McCarthy, Dennis J., 82

McConkie, Bruce R.: on spiritual gifts, 34, 176; on callings to serve, 37; on Church of Firstborn, 124; on salvation, 139; on name of Jesus, 148; on mortal ordeals of Christ, 155; on temptations of Christ, 156; on preexistent traits, 161; on charity, 172–73; on prophecy, 174; on sin, 183; on Peter's experience with Cornelius, 195

McConkie, Joseph Fielding, 114

McKay, David O., 175–76

Mediterranean Sea, 97

Melchizedek Priesthood, 124

Mercy, 27

Metaphor of adoption, 82, 86

Meyers, Eric, 61

Miller, Stuart, 61–62

Millet, Robert L., 124
Miracles, 39–40, 119; gift of working, 169
Mishnah, 55
Missionary: support of Paul as a, 14; instruction to Twelve, 23; training of, 74, 76; work done among non-Jews, 96; Acts records, work to Jews, Samaritans, Gentiles, 97–98; extending Church, system, 101; Brigham Young on being a, 188; focus of Church on, work, 189
Mission: of church of Christ, 121; to Gentiles, 193
Montefiore, C. G., 48
Moore, George Foot, 49
Moral: law, 166; overview, 19, 28; perfection, 135; sins in Corinth, 167
Moroni, 34–35
Mortality: as arena of opposites, 118; and natural birth, 144; of Jesus Christ, 151–52
Mortal Messiah, 151; Paul's teachings on, 154
Mosaic law: dietary requirements of, 18, 200; requirements of circumcision and table fellowship in, 195, 198–99
Moses, on experiences with God and Satan, 118
Mount of Olives, 15; great commission delivered on, 189, 193

Name, new, 81–83
Name changing in Old Testament, 83
Natural birth, 144
Near East, renaming in ancient, 83–84
Nephi, 75
Nephites, 76, 141–42
Nero, 178–79
Neusner, Jacob, 55
New Jerusalem Bible, 26
New Testament: covenant making in, 84; missionary service of apostles recorded in, 97; proselytes in, 99

Nibley, Hugh, 40–41; criticizes rhetoric, 66–68
Nicolas, 100
Nonretaliation, 19

Oaths, 27
Old Testament adoptive-redemptive model, 80–81, 89
Old Testament Yahweh, 81
Olivet prophecy, 15–16; Paul follows pattern of, 17; segments of, in Paul's writings, 23
Opposites, 118
Oracles, 25; Matthew kept record of, 28
Oral: tradition, 28; transmission of stories, 4, 12
Oratory, 65–66
Ordinance of sacrament, 11
Ordinances, Paul received, 129–30
Organic evolution, 109
Orr, William, 59

Pace, Glenn, 143
Packer, Boyd K., 124
Palestinian Judaism, 49, 53–54
Papias, 24, 28
Parables, 16
Parmenas, 100
Patience, 123
Paul: letters of, 3–4, 17, 22, 178; vision of, 8, 28; writings of, on Christ, 11–12, 21–22, 23; and resurrection appearances of Christ, 12–13; atonement of, 13; appeals for charity, 17, 21, 34; evaluation of love, 21; speaks with authority of Christ, 22; vision of, on road to Damascus, 23–24; and faithfulness, 30; and gifts of Spirit, 34, 42–43; instructions of, to Saints at Corinth, 34; on word of God, 37–38; healing by, 39; curses Elymas, 40; bitten by snake, 40; as a prisoner, 41; on divine assignment of gifts, 44; language of, 47, 58–59;

relationship of, to Judaism, 48;
Jewish upbringing of, 52;
conversion of, to Christianity, 52;
Greek education of, 59, 62;
adoptive redemption in writings
of, 84–85, 87; Acts records
conversion and ministry of, 97;
Protestant Reformation based on
writings of, 98; confers Holy Ghost
on converts, 100; proclaims
testimony of Christ, 101; as a
special witness of Christ, 110, 145,
151, 161; as a type of Christ, 111;
content of writings of, 111;
physical appearance of, described
by Joseph Smith, 116; opposed by
Satan, 117–18; and healing power
of priesthood, 119; casts out
devils, 119–20; witness of
resurrection of Christ, 123; hold
keys, 123; seals testimony with
own blood, 125–26; martyrdom of,
126–27; received ordinances,
129–30; doctrinal themes of,
132–33; on salvation through name
of Christ, 147–48; love of doctrine
of, 148–49; as chosen vessel, 149,
196; teaches Philippians of divinity
and mortality of Christ, 152; on
Christ as Creator, 153; on divinity
of Christ in mortality, 160; on less-
visible gifts, 172; on gift of
tongues, 174; on listening to
prophets, 174–75; admonishes
Timothy, 175, 185; farewell of,
185–86
Paulus, Sergius, 40, 68–71, 75–76
Persuasion, 77
Peter: testimony of, 5–6; Christ's
appearance to, 8; death of, 10;
confers Holy Ghost on converts,
100; baptizes Cornelius, 101
Petition of Christ, 152–53
Philetus, 181
Philip, 100
Physical suffering of Christ, 156–57

Plan of salvation, 153, 156
Polyhistor, Alexander, 57
Preaching, 29
Premortal: glory of Christ, 153; life,
159–60
Pride, 183–84
Priesthood: authority, prophets and
apostles preach with, 97; healing
and, 119; keys, 101; power, 73
Prisoner, Paul as, 41
Proclamation of gospel, 133
Prophecy: gift of, 34, 40, 144, 169,
171–72; more sure word of, 128
Prophets: characteristics of, 111–12;
false, 17; given all spiritual gifts,
171
Proselytes: baptism of, and
circumcision, 85; meaning of, 99;
conversion of, 194
Protagoras, 67
Protestant Reformation, 98
Proto-Gospels, 30
Public speaking, 76. See also Rhetoric
Purification, 18

Questions, 182
Quorum of the Twelve: vacancy in,
99; members of, speak in tongues,
99; ministry of, among Jews, 100

Rabbinate, 54–56
Ransom by Christ's blood, 89
Redaction, 6
Redeemer in ancient Israel, 81
Redeemer-kinsman, 81, 84, 86, 93
Redemption: and adoption, 80–81;
meaning of, 85–86; in Ephesians,
87–88; in Christ, 88; eschatological
sense of, 89
Refining process, 117
Reformation, Protestant, based on
writings of Paul, 98
Remarriage, 13
Renaming, 81, 83, 84
Restoration, 41; records preserved for
benefit of, 97–98; truth of, 121;

significance of scriptures in,
  184–85
Resurrection: appearances of Christ,
  8, 24; Paul's writings on, 23; Paul
  as witness to, 123
Revelation: and rhetoric, 65, 67;
  confronts tradition and custom,
  109
Revised English Bible, 26
Rhetoric: and revelation, 65, 67;
  criticism of, 66, 76–77; Lord gives
  pattern for, 74, 77
Rhetorical education of prophets, 76
Righteousness, 27; terminology, 50;
  necessity of, 136, 138
Ritual: purity, 18, 23; baptism, 86
Robinson, Stephen E., 3, 156
Romans, adoption in epistle to, 89–90
Romans-Matthew correlations, 28

Sacrament: Christ established, 11, 13;
  Paul's writings concerning, 23,
  28–29
Salvation: in Christ, 134, 138–39,
  147–48; working out our own, 142;
  accomplished only if bands of
  death are broken, 157
Samaritans: Church established
  among, 100; Jesus forbade
  disciples to enter cities of, 193
Sanders, Ed, 49–50
Satan, 16, 118
Saul: witnesses death of Stephen, 100;
  converted to Jesus Christ, 100–101,
  145; goes to Antioch, 102;
  conversion of, 112–13; received
  gift of Holy Ghost, 114–15; vision
  of, of risen Lord, 115–16; baptism
  of, 116. See also Paul
Savior. See Jesus Christ
Schweizer, Eduard, 193
Scott, Robert, 56
Scriptures, relying on, 184–85
Second Comforter, 127–28
Second Coming: prophecy of, 15–16;
  Paul on, 17

Second Sophistic, 66–67
Second Timothy, 178
Semitic, anti-, position of churches, 51
Seneca, 68
Sermon on the Mount, 18–19, 23; as
  test of Nephite record, 26;
  righteousness taught in, 27; James
  adapts, 30
Sermon on the Plain, 18–19, 27
Service, 169–70
Seventy, the, 14
Shepherd, Massey, 28
Signs, miraculous, 119
Silas, 105
Sin: deliverance from, 90; put to
  death through baptism, 116;
  conceived in, 134; forgiveness of,
  148
Smith, Joseph: Bible translation of, 26;
  healing by, 39; on power over
  spirits, 41–42; on gift of tongues,
  43, 173–74; on priesthood power,
  73–74; restores fulness of gospel,
  98; explains Holy Ghost, 101;
  describes Paul's physical
  appearance, 116; on refining
  process, 117; healings by, 119; and
  divine nature, 122; on resurrected
  beings, 125; on sealing testimony
  with blood, 126; martyrdom of,
  126–27; on Second Comforter,
  127–28; receives divine
  approbation, 129; on fulness of
  Christ's glory, 152; on gifts given
  to man, 170, 172; Wentworth
  Letter of, 188
Second Coming, 182
Selfishness, 183
Socrates: in defense of Paul, 60–61
Soothsayer, 42
Sophistic, Second, 66–67
Sophistry, 72
Souls, worth of, 121
Sperry, Sidney B., 25–26, 121; on
  being justified, 137

Spirit: gifts of, 34, 173; of adoption, 80; manifestion of, 170
Spirits: false, 41; evil, rebuked, 42
Spiritual: birth, 144; death of Christ, 159; endowments, 36–37; elitism, 35; salvation of mankind, 157–58; suffering of Christ, 158–59; transformation, 143
Spiritual gifts. *See* Gifts of Spirit
Stendahl, Krister, 51
Stephen, 100
Stevenson, Edward, 126
Stott, John, 142–43
Strife as a tool of devil, 180
Suzerains, 83–84
Synoptic Gospels, 2, 23
Syro-Phoenician woman, 192

Table fellowship, 203 n.6
Tacitus, 68
Talmage, James E., 65; on veil of forgetfulness, 160; on Nero, 178–79
Tannaites, 55
Tarn, W. W., 55
Taylor, John, 125
Teachers, 75
Temperance, 121, 123
Temptations: of Christ, 155–56; plan of salvation includes, 156
Tertullus, 69–70
Testimony, 37, 168
Thackeray, H. St. John, 48
Theophilus, 96
Thessalonian letters, 23
Thessalonians, Second, 16
Third heaven, 112
Thomas, W. Ian, 140–41
Three degrees of glory, 121
Timothy, 107; Paul admonishes, 179, 185

Titus, 106
Tongues: gift of, 34, 42–43, 170, 171–72; Twelve speak in, 99; Paul exercises gift of, 120
Tradition and custom, 109
Truth, resisting, 183
Twelve: missionary service of, 97; as special witnesses of Christ, 161 n.3

Uncleanness, 135
Ungodliness, 181
Unity: in Church, 35; in Christ, 168–69; essential to reception of Holy Ghost, 180; through diversity, 201
Urim and Thummim, 126

Vain babblings, 181
Vassal kings, 83–84
Virtue, 123

Walther, James, 59
Wedding feast of the Lamb, 114
Wentworth Letter, 188
Wickedness, 16, 124
Wisdom, 144
Witness of Christ, Paul as a, 110, 145–46, 151, 161
Witnesses, 23, 36
Woodruff, Wilford, 39
Word of God, 37–38
Works, faith manifest in righteous, 139

Yahweh, 81
Young, Brigham: on speaking by power of Spirit, 66; on being a missionary, 188
Youthful lusts, 181